▶ Hydnophytum
Hydnophytums enjoy "mutual benefit" living arrangements with ants. Tree-dwelling species of the South-east Asian jungle, they have fleshy tubers in which ants tunnel dwelling chambers. In return for shelter and nectar, the ants protect the plants against intruders, and transport their seeds to new sites.

▼ Venus Flytrap
The carnivorous Venus's Flytrap (Dionaea muscipula) operates a hair-spring trap to catch its prey. The bristle-edged leaf lobes each have three trigger hairs on the surface. If one is touched, nothing happens; but if two or three are, the trap closes within a quarter-second.

▲ Bladderwort
The aquatic Bladderworts (Utricularia) carry tiny traps like miniature lobster-pots on their submerged stems. If a water-creature, like Daphnia, brushes an external trigger-hair, an airtight lid on the pot opens inwards and the prey is sucked in.

▲ Butterwort
Insect-eating Butterwort (Pinguicula) invented fly-paper before we did – small insects alighting on this bog plant's sticky leaves are stuck fast. Glands on the surface then exude more sticky juice, and an acid fluid which dissolves the prey. Meanwhile, the edges of the leaf curl slowly inwards, and enclose the insect.

▼ Nepenthes
Plants of several families have "pitchers" to trap insects. Nepenthes have lidded pitchers at leaf-ends to entice with an attractive odour and nectar-like fluid on the rim. But down-pointing barbs and waxy walls ensure a one-way trip into a digestive liquid at the bottom.

▲ Sundew
Sundews (Drosera) make doubly sure of their victims: the red hairs covering the leafpads each carry a glistening drop of very sticky clear fluid. Any insect attracted by these droplets, like the lacewing here, becomes stuck fast, while other hairs gradually bend around and pin it to the centre of the leafpad, which bears acid-secreting glands. Biggest of the sundews, D. regina from South Africa has leaves 60 cm long.

▼ Bucket orchid
The bizarre Bucket Orchids
(Coryanthes) show how to
make an insect pollinator look
ridiculous! Bees suck attractive
fluid on the edges of the huge
lips, become inebriated, and fall
into the liquid-filled "bucket".
They can only escape by
squeezing under the flower's
sexual organs: it may take a bee
thirty minutes to wriggle out –
yet it will return and so carry
out cross-pollination. The
Orchid family has the most
complex pollination method of
any family, usually involving
one species of insect to each
species of orchid.

▶ Bee orchid
Bee Orchids (Ophrys) depend
for pollination on deluding male
insects into mistaking their
flowers for desirable females:
they have the right odour,
pattern and degree of hairiness.
Once alighted on a flower, the
male insects attempt to
copulate.

◀ Arum maculatum
When ripe for pollination,
Lord-and-Ladies (Arum
maculatum), give off a
powerful odour to attract
insects. Midges crawl on the
female flowers at the base of the
tube (the males are above). The
central hairs allow midges to
enter, but not to leave until the
pollen is shed on them.

▶ Ceropegia
Ceropegia haygarthii waves a
hairy, club-shaped organ to
attract insects. Odour then leads
them to the slippery chute of the
flower proper, which restrains
them till their pollinating work
is done, when the bloom tips to
release them.

▼ Rafflesia
One species of Rafflesia wins
the record for the biggest flower
in the world. A metre across, its
size is doubly amazing because
it is a totally leafless parasite,
the huge flower usually
emerging from the liana host's
roots but sometimes from high
up its stem. The evil-smelling
flowers are pollinated by flies,
and the seeds dispersed by ants.

GREEN INHERITANCE

GREEN INHERITANCE

The WWF Book of Plants

Anthony Huxley

Foreword by David Attenborough

Gaia Books Limited

A GAIA ORIGINAL

This book was written by Anthony Huxley with the
help of the World Wide Fund for Nature and the
International Union for Conservation of Nature
and Natural Resources.

Editorial	Elizabeth Hoseason
	Juliet Bailey
Design	Bridget Morley
	Tony Spalding
Picture Research	Elly Beintema
Direction	Joss Pearson
	Patrick Nugent

® This is a Registered Trade Mark of Gaia Books Limited

First published in the United Kingdom 1984
by William Collins Sons & Co. Ltd.
This edition published in 1991 by
Gaia Books Limited
66 Charlotte Street
London W1P 1LR

Filmset by SX Composing, Rayleigh, Essex, England.
Reproduction by Rommerstsen van Santen BV, Netherlands.
Printed and bound in Hong Kong by Mandarin Offset.

British Library Cataloguing in Publication Data
Huxley, Anthony 1920–
    Green inheritance : the WWF book of plants.
    1. Plants useful to man
    I. Title   II. World Wide Fund for Nature
    581.61
ISBN

8895

For Zoë
who is part of the future

The aim of this book is to show, before it is entirely too late, just how rewarding our green inheritance is to mankind – to demonstrate the wonder and worth of plants, and their great potential, to explain why they cannot take any more punishment, and to point out how those that remain can be saved. And indeed, we must save them, because each plant that becomes extinct represents a loss to ourselves.

Plants have fed the world and cured its ills since life began. Now we are destroying their principal habitat at the rate of 20 hectares every minute.

Because many important and valuable wild plants and plant communities are endangered, the World Wildlife Fund and the International Union for Conservation of Nature have launched an international programme for plant conservation – to save the plants that save us.

Contents

Foreword

The need for this book has never been greater. Never has it been more urgent or more important that the message it carries should be widely heard and understood. For what it makes marvellously and soberingly clear is the extent of our dependence upon plants.

Plants provide us with power. In many places, people burn them to cook their food and to keep themselves warm. Even in industrialised parts of the world, fossilised plants, in the form of coal and oil, give us most of the energy with which we run our machinery and illuminate our cities. Nearly half of all our drugs are based on substances that are derived from plants. Plants maintain the level of oxygen in the very air we breathe. And who can quantify the joy that their beauty brings to our spirits?

Indeed, animals could not exist without plants, for all – including humans – rely upon them for food. Even the lion that lives on antelope is eating plants, as it were, second-hand. As the Bible says, all flesh is grass. Putting that truth into different words, plants alone have the ability to combine atoms of carbon, oxygen, hydrogen and nitrogen and produce the complex molecules that are the building blocks of living tissue and the essential food of animals. So plants not merely sustain all forms of life, but continuously re-enact the ultimate and fundamental miracle of turning the non-living into the living.

Obvious though our dependence upon plants may be, we have, it seems, taken it for granted that they will continue to exist in all their variety no matter how we treat them and the land on which they grow. The initial concern of many conservation organisations was to protect rare animals. Maybe it was the very mobility of birds and mammals that first attracted our attention to them and diverted our care from the green organisms that remained stationary, rooted to the ground. But slowly, people began to realise that the survival of the animals about which they were concerned depended on the continued existence of plants – and, nearly always, upon particular kinds. If you want the yearly delight of butterflies in a garden, you must grow special things – buddleias and nettles, honeysuckle and bramble. And if you want to keep giant pandas, you have to grow bamboo!

Initially, the main problem seemed to be with preserving the butterfly and not the nettle, the panda, not the bamboo. Many plants, after all, can be kept as seeds in a packet, transported from one site to another by post if needs be, and brought to life by a little judicious watering. Surely *they* could not be endangered too. Now, to our cost, we know better.

No one is certain exactly how many different species of plant exist. A reasonable guess is that there are about a quarter of a million flowering plants alone. Two thirds of these grow in the tropics. Yet it is precisely there that their destruction is proceeding the fastest. We need no longer guess at how quickly that is happening. Satellites can show us only too clearly. The photographs they produce differentiate between forested and unforested land, and every year ten thousand square kilometres of trees are disappearing. Of the 80,000 species of plants growing in South America, only about 1 per cent have been examined to see what value they might have as food, or for medical or any other purpose. So, year after year, we are destroying species without even knowing what we are losing. All over the world, we are draining marshlands, felling mangrove forests, ploughing up grasslands, and spreading lethal plant poisons. Worldwide, there are, at the moment, about 25,000 species in imminent danger of extinction.

The World Wide Fund for Nature and the International Union for Conservation of Nature have decided to make a sustained effort to halt this devastation and are involved in a world-wide campaign to save the plants that save us.

selected from, among other sources, the rich library of drawings assembled by the premier Botanical Gardens in the world at Kew, in England; many of its facts have been supplied by research scientists belonging to the IUCN; and the whole has been put together by Anthony Huxley, a botanist who is as knowledgeable about the nature, distribution and value of plants as he is skilled in actually growing them, whose breadth of vision is matched by his invaluable ability to express the findings of his science in the simplest of words. You will not find here strings of those baffling adjectives – glabrous and glaucous, oblanceolate and indehiscent – to which so many botanists are attached and which so many non-botanists find such a barrier to comprehension. In chapter after revelatory chapter, Anthony Huxley unveils the beauty and wonder of the plant kingdom and shows just how intimately our lives are bound up with it. Perhaps his wisdom and his vision will at last persuade us to set about the task of protecting what he describes with such clarity. It will not be before time.

Each specialised habitat on earth has plants adapted to life there, like the cordgrass on this North Carolina saltmarsh.

The Green Inheritance

Plants are very familiar. They tend to be taken for granted and regarded with placid affection rather than with the fascination and interest they deserve. For most people they are part of the view, whether open country, farmland, or townscapes with street trees. Yet they are unique among the organisms with which we share this planet, for they alone contain the pigment chlorophyll which allows them to derive their energy from light. Outwardly, "They toil not, neither do they spin", but inwardly they are highly active and amazingly complex chemical-producing factories.

There is more than one view of plants. To the more comfortably off they include garden or park plants for leisure and pleasure, and the indoor pot plants which provide for town dwellers that contact with the green wild world that seems to be an instinctive need.

By contrast, many people in developing countries depend very heavily on plants, but look at them hardly at all from the standpoint of beauty or solace. Crops are there to be cultivated, often with extreme sweat and toil, and wild plants to be exploited directly. The overwhelming need for fuelwood and grazing for animals is frequently totally unselective.

We use plants in every field of life and have long ceased to rely on those native to our own area. The average Northerner has foods, products, and material contributed by plants from all over the world, many grown far from their original homelands – exotic hardwoods from the tropics for TV sets and tennis racquets, fruit and vegetables from around the world, insecticides from chrysanthemums, medicine from the Himalayan Opium Poppy or the Andean Coca, spices from the East, dyes from Asia, polishes from the jungle, toiletries from Jojoba, grown in the desert; pot plants from the tropics, oils from the Mediterranean Olive; Soya from Brazil; Cotton, Sisal, Rubber – the list is almost endless.

Not very long ago, the plant world seemed inexhaustible, always reasonably renewable. Today it is all too clear it is not. Nevertheless, we continue to wrench plants from the ground or destroy their environment and, whether for reasons of pressing immediate need or for greed, eradicate natural plant life as we do so. It is a sad fact that few people, whether the local tiller of soil or the modern entrepreneur, have any real regard for the world of plants, either for the plants' sake or for their own. The wild plant is in deep trouble; there is no mistaking that.

Numbers and Niches

Plants often surprise people by their diversity. Few people realise that there are as many as 380,000 different species – or kinds – of plants. There are many more plants, in fact, than higher animals: the vertebrates – animals with backbones – consist of 46,000 species of which about half are fish, about 4200 mammals and 8700 birds. But in contrast there are far fewer plants than invertebrates, of which a staggering 1.4 million have been described and many more await discovery.

The number of plant species in the world can only be an estimate rather than a known total. As new areas are explored, botanists continually find plants never seen before; one expert believes that there may be about 10,000 undiscovered plants in Central and South America. Indeed, for some parts of the world, knowledge of plants is still at a rudimentary level. For example, there is no book that describes or even lists the plants of Colombia despite the fact that it is one of the richest of all countries for plants. Botanists all over the world are working feverishly to catalogue and describe plants; as vegetation disappears it has become a race against time. In fact, whereas most of the plants grow in the tropics, most of the botanists live in the temperate realm where plant life is much less diverse and thus better known. However hard botanists work, many plants will inevitably become extinct before they have been seen and described, let alone saved for the future and screened for useful products.

Of the 380,000 species of plant, about 250,000 are "higher" plants in evolutionary terms. There are two main groups: the angiosperms ("enclosed-seeded") which include the flowering plants; and the much less numerous gymnosperms ("naked-seeded") which include the conifers and the more primitive, palm-like cycads.

Of the other 130,000, in order of evolutionary development, 10,000 are ferns, horsetails and clubmosses; 16,000 mosses and liverworts; 50,000 fungi; 18,000 lichens; and 25,000 algae, a group which includes seaweeds. The marine algae form an integral part of the sea's life-system, providing home and nutrition for huge numbers of organisms, and releasing no less than 70 percent of the world's atmospheric oxygen.

Some seaweeds are extraordinary, often having fronds 15 metres long, while the giant kelp, *Macrocystis pyrifera*, is reputed to reach 200 metres long, including its deep-fastened stem.

It is fascinating how all the stages in plant evolution – the different groups which reached standstill at various points on the evolutionary road before the flowering plants appeared – now exist together on the land surface, each occupying niches according to their capabilities. These often overlap – both ferns and orchids, for instance, co-exist as epiphytes on the trees of the tropical rainforest.

Which plants grow where is controlled by many factors including climate, temperature, light, water availability, soil composition and acidity. The botanist classifies the world's vegetation into a range of zones which reflect the local climate. In each a unique set of relationships is built up, the plants always forming the basis of each life-system or ecosystem, supporting all its diverse inhabitants. In few cases could animal life of any kind exist without plants, even temporarily.

In the bleak tundras, below freezing for much of the year, the primitives, lichens and algae covering bare rock surfaces, are the only plants close to the ice-caps; they also occur on high alpine rocks beyond the level of flowering plants. But in both arctic tundra and alpine zones below the bleakest levels grasses, sedges, herbaceous plants and dwarf shrubs thrive; the flowering plants demonstrating their adaptation to the environment by creeping flat on the ground or in cushions, with roots often extending widely in shifting scree or permeating rock crevices.

Throughout the different zones one can see plants specially adapted to each set of circumstances. In hot, moist, "lavish" climates tree leaves will be large. In cold climates, leaves are often small, needle-like and evergreen losing their moisture very slowly by having thick cuticles and breathing pores (stomata) in deep pits. These occur, for example, in the conifers of very cold forest zones with short growing seasons and in the characteristic heath forest of some tropical areas where soils are very poor and drain very freely, so that water conservation is equally essential. In Mediterranean climates, where the summers are hot and dry, leaves tend to be evergreen, small and leathery.

Some of the most obviously remarkable adaptations are found in arid semi-deserts. The cacti, almost all American, and the succulent spurges from Africa, have mostly abandoned leaves, transferring their duties of photosynthesis to the stems which have become enlarged into the typical sphere and cylinder shapes, those in which most water-retaining volume can be fitted into the least surface area capable of losing moisture by evaporation. Cacti and spurges form an example of parallel evolution – plants ancestrally quite different becoming superficially similar because they live in similar environments.

Most other succulents have not lost their leaves but have developed them into comparable swollen shapes. In one family, the mesembryanthemums of Southern Africa (Aizoaceae), one can trace a whole range of genera in which the fleshy leaves grow closer and closer together, finally reducing in number to three or four tight-packed pairs, a single pair, and a coalescent pair making a "plant body" as in the stone mimics (*Lithops, Conophytum* and so on). In this way the character of having separate leaves is transformed to resemble rounded cacti.

Each vegetation zone has its special needs and its unique set of relationships between different kinds of plant and between plants and animals. The most complex is undoubtedly that of the tropical rainforest which originally girdled the earth around the equator. Here there are often no marked seasons, and days and nights are roughly the same duration. Rainfall is large, often coming in prolonged drenchings, and fairly evenly spread through the year. Rainforests usually exist on a very shallow humus layer, almost all the vegetable matter – the biomass – being in trees and other plants. Among the trees, which occasionally reach a height of 60 metres, the variety of niches ranges from low shade-tolerating plants on the ground to the lianas which clamber towards the light, devoting minimum energy to supporting mechanisms, and the epiphytes which cluster on upper branches with no connection with the soil, clinging by aerial roots which absorb moisture from the air. Many larger-leaved plants are covered with a scurfy film of minute hanger-on plants called microphylls.

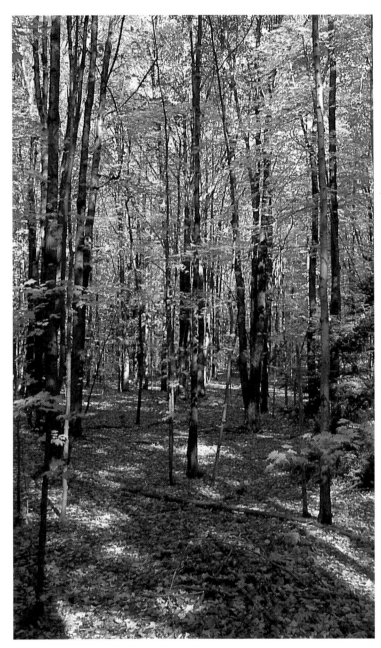

The Olympic peninsula at the north-west extremity of the United States has the most northerly example of temperate lowland rainforest, with average annual rainfall of 350 cm. Tall conifers and lesser deciduous trees are draped with mosses, clubmosses and ferns which thrive in the very humid conditions.

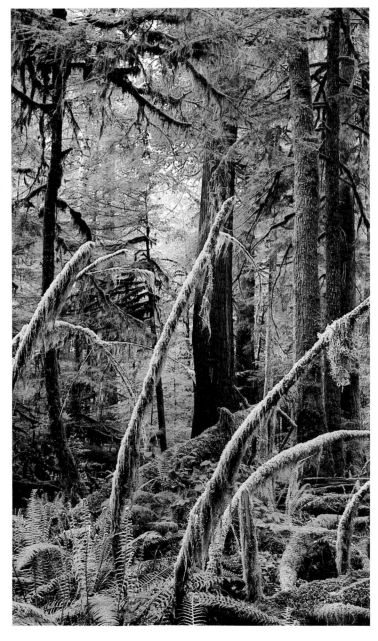

Many landscapes which we think of as natural have in fact been modified by past human activity. This New Hampshire woodland of oaks and maples has a different – poorer – mixture of species from its pristine composition because of selective cutting over the centuries.

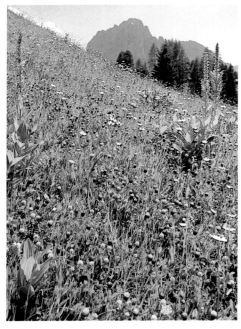

The characteristic high-altitude vegetation of the Northern Andes (over 3000 metres), called paramo, above, is composed of bunchgrass, sometimes with small bamboos, many small-leaved shrubs, and rosette plants like the espeletias which dominate this Colombian view. This natural plant complex can be compared with that of European mountains, near left, which are often modified by the grazing of domestic animals that are moved to the high grassy alps in summer, while in the lower reaches the lush meadows are cut for hay. However, the wild plants continue to thrive under these circumstances, in total contrast to terraced rice paddies as in Nepal, far left, where the original vegetation has been entirely removed and the topography transformed.

Distribution and Diversity

Plant species are unevenly spread over the land. In general terms there are far more in the tropics than in temperate regions. Of the estimated 250,000 species of flowering plant, 90,000 occur in Central and South America with 35,000 in Brazil alone; tropical Africa accounts for 30,000 and the island of Madagascar another 10,000. As one might expect, going north towards the Arctic reduces the number of species; Great Britain has only around 1,800, though Mediterranean Greece, five-eighths of its size, claims 6,000. Greece has a high proportion of endemics – plants found nowhere else – but perhaps the highest ratio is found in the Hawaiian Islands where 96 percent of plants are endemic. A great many plants are very local indeed, especially on islands or isolated mountains where independent evolution has continued, and these are often the most endangered.

Many such plants are, not surprisingly, highly adapted to a particular environment, but this does not always mean that, if transferred elsewhere, they will not grow happily. Many maligned plants have spread widely after transfer, usually as a result of being introduced to gardens as ornamental plants, like Bermuda Buttercup (*Oxalis pes-caprae*), Prickly Pear (*Opuntia*) and Water Hyacinth (*Eichhornia crassipes*), none of them particularly strong colonisers in their original habitats. Some introduced colonisers swamp and destroy native vegetation – Hawaii is in process of having its endemics choked by lantana: a staggering 822 species are in imminent danger of extinction, many reduced to a handful of individuals. Others spread rapidly as weeds of cultivation. Many such weeds can be said to be gifted with an innate ability to take advantage of the disturbed areas that follow cultivation, road building and the like. Such adaptability characterises other plants which are naturally widespread cosmopolitans, like bracken – one of the most powerful invaders of all kinds of terrain. A bracken plant seems immortal and immeasurable, spreading as it does from underground growth buds at a rate of one metre a year.

Since the world is full of vastly differing habitats for plants and climates in which they grow, it is not surprising that plants exhibit an equally vast range of form. Within the gymnosperms and flowering plants alone they range from the minute duckweed under a millimetre across, to huge forest trees; the tallest accurately recorded was a *Eucalyptus regnans* of 114 metres, though "Howard Libbey" is the tallest tree living today; it is a Coast Redwood growing in northern California and about 112 metres high. Flower size varies from the fraction of a millimetre of the duckweed to the near-metre of the parasite *Rafflesia*; seeds range from those of epiphytic orchids which weigh in at 1,000 million per gram to the Double Coconut, which can weigh 18 kilograms.

Even more remarkable are plant construction, metabolism, and specialised devices. Consider for instance the engineering which enables a tree to hold itself up and withstand all but the fiercest winds; the internal plumbing system that ensures that every part of the plant from the top down to the roots receives products of the photosynthetic energy generated in the leaves and, in reverse, that the leaves receive supplies of water, essential for photosynthesis, from the roots; the force needed to pump water up a 100-metre tree is enormous.

Above *Barley is one of the more remarkable of our cereal crops because, though originally a plant of arid lowlands in the Near and Middle East, it will thrive in mountain areas, as here in Nepal, into the Arctic, and even in saline desert conditions, often in places where other crops refuse to grow because of drought.*

Top *When unaffected by severe drought and both animal and human over-population, the African savannah, as seen here in Tsavo Park, Kenya, provides a perfect environment for a wide variety of creatures large and small. Dominated by acacia trees, the surrounding grassland becomes lush in the rainy seasons and dries up in between.*

Above *The Joshua Tree, a branching species of yucca, is characteristic of many North American deserts. Unlike the cacti with which it often grows – which have lost their leaves and developed fleshy water-retaining stems – the Joshua Tree protects itself against drying out by well-insulated, spiky leaves.*

17

Every plant is a chemical factory for complex substances which exceeds any human capability; even a bacterium can outperform us in this respect. In their seeds plants invented aerofoils aeons before the Wright Brothers; in their bulbous roots they were well ahead in devising winter larders. In their poisons, antibiotic agents, prickles and foul tastes, they developed defences against attack long before human stockades and pesticides. Their anti-exposure devices are manifold. The typical insulation is of hairs, often dense and furry, of waxy cuticle, or layers of lifeless, air-filled cells under the surface. The extraordinary giant lobelias of central African mountains have long woolly leaf bracts which fold over the developing shoot or flowerhead at night. In addition, the shoot tip is itself surrounded by a liquid; at night the top 2-3 cm of this freezes, but around the shoot tip the liquid remains just over freezing point. The nearby Tree Groundsels protect their trunks by retaining their old leaves, as a dense layer of lagging.

Bark is the standard insulator for trees, sometimes thick and corky, as in the Cork Oak, to combat heat and dryness, or in the Hawaiian Ohia Lehua which resists red-hot cinders from volcanic eruption. A dramatic example is Giant Sequoia (*Sequoiadendron giganteum*) from California: its branches start 60 metres from the ground, so when forest fires rage below, its 60cm thick bark keeps it unaffected.

It is because plants cannot run away from their predators that they have had to develop convincing deterrents: all manner of spines and thorns; the stinging hairs of nettles which resemble a hypodermic syringe in action; saw teeth on leaves; bitter or blistering sap; and leaf cuticles reinforced with abrasive silica. A few plants protect themselves by mimicry, notably the many kinds of "living stones" in South Africa, resembling the pebbles in which they grow, brown, grey, or white and quartzy. Other succulents, like some *Anacampseros*, look like nothing more than bird droppings.

Some plants have taken to eating meat: Butterworts and Sundews have sticky surfaces or tentacles which trap and enfold insects. Venus' Flytrap (*Dionaea*) has a pair of spine-edged pads with sensitive hairs in the centre – an insect tripping them is instantaneously shut in and then digested. *Nepenthes* and *Sarracenia* have pitchers with an attractive odour, barbed hooks and slippery edges at the top, and a reservoir of digestive fluid at the base. All these plants live in nitrogen-deficient habitats like bogs and need flesh to supplement their diet.

The movement of the Venus' Flytrap is one of the fastest in the vegetable world, but many plants can move some of their organs in response to stimulus. Most familiar is Sensitive Plant, whose leaves and stems collapse at a touch. Plants with tendrils move these around supports very rapidly when contact is made. To aid pollination some plants have moving stamens or other devices in the flower.

Pollination provides the most numerous and amazing, highly-tuned devices for ensuring that an insect, bat, bird or, sometimes, small mammal transfers pollen from one flower to another. Odours are the most obvious bait – not just the sweet ones which typically attract bees and moths but, to us, odious ones for insects like flies. Stapelias and their kin smell of decay and their lurid red, brown and yellow tones resemble rotting meat; some even have hairs to mimic mould. Flowers which attract bats for pollination have strong odours, typically musty, fishy or foxy.

Plants of several distinct families have become flesh-eaters, an adaptation to living in nitrogen-deficient conditions such as boggy or peaty areas, and so needing to balance their diet. The tropical pitcher plants of the genus Nepenthes are climbers; the pitchers are developments of the tendrils at the leaf ends. Nectar at the edge of the pitcher attracts insects; down-pointing barbs over ice-smooth inner walls help insects down but prevent any escape, so that they fall into an enzyme-rich digestive liquid at the pitcher's base. Biggest of all is Nepenthes rajah; its capacity is 2 litres – big enough to contain a pigeon! Nepenthes are widely cultivated though some are endangered in nature.

An extreme of the evolutionary process is shown by the many plants which parasitise others. The dodders, which often infest large trees in the tropics, germinate normally in soil, but once they have found a host, plunge sinkers or "haustoria" into its tissues and lose their own roots. All their nourishment is then derived from the host, their own leaves being reduced to scales.

The African succulent stapelias are called carrion flowers because they simulate rotting meat in order to attract the blowflies which pollinate them. They have the lurid colours and odour of decay, and many carry fine hairs which move in air currents and mimic moulds. Flies are often so thoroughly deceived that they even lay their eggs on the blooms.

The leaves and stems of the Sensitive Plant, (Mimosa pudica) collapse at a touch at a rate of about 3 cm per second from the point of contact – perhaps to discourage browsing animals, which see their lunch disappearing as they brush it. At night the plant folds its leaves into a "sleep" position – a habit shared with a number of other plants, the purpose of which is unclear.

The leaves of the giant waterlily, Victoria amazonica, are a wonderful example of plant engineering. Underneath they have an array of girder-like radial and transverse ribs which keep the two-metre-wide surface rigid and, since they contain air spaces, afloat. A big leaf can support a child's weight. Large prickles on the underside probably deter predatory watersnails.

The orchids are the most highly adapted plants of all in this respect, one species usually pollinated by a single species of insect. The huge lip of the Bucket Orchid (*Coryanthes*) is, literally, a squarish bucket with a trough-like spout filled with liquid from special glands. Its edges are edible and highly attractive to bees, which become inebriated; they fall into the bucket, from which the only escape is under a rod-shaped organ bearing pollen on its stigmatic surface. The Mediterranean bee orchids, *Ophrys*, are pollinated by male wasps because they smell, look and feel like female wasps – the males "pseudocopulate" with the orchid, deceiving themselves but achieving success for the flower.

Plants which Serve Us

Plants are remarkable, then, in their own right – as objects for study, to amaze us the more we learn about their lifestyle. Many are prized for their beauty and cultivated accordingly; others have innumerable utilitarian applications which technology shows no sign of superseding.

Every year, our farmers have to find food for more people; our forests have to provide more timber and fuel; our chemists have to supply more medicines; our industrialists need more raw materials to meet human needs and demands. Unless the population stabilises, which on present projections may not happen before the twenty-second century, and some kind of equilibrium is reached, this battle to squeeze ever more out of the living world will intensify year by year. And right in the firing line are the plants – the green inheritance on which we, and all animal life, depends.

Some plants are pre-eminently valuable. The Cotton plant, *Gossypium*, (opposite) is a striking example of the "multipurpose" plant, and other members of its family, Malvaceae, demonstrate how many surprising uses they have. This, the Mallow family, includes familiar garden plants like Hollyhocks (*Althaea*), Hibiscus and various mallows. A great many of these have strong stems which produce fibres of various qualities, some fine, some as strong as Jute. They contain mucilaginous substances which make them valuable in soothing medicines (Hollyhock flowers, for instance) and also in sweetmeats of various kinds; marshmallow is an ancient confection which used to be made from the root of *Althaea officinalis*.

We easily forget how often we use plants. Cotton is just one example. In Norman Myers' words, we benefit from plant materials every time we apply a shampoo or sunscreen lotion, paint a wall or varnish a table; every time we use a golf ball or jet engine or oil-drilling equipment; every time the dentist makes a mould of our teeth or the doctor gives us a vaccination. The plant kingdom is truly a part of our industrial and social jungle.

The Web of Life

The richest web of life, the greatest concentration of species, is found in the world's rainforests like those of Amazonia. Plants are the rainforest's fabric: a great assemblage of trees, ground-living plants, epiphytes perched higher up, and lianas bridging the gap between floor and crown.

To most of us cotton is just a fibre, useful for all kinds of thread, clothing and fabric. About 95 percent of world cotton production is taken from the seed fibres of Gossypium hirsutum – a medium-long-staple species grown mainly in the USA and USSR. The extra-long-staple G. barbadense, from Egypt and the Sudan, is shown being harvested here. The short-staple G. herbaceum and G. arboreum, accounting for only about one percent, come from India and Pakistan. The fibre has many uses: for cordage, carpets and rubberised fabrics, and as cotton wool, used both in surgical dressings and cosmetic cleansing. The wool is the sterilised fibre cleared of its natural oiliness.

And fibre is not the limit of the plant's usefulness. The seeds are rich in oil for cooking, salad oils and lard substitutes, for margarine, soap and soap powders. The oil cake left after the oil has been pressed is valuable for cattle fodder, fertiliser and as a dyestuff. The seed cases or hulls also have many uses; fodder and fertiliser again, but also as a basis for explosives and alcohol, and in lining oil wells. The stems, if not burnt for fuel, are fibrous enough for paper-making. The root bark has medicinal properties including that of stemming bleeding. The flowers are a good source of honey and, in India, a yellow or brown dye is obtained from the petals.

Even today, the Cotton plant may not have exhausted its repertoire: its seeds may be able to supply us with the elusive "contraceptive for men" (p. 123).

In the dim world under the layers of vegetation insects are to be found everywhere, from the microscopic to the great cockroaches and brightly coloured beetles; often of weird shape or mimicking leaves, twigs, thorns, seeds or bird droppings. Bees and fierce wasps make large colonial nests. Others like the mantis prey on their relatives, while spiders lurk at every point and level, trapping, snaring or pouncing and culminating in the enormous hairy bird-eaters. Apart from midges and mites which can madden the human visitor, butterflies are prominent – great blue Morphos flitting slowly, others shaped more like dragonflies, some with almost transparent wings. Their caterpillars, and those of moths, feed on the leaves; their adults help to pollinate the trees' flowers.

Ants are everywhere, from large, aggressive army ants to smaller leaf-cutters carrying pieces of leaf from selected trees for hundreds of yards in endless streams, to underground caverns where they grow fungi on leaf compost to eat. Termites (similar in appearance to ants but biologically closer to cockroaches) are concealed in large nests of chewed wood and saliva up the tree trunks, travelling to soil level via tunnels to feed on debris. Together with the innumerable fungi, they are the most important agents of decay in the forest and are responsible for the release of plant nutrients back into the system.

In their turn insects are meat for small rodents, lizards, frogs and birds. Birds are surprisingly difficult to see but they are there in plenty; puffbirds and jacamars catching butterflies on the wing, and antbirds on tree-trunks or on the ground, while hummingbirds suck nectar high up in the flowering canopy. Fruits and nuts are consumed by huge-beaked toucans, gaudy macaws and other parrots, all adapted with short wings for inter-tree flying and equipped with pincer-like feet for clambering. High up there may be primitive, ungainly hoatzins, a bit like pheasants, which eat aroid leaves; heavy fruit-eating curassows which clamber up trees before gliding down again; and, on the ground, flocks of aptly named trumpeters. With extra luck one may see a number of brilliant gold male cock-of-the-rock leaping and bobbing to attract mates.

Bats are mainly (apart from the blood-sucking vampires) fruit and nectar eaters. The teeth and muscular tongue of the Corollia enable it to crush every bit of goodness from a fruit and then to spit out skin and seeds to help dispersal. Pollination is helped by such species as the long-tailed bat which sucks nectar from flowers: such bat-encouraging blooms are large and sturdy, as indeed they must be to stand up to the weight of the bats hooking on to them to feed.

Birds of prey, notably the spectacled owl and the huge harpy eagle, mainly attack the tree-inhabiting mammals. Most spectacular of these are the monkeys – small chattering capuchins, woolly, spider and well-named howler monkeys, all with prehensile tails (unlike monkeys in most other parts of the world) which enable them to spend almost all their time in the airy branches. Here too are furry little kinkajous, feeding on fruits or honey, and tree porcupines eating fruits and leaves: both have the invaluable prehensile "fifth limb".

High in the trees live the various sloths, hanging upside-down and motionless much of the time, camouflaged by green algae growing on their damp hair; they come to the ground only to defecate. The related dwarf anteater is almost as sluggish. Like the larger tamandua it has a prehensile tail and feeds by scratching out ant and termite colonies.

Many warm-blooded creatures forage on the ground – small deer, tapir, peccary, giant anteater, and the herbivorous rodents, agouti and paca. These search variously for roots and tubers or for the multifarious life in the leaf litter – insects, molluscs, worms and crustaceans. Coatis, their groups up to forty-strong, are omnivorous, eating animals and fruits, and scrambling in the lower branches as well.

These foragers, as well as birds, lizards – anything for a mouthful – are sought by carnivorous cats – ocelot, margay and jaguar, this last dropping silently out of the trees onto its prey. Jaguar will also fish, using its tail as a lure. Tayra and grison also attack; they are sometimes tamed by Indians to flush out agoutis. Packs of the stumpy bush dog hunt the large rodents too.

The giant anaconda is yet another hazard to mammals, while the emerald tree boa eats smaller prey such as young birds. Both kill by strangulation; venomous snakes are few. Smaller kinds creep up the trees, pouncing on insects, lizards and frogs.

Frogs are mostly small and often brightly coloured, like the viridian arrow-poison frog which, after its eggs hatch, transports its tadpoles on its back to the safety of the water reservoir of an epiphytic bromeliad. In these "urn plants" or "tank epiphytes" there is indeed an amazing miniature ecosystem. Tiny crabs and mosquito larvae feed on protozoa in the water and dragonfly larvae feed on these. Carnivorous bladderwort plants often establish themselves in the water reservoir. Beside the frogs – some of which spend their entire lives within one plant – snails, worms and salamanders appreciate the moist shelter, and these are prey for birds and mouse opossums as well as large insects attracted by the water.

It is a sobering thought that when the jungle is destroyed hundreds of species of birds, bats and large animals, and tens of thousands of insects and other small creatures, disappear forever. Without the ambience of the forest they cannot survive.

The jungle took millenia to develop; a tree can be destroyed in minutes. Important and fascinating as it is, however, the jungle is but a part of our green inheritance. This – the genius of evolution and plant survival strategies, and the genius of thousands of human generations – is the capital on which we live today. The bowl of rice on your table is a gift of the ancestral wild rice, of the centuries of rice growers, of the skills of modern botanists, of the disease-resistance of a wild relative recently "borrowed", of the work of soil micro-organisms. What should we do for rice today if the first wild rice ancestors had been ploughed under by a bulldozer to make way for a neanderthal holiday resort?

We have loved plants, and sometimes worshipped them, all through history. Far more than animals, plants have been symbols of the earth's life force and have provided solace to the human race. Yet we are squandering this inheritance in ignorance, in thoughless impatience and greed, failing to appreciate either the beauty or the value of what we destroy. The aim of this book is to show, before it is entirely too late, just how rewarding our green inheritance is to mankind, what potential it has, how it cannot take much more punishment, and seek to ways to save what remains.

Hot sulphurous springs in Yellowstone National Park are colonised by brilliantly coloured bacteria.

Guardians of the Environment

Plants are continuously active, by day conjuring the food they need out of sunlight, water, and gases around them, like magicians pulling rabbits out of a hat; by night and day, using the stored energy for growth and life. This miracle of living alchemy is called photosynthesis. Without it, virtually all life on this planet would cease.

In essence, a plant taps the energy of sunlight to make carbohydrate out of carbon dioxide gas and water. The plant then uses this carbohydrate for energy, and as a building material to synthesise proteins, fats, and all the complex chemicals of life, drawing also on minerals in the soil.

Plants are self-sufficient, able to colonise new terrains and survive by photosynthesis, where animals could not. They were the first organisms to emerge on dry land, in the course of evolution. In the Arctic, the algae are the first colonisers of rocks and debris, their slime creating a toehold for other microscopic organisms. Multicoloured single-celled algae grow on snow; at the other extreme, blue-green algae can live in temperatures of up to $35°C$. Plants, too, are the first recolonisers of damaged, hostile environments, from devastated wasteland to natural salt land and lava flow. Of all the benefits plants can bring, perhaps the greatest is the potential to repair the harm we have already done.

Plants produce food: animals consume it. Without plants, animal life could not exist. The range of plants, from single-celled algae to great forest trees, is food for vast numbers of creatures in the sea and on land; these creatures are themselves food for carnivores. This is the food web we all understand, with humanity at its centre, omnivorous but relying to a large degree on food derived directly from plants. At each point up the chain, there is a great drop in the number of organisms: one whale depends on millions of krill; one person eats the bounty of perhaps millions of plants and thousands of animals in a life-time.

Plants provide the fabric of our landscape, the home for all animal life. In the era before human dominance, natural vegetation flourished as a green tapestry over the earth, endlessly varying from tall forest to waving grassland, from tropical savanna to arctic tundra, reflecting changes in climate, soil and terrain. It formed a natural security blanket on the surface of the earth, helping to maintain the balance of gases in the air and nutrients in the soil, stabilising climate, river flows and soil cover.

Guardians of Air, Climate, and Soil

While busily converting carbon dioxide and water to carbohydrate, plants give out oxygen, a by-product to the plant but essential to all human and animal life. (Interestingly, over 70% of the oxygen in the atmosphere is produced by sea algae, mostly microscopic plant-plankton.) They also catch carbon, returning some to the air, but passing some into food chains, and also into the soil.

Another vital element, nitrogen, makes up almost four-fifths of the air. As a gas, however, nitrogen is unavailable to plants. It is brought into their life cycle mostly by microbial organisms; some of these fix nitrogen and synthesise nitrogenous compounds in symbiotic association with certain plants – mostly legumes. When such plants and bacteria die other bacteria convert their protein to compounds of ammonium, which can be absorbed by plant roots from the soil solution to build up their proteins.

In addition to nitrogen, plants take phosphorus and potassium from the soil – the N, P, K of the fertiliser packs – as well as calcium, magnesium, and trace elements. These then find their way into the food chains and, via decomposers, back to the soil.

We have always taken for granted these services of plants in maintaining the "life-support systems" of the planet. Plants are life-givers: it was the emergence of green plants, long ago, that gave us the air we breathe – the primeval atmosphere would poison present-day organisms. Our oxygen-bearing atmosphere was a by-product of early photosynthesis, mainly by marine algae; these ocean plants still provide the bulk of our oxygen. All plants are involved in maintaining constant oxygen and carbon dioxide levels, their ceaseless exchange of these gases playing its part in the global cycling of gases between air, ocean, rocks and soil.

Throughout evolutionary history, temperatures on our earth have remained generally favourable to life (if less comfortable during Ice Ages). The level of carbon dioxide in the air has provided one form of temperature control; the gas acts as an insulating blanket, trapping much of the heat energy radiated from the earth, which would otherwise be lost to space. Water vapour in the air is important too. Plants assist in the cycling of water through soil and air, transpiration from their leaves providing humidity which encourages rain – over the great moist tropical forests, clouds can be seen gathering, to stop short where the lush greenery ends. Plant and cloud cover affect the earth's "albedo", a measure of its shininess or tendency to reflect sunlight (and heat) back into space – another temperature control.

Today, the world's green mantle is disappearing fast; forests are felled, erosion spreads. One has only to enter a barren area to realise what the immediate consequences may be. In plantless lands, the sun beats down, reflecting back from the bare ground; at night, temperatures plummet,

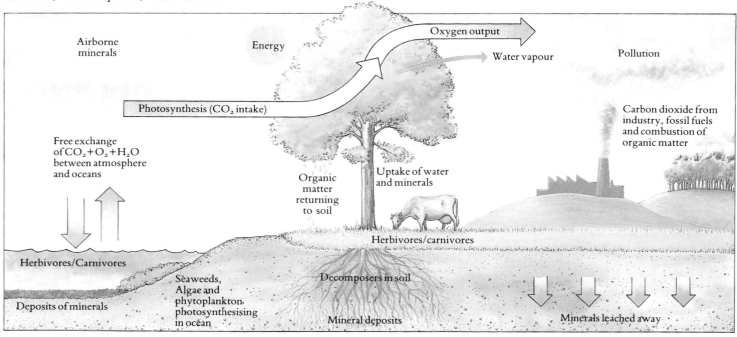

since no heat is retained. The air is extraordinarily dry, and so is the soil; it rarely rains, and when it does the unprotected soil is rapidly washed away. Such conditions are inimical to life. Although many deserts are natural and some are very beautiful, loss of vegetation, through overgrazing and other human pressures, is more and more often a prime cause of desertification. As plant cover goes, climates change and soil is eroded.

If the forests are lost, a link in the carbon cycle is weakened because, in their photosynthesis, plants catch carbon. Carbon dioxide levels in the air are rising; they have increased from 300 to 330 parts per million during this century so far, and may top 376 ppm by the end of it. (Combustion of fossil fuels is a major source, but some scientists suggest that burning of tropical forests is significant too.) It is argued that this may lead to a rise in the earth's temperature – the so-called "greenhouse effect" – causing the world's climate zones to shift, perhaps making some equatorial regions uninhabitable, and melting the polar ice-caps. This would radically shift the food-producing areas of the world, and drown low-lying coasts including many great cities. Ultimately, the newly enlarged oceans might reflect so much more sunlight back into space that long-term cooling would set-in, and an Ice Age might follow.

Even if this greenhouse effect never materializes, changes in the planetary albedo caused by deforestation and desertification may upset temperature control. Loss of forests causes loss of cloud cover, which accounts for three quarters of global albedo value. Desertification increases reflection considerably; this may in turn create greater stability in the atmosphere, and hence reduced rainfall. In total, perhaps 17 percent of the land has been modified in terms of albedo. Various climatic models predict a 1° cooling of the planet from human handiwork, including atmospheric pollution.

We know too little about the incredibly complex, inter-related mechanisms of atmosphere, climate, and plants to resolve such conflicting theories. We do know, however, that human modifications of plant cover already have significant effects. Cutting down forest in Brazil not only reduces rainfall locally but also affects the unnatural spread of deserts in nearby Peru. How far the effect reaches is not known, but some concern is expressed for the US grain belt. We should be very cautious in what we do.

Plants stabilise the atmosphere and climate: they also create and protect the soil, perhaps our most precious resource. Soil is a mixture of mineral particles and humus. Mineral particles are largely made available by weathering of rock by heat, cold and water, especially acidic or fast-running water; plants help this process only in a small way. Humus on the other hand results from the decomposition of organic matter (both vegetable and animal). It is jelly-like, coating the soil particles, swelling when wet and shrinking when dry; it stabilises soil structure, holds water, but allows air to percolate. It contains all the soil's reserves of nitrogen and holds many other essential nutrients.

Roots of plants both secure them in position and absorb nutrients; questing through the earth, they create channels valuable for drainage and aeration, and may tap minerals and water from layers of rock below. The amount of minerals required by different plants varies enormously. In the rain forests, epiphytic orchids, bromeliads and ferns live high on the trees, with very little mineral supply at all; cacti and succulents, by contrast, inhabit semi-deserts where the proportion of humus is minute, but the quantity of minerals is large. Plants, it seems, can grow anywhere; no matter how impoverished, imbalanced, or toxic a soil, plants will be found there with leaves, root structure and chemistry tailored to fit.

Roots of desert plants typically spread widely and shallowly to benefit from dew (it has been said that, if turned root-side-up, a desert would appear fully inhabited), though some have long taproots which penetrate to deep underground water. Many desert trees do the same – Tamarisk roots have been recorded (during the building of the Suez Canal) to the depth of 50m. In temperate dunes, grasses with long creeping stems bind the sand. On tropical mudflats, mangroves grow stilt roots for stability.

In cacti and many other succulents, leaves have vanished, to be replaced by spines. The growing of spines, thorns or prickles is a common response of trees and shrubs in arid places – savannas, Mediterranean low scrub, and Asiatic steppe. Loss or reduction of leaves curtails water loss by transpiration; spines also act as a measure of insulation against the sun, help to collect dew, and discourage grazing animals. Plants of salty dunes and pebble beaches, by contrast, may be fleshy, like the aptly named Saltwort, and the Sea Rocket. These plants adapted to very difficult substrates – deserts, salt-lands, dunes or coasts – are obviously of great value: their guardianship of fragile lands is vital (p.36). Equally fragile, however, are the soils of the tropical rainforest, for all their lush greenery and year-round growth.

In northern Europe, and in much of North America, most of the lowland forests have long been cut down. In their place are rich productive farmlands and, where prairie agriculture has not taken over, a pleasant and sustainable landscape. In contrast, however, when landless peasants from the poverty-stricken north-east corner of Brazil move thousands of miles

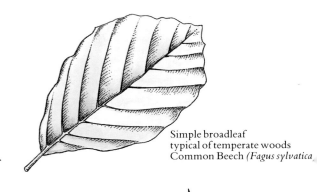

Simple broadleaf typical of temperate woods Common Beech *(Fagus sylvatica*

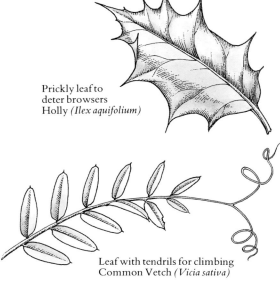

Prickly leaf to deter browsers Holly *(Ilex aquifolium)*

Leaf with tendrils for climbing Common Vetch *(Vicia sativa)*

Left *Leaves and root systems may be integrated to ensure maximum efficiency. In the Caladium, far left, the absorptive rootlets grow just below the points of the outward-sloping leaves where rain drips. By contrast Rhubarb leaves slope inwards and channel the water to the central root-stock from which the rootlets emerge.*

Insectivorous leaf to
supplement nutrients
Venus Flytrap
(*Dionaea muscipula*)

Cup-shaped reservoir
formed by leaf bases
Bromeliad (*Vriesea*)

Jungle drip-tip
to shed water
(*Philodendron hastatum*)

False leaves, actually
modified stems with
flowers Butcher's Broom
(*Ruscus aculeatus*)

Leaves much reduced
to prevent moisture loss
(*Casuarina*)

Trample-tolerant, flattened
rosette with thick parallel ribs
Plantain (*Plantago major*)

Waxy succulent leaves
to conserve moisture
Stone crop (*Sedum anglicum*)

Water-repellent with pores
only on upper surface
Yellow Waterlily (*Nuphar lutea*)

into the depths of the Amazon forest, clear a few hectares and start to grow crops, disaster often ensues: the plants barely grow, what does is eaten by plagues of insects, and torrents of rain wash away the thin soil. They find that a tropical forest without its trees is not a lush paradise but an unproductive and hostile place.

Of course, this stark contrast is not universal; but it is a common enough experience to create a great political dilemma. What right, the policy-maker in South America may say, have western experts to advise him not to fell his forests? After all, they have felled theirs over the centuries and are now happy and prosperous! Western concern over deforestation can seem like a move to retain economic dominance. The consequences of this dilemma may be political, but its causes are biological.

Forests and their Soils

The typical forest in a temperate country is usually on deep soil, which allows the tree roots to penetrate far down. There is plenty of leaf litter, which forms the humus. Under the newest, dry leaves there is a deep fine nutritious layer that readily supports small plants. Under the litter the soil is

29

Above *In the tropical rainforest the layer of nutritious organic matter produced by leaf litter is extremely shallow, for its decomposition is hastened in the hot humid conditions. The weathered rock below is devoid of mineral nutrients, so roots do not penetrate it, as the picture shows.*

Right *Tropical forests contain a great diversity of species, often arranged in more or less distinct "storeys" according to size and the amount of light needed. Individuals of each species may be very widely spaced out, perhaps only one or two occurring per hectare. The diagram represents an area 75 metres square.*

rich in minerals, left by the Ice Ages: either glaciers brought plenty of newly weathered particles, or old soils became well mixed with rock particles as ice froze and thawed within it. In tropical rainforest, by contrast, trees do not need deep or extensive roots – they get ample nutrition from the decomposing leaf litter on the ground, and sufficient moisture through their leaves. Beneath the litter is often found sand or clay. Unweathered rocks usually exist only at considerable depth, and most mineral content has been leached away.

Although leaf fall is virtually continuous, the layer of decomposing matter is shallow – heat and moisture accelerate the process of decomposition by fungi, microscopic animals and termites. The trees glean all the nutrients they can from the layer of decomposing litter, very little from further down, and hold the nutrients within themselves. Every bit of litter which drops is almost immediately sucked up again by this vast tropical vacuum cleaner. In effect the tropical forest is a closed, nearly leak-proof system, millions of years old. Almost all the phosphorus, for example, is held in the vegetation rather than the soil, compared to half and half in a temperate oak wood; a good third of the nitrogen, as against a tiny fraction; and nearly half the magnesium, as against a sixth. Burning or felling the trees thus removes far more of the nutrients in the ecosystem than it does in a temperate forest.

In fact the fertile soil layer itself is so shallow that, without the trees, tropical downpours may remove it entirely, within one or two seasons. Gullies and serious erosion follow. The weathered rock particles, once exposed, can become like cement, forming an impervious layer of hard rock, called laterite. The peasant loses his crop; the forest may not be able to regenerate, especially if large areas have been cleared. Even if it does, it will not contain the species diversity of the original forest. This, greatly simplified, is the tragedy of tropical deforestation.

Guardians of Diversity

The rainforest vegetation found throughout the tropics is amazingly complex. For one thing, there is usually no particular plant that predominates. A hectare and a half of Malayan forest, for example, has been found to contain 227 kinds of tree – but there might be only one or two individuals of a species. A similar area in deciduous woodland in Michigan could contain as few as 10 species, but many individuals of each: in coniferous forest near the Arctic Circle, it might contain one tree species only.

A second level of complexity derives from the vast quantities of plants and the diversity of ways in which they exist. For support the trees may have stilt roots in wigwam arrangement; curiously enough many of these lose the original central stem of the seedling tree when they grow to any size. The alternative method of support is the buttress root. If one sees an uprooted buttressed tree, it is astonishing to observe how its feeding roots jut down from these buttresses for as little as 50 cm. Many other trees have no such architecture and are supported by each other. If a transect is cut through the forest, the ordinary thin-trunked trees just fall over into it: their roots have no anchoring capacity.

Most rainforest trees have such shallow root systems that they effectively support each other. Some have special ways of ensuring stability: they may have stilt roots produced from the lower part of the trunk, as shown above, or thin, wide-spreading flange-like buttresses, below. These dramatic buttresses send down thin vertical feeding roots, only 50-100 cm long, into the shallow soil layer.

Right *Epiphytes of the tropical rainforest include many orchids like the Brazilian Maxillaria picta. They cling to tree branches with aerial roots and absorb sufficient moisture through these from the air, and debris which accumulates around them, which will include nutrient minerals. Water reserves are held in the fleshy "pseudobulbs" at the base of the leaves.*

Below *A curiosity of tropical jungles is the strangler. A number of different trees are involved. Their seed germinates in the debris-filled crown of the "host"; as it grows the strangler sends down roots which eventually reach the ground and thicken, often meshing together around the host's trunk. Eventually this prevents the latter expanding and will choke it to death.*

Below *Rainforest vegetation can occur at altitudes from sea level to mountains, as in this Andean example at about 3000 metres; at such high altitudes it may be known as cloud forest. High air humidity is common to both, encouraging epiphytes and ferns as seen here, together with fungi which play an essential part in the forest's life cycle by decomposing dead vegetation into humus.*

Above *Bromeliads like vrieseas — relatives of the pineapple — are found on trees and cliffs in areas ranging from very hot to quite cold in much of South and Central America. They are mostly epiphytes with minimal roots for attachment, and a unique system for ensuring water supplies — the leaves form a central reservoir in which rain collects, with special water-absorbing cells at their bases.*

The rainforest contains some very large trees, maybe 50 metres tall, and varying layers, or storeys, not always clearly defined, of lesser trees below. The tallest trees are called emergents, and between them the space is filled by the wide crowns of the main canopy trees. A layer of smaller trees, or youngsters of the taller ones, is typically found at around a quarter of the height of the emergents. There is then a shrub layer – some seedling trees, but mostly mature low-growing species adapted to the reduced light; around them will be herbaceous plants of many kinds.

Within this deep forest the level of air humidity increases fourfold from top to floor; but wind, rainfall, and temperature (and temperature fluctuation) are at their lowest on the floor, and greatest above the canopy.

Climbing plants germinate on the floor and ascend the trees in various ways. Thin-stemmed species like philodendrons attach themselves to trunks with aerial roots (just like ivy in temperate climates). Once into the canopy, they send down vertical aerial roots which absorb moisture from the air and finally anchor themselves in the ground. The lianas (like temperate clematis) have thick stems, sometimes round but more often flattened, twisted, or pierced and ladder-like; they twine round trunks and branches. In the Far East, there are rattans or climbing palms with downward-pointing spines to prevent the thin, upward-thrusting stems from slipping down; they are like the giant clambering roses of the Himalayas.

The converse of the climber is the strangler. These are trees – the familiar houseplant *Ficus benjamina* is one – which will grow in debris in another tree crown, if their seeds have germinated there, and send down roots that eventually reach the ground. Criss-crossing round the trunk of the host tree, these roots coalesce and thicken, and literally prevent the host from expanding its trunk, while the strangler's leaves crowd out the host's. After a century or so, the host dies and decays, to leave just the woody cylinder of the strangler's root system its sole support.

On the spreading upper branches of the canopy trees especially there will be a dense growth of ferns, orchids, bromeliads and other epiphytic plants, content with a limited amount of moisture absorbed from the air and in debris which accumulates around their fixative aerial roots. Some grow lower down, notably great ferns like the "birdsnests" and "stagshorns".

Lichen, mosses and algae colonise all levels of the forest, treating tree trunk and rock the same. And everywhere on the floor, growing on fallen leaves and tree trunks, there will be fungi in an amazing array of form and colour. They serve to break the dead matter back into its constituents, to feed both the old inhabitants of the forest and equally the young seedlings emerging and hoping for a break (in both senses of the word) so that they can reach the desired light level without being choked.

Kapok (Ceiba pentandra) is an important component of both old and new world tropical forests, especially in areas where there is a dry period; the forest type (in contrast to that of the savanna) is a large tree with buttress roots. The seeds are surrounded by very light fibre, at one time of considerable commercial importance but now partly replaced by synthetics.

Guardians of the Water Cycle

People have cut down the trees around them for a very long time. The civilisations of Mesopotamia and the Indus Valley foundered because of excessive deforestation. In Greece, in the fourth century BC Plato wrote that "Compared with what it was, our land is like the skeleton of a body wasted by disease. The plump soft parts have vanished, and all that remains

Trees on mountain watersheds safeguard the soil on the steep slopes by binding it with their roots, and absorb most of the rainfall. If the trees are cut, or killed by excessive tapping for resin, this guardianship of the terrain is entirely lost. Soil is washed away, rain gouges out ravines, exposing the underlying rock, causing landslides, and creating all the horrors of erosion in valleys lower down, as in this all too typical scene in the highlands of Nepal.

In India floods caused by deforestation in the Himalayas mean that an estimated 6,000 million tonnes of soil containing a million tonnes of nutrients are lost every year. The 1979 monsoon did over two billion dollars worth of damage: in Bihar, West Bengal and Uttar Pradesh 3,000 people and at least 200,000 cattle were killed by floods, and the following drought destroyed 35 million hectares of crop land. Loss of India's forests is now a major political issue.

is the bare carcase''. Whatever the reasons behind the present accelerating rate of forest clearance, the removal of the trees usually demonstrates how essential they are – or have been – as guardians of the environment. Trees safeguard the soil on the steep slopes of mountain watersheds, where rivers have their sources. Cut the trees and the soil is washed away off the underlying rock, sometimes gouging deep ravines. Landslides occur. The water rushes into rivers which cannot contain the sudden onslaught and overspill their banks downstream. When the floods eventually subside, there can be long periods when the rivers are dry, for the slow-releasing sponge of the forests is no longer there to trickle moisture into the streams.

In China disastrous floods in 1981 killed thousands of people and made one and a half million homeless. Deforestation of the upper reaches of the Yangtse River was publicly acknowledged as the cause of the tragedy. Surveys indicate that the huge volume of silt being washed down from the denuded hillsides is blocking the major artery, making flood prevention schemes useless, impeding navigation and destroying irrigation.

Trees intercept and hold water. Moist air is continuously produced over them, clouds form, rain regularly falls. Estimates for the proportion of water vapour recycled in rainforests range from 15 to 75 percent. What is becoming apparent is that without the forest, rainfall becomes reduced. At Mahabeleshwar, south of Bombay, where the surrounding hills have been severely logged, annual rainfall has decreased from 1000 cm a year to a little over 600 cm, and the pleasantly warm summers have become oppressively hot. When virgin forest was originally cut in Malaysia to plant rubber, rain clouds were seen to stop precisely at the edge of the tall forest and left the young rubber plantations dry.

The rainforests occupy a large part of the tropics (30 percent of the land area of the 20° equatorial belt lies in the Amazon region, for instance), and the air masses associated with them are globally very important. Upsetting their hydrological balance is likely to cause world-wide disturbance to the weather system.

Indonesia, however, provides an example of how watershed forests can be protected. The World Bank had sponsored a massive irrigation scheme to grow rice in the Dumoga valley of Sulawesi. The authorities realised they would have no water unless they protected the watershed on the hills above the valley. The Bank asked WWF for help; the result was the massive 320,000 hectare Dumoga-Bone National Park (funded by a loan from the Bank) which not only protects the watershed but also conserves many of the unique plants and animals for which Sulawesi is famous. Similar projects are afoot in Thailand and in Madagascar.

India is also showing the world a new way of combatting deforestation. When contractors arrive to cut timber, women from the villages, following an age-old precedent, embrace the trees, hoping to save them from the axe. Women died in early massacres. This grass-roots movement, called Chipko or "Hug-the-Trees", is proving extremely effective in protecting the Himalayan forests. It is mainly a women's movement as the women suffer most from having to go further afield to graze their cattle, to gather firewood and to find wild fruits, nuts and honey. Now the women are starting to replant some of the forests, including the many wild plants that they use in daily life. Chipko also influences government: Chipko leaders

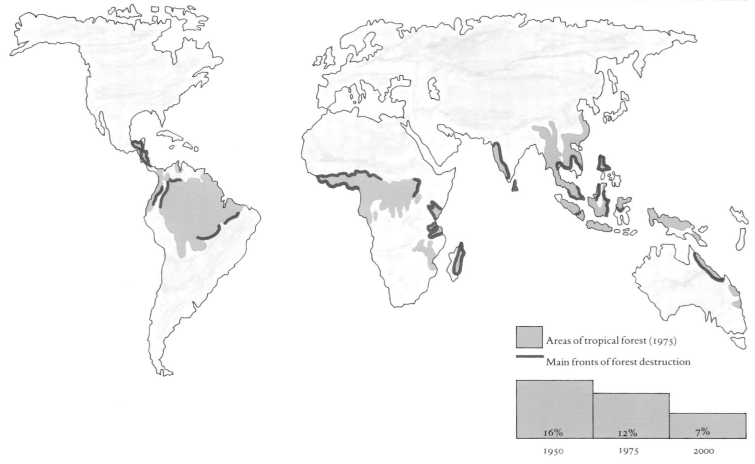

Areas of tropical forest (1975)

Main fronts of forest destruction

16% 12% 7%

1950 1975 2000

Grazing animals in excessive numbers are a prime cause of almost irremediable damage and desertification: in the Mediterranean the goat is the major culprit, especially as it can readily climb into trees like this carob. Cattle and camels are the other main culprits.

Chipko leader, Sunderlal Bahaguna, has said, "In one of our religious books it is written that a tree is like ten sons. It gives ten valuable things: oxygen, water, energy, food, clothes, timber, medicinal herbs, fodder, flowers and shade."

Until the middle of this century the tropical rainforests were hardly affected by human activity. Slash-and-burn cultivation was on a limited scale and adequate regeneration took place. Since then destruction has occurred at ever-increasing speed – for cultivation of crops and utilitarian trees, timber extraction, mineral and oil exploitation, and in some places for ill-conceived ranching schemes. The block diagram above indicates the percentage of rainforest in relation to total landmass in 1950 and 1975 and as projected for the year 2000 if annihilation continues at present rates. The map shows the extent of tropical forest in 1975 and, in red, the main fronts of its felling and burning.

35

■ Basin peat
▨ Peaty and humose gley soils
□ Upland soils

Above *Removal of hedgerows to give scope to huge agricultural machines, the resulting creation of extremely large open fields, and the drainage which dries out the top layer, have resulted in parts of the fertile peatlands of East Anglia, England being blown away by winds howling across the flat countryside. These maps show the projected change between the mid-1960s (top) and mid-1980s (above) – often 60 cm of peat loss.*

Facing page *This astonishing photograph of the edge of the Gibson Desert in western Australia shows trees maintaining individual patches of fertile ground around them: their leaf litter produces organic matter in which soil organisms can multiply and humus be created, thus retaining the very limited amounts of moisture available for continued root growth.*

persuaded Mrs Gandhi to ban felling on steep Himalayan slopes and the state of Uttar Pradesh has now banned all commercial felling in the hills.

Guardians of Fragile Lands

The world perhaps first woke up to the devastating consequences of destroying the natural guardians of the soil, when the dust-bowls of the American Middle West were created in the nineteen-thirties, with results on land and people so poignantly described in John Steinbeck's novel *The Grapes of Wrath*. These were areas where the natural vegetation had been removed for growing crops, mostly cereals, with the addition of fertiliser but no humus-forming matter. After a relatively short period of heavy cropping and annual ploughing, the soil of the arable prairies simply crumbled to dust and blew away.

Agricultural land commonly has soil erosion rates at least five times the natural level; removal of hedges and trees, and lowering of water tables (as in fenlands) make matters worse. Even Europe, the continent least troubled by soil erosion, is calculated to be losing close to a billion tonnes a year. In parts of the world where forest cutting and pressures on the land are severe, the rates are far higher – one estimate suggests that human disturbance may have increased the global denudation rate from 20 million to over 50 *billion* tonnes a year.

The most vulnerable soil of all is that of the world's drylands – areas where rainfall is low and the climate usually harsh. Covering about a third of the earth's land surface, their natural vegetation includes grassland, low woodland of scattered trees with grass, and steppe. About 20 million sq km of dryland, an area twice the size of Canada, is now threatened by desertification – the process by which overgrazing and cutting of the trees for firewood gradually removes the plant cover. As the plants are eaten away, the climate grows drier, while the pressures from hungry herds of livestock intensify – a vicious circle that ends in barren lands. The livelihoods of hundreds of millions of people are threatened.

The combating of erosion and degradation of lands that once provided a livelihood is one of the most urgent tasks facing humanity – and one in which plants, particularly those tailored by nature to survive in fragile lands, play a crucial role.

Hardy acacia species, for example, planted in the path of shifting dunes, are helping to halt the desert's march. Trees in desert conditions have a hard time, but if they can be established they both bind the sand and gradually accumulate soil, resulting from the decay of falling leaves around their trunks. Stockproof fences are erected and the sand stabilised by "planting" rows of dead brushwood, after which the acacias and other trees are planted closely and provided with enough water for establishment. This method resembles those being tried in British peatlands, where erosion is being halted by planting rows of straw, or by drilling seed into the unploughed stubble of a previous crop.

There are other possibilities. Alginates (product of seaweeds) and granular synthetic polymers are substances that will absorb many times their own weight of water – one polymer now in experimental use absorbs up to 30

times as much. When these are worked into the upper layer of sand and watered, annual weeds usually sprout which can be ploughed into the soil to start the humus cycle, or crops or trees can be planted directly.

It is amazing what can be achieved by tree planting. The Chinese are perhaps the greatest present-day example; literally millions of trees have been planted in the last few decades. Even in the stony wastes of the Gobi Desert plantings of poplars amaze the visitor.

With modern technology, crops can be conjured from the most barren lands. Saudi Arabia has demonstrated this, producing more than 600,000 tonnes of wheat in 1983 and nearing self-sufficiency. Deep beneath the arid crust lies a hidden treasure of aquifers stretching eastward from the Arabian Shield to the Gulf. But the water is a fossil resource; it fell 15,000 to 30,000 years ago, and though it is calculated to last at least 100 years, like oil it cannot be renewed.

Israel has a different approach to desert agriculture. Essential low-value commodities such as grain and sugar are imported, and the desert is used as a huge natural hothouse providing goods such as fruits, vegetables and cut flowers for luxury markets. Israel, too, draws on underground water sources, but has an advanced system of management, with less than two per cent of all run-off allowed to flow to the sea unused.

Comparable aquifers and high water-tables exist in many countries, but where they are being tapped they are falling at a more or less desperate rate. In the American south-west arid-land agriculture is clearly beginning to disintegrate. Water is pumped out at such a rate that the ground water level near Tucson, Arizona, has fallen by more than 60 metres in 35 years and it may run out by the end of the century.

Allocating water resources in the western United States has now become an issue of contention between California and other arid western states. The argument centres around the question, how much water can each state, with its city-dwellers and farmers, take from the great rivers, like the Colorado River, which flow from the Rockies to the Pacific? With limited resources and virtually unlimited demand, there is no easy answer.

One way and another, we may be able to overcome these problems, but at what cost? Is it really worth the huge input of energy and technology to force the deserts to bloom unnaturally with carnations and cabbages? Some believe the way forward is to adopt new crops using plants native to arid lands, such as the Jojoba bean of northern Mexico and southern USA. Jojoba produces a high quality oil and grows well in poor soils.

Super-salt-resistant plants may also be valuable: large areas of formerly agricultural land cannot now grow crops because of a build-up of salt following short-lived irrigation schemes; other areas are naturally too salty for normal crops. But for example, the Tamarugo tree from Chile can survive in exceptionally salty conditions and (according to the US National Academy of Sciences) its highly nutritious pods and leaves allow sheep to be stocked at rates close to those of good grassland.

The deserts are ripe for the new wonder crops, but there is still plenty of scope for traditional methods. Savanna and desert scrub have been cultivated for centuries without ecological failure, and it does not take new crops to end the profligate use of water. And the social fabric of a region will be much less disrupted by modifying old technology.

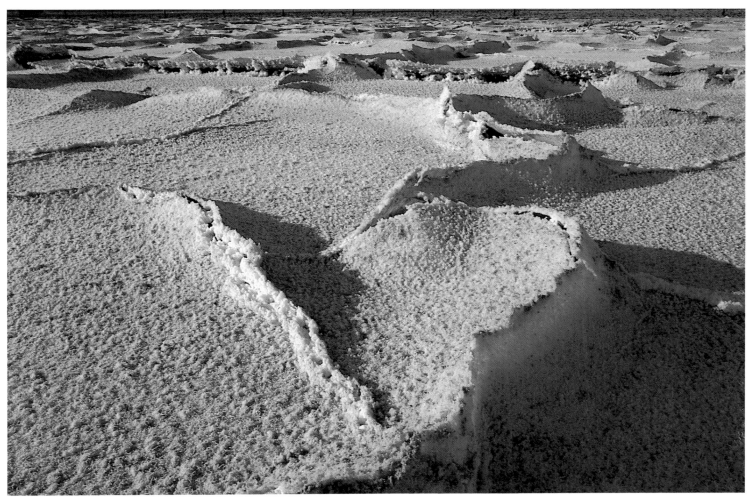

Above *The Great Salt Lake Desert in Utah, USA is a land encrusted with salt crystals, dramatic but lifeless. Little can be done with deserts as salt as this one, but potential crop plants are being developed for saline situations – often the result of faulty irrigation techniques – so that terrain once thought totally unproductive can some day be made productive.*

Right *Subterranean aquifers may contain huge amounts of water but they are non-renewable resources. Pumping them out is usually of short-term value, made ridiculous in situations where hot climates quickly evaporate the water. In Jordan run-off from irrigation systems is returned to the aquifers together with surplus winter rain, but chemicals are beginning to accumulate in the subterranean reserves with potentially alarming results.*

For example, the Sudanese have adapted a natural ecosystem with Acacia-grassland as the cultivation-climax, to produce gum arabic as their second largest export. Native farmers clear the scrub and the cleared land is planted with Millet, Sorghum and Sesame until after a few years the poor soil is exhausted and the land is left fallow. Among the native flora that regenerates and restores fertility is *Acacia senegal*. This is tapped for gum arabic in the latter half of the soil-resting period.

Unfortunately this ecologically balanced cycle has broken down in most places because under the pressure of a growing population the cultivation period has been óver-extended, severe grazing is preventing seedling establishment, and mature acacia bushes are lopped for firewood. However, the system has been further modified: *Acacia senegal* has been included in shelter belts around towns, where people are licenced to collect gum.

Plants which, like the acacia, are adapted to difficult conditions, offer great hope for land reclamation. Many plants are superbly adapted to the sites where they grow wild. Desert species often have mechanisms for searching out, storing and conserving water. Those on the seashores and dunes may be adapted to similar problems of physiological drought, because the strongly saline conditions prevent the roots absorbing water readily. Here too, plants act as guardians, like the Marram Grass stabilizing dunes along temperate coasts. Colonisation of shores by the saltmarsh and sand dune plants finally enables enough soil to accumulate to bear more orthodox plants. Samphire and Cord Grass, for example, garner particles on the retreating tides, and so slowly build marsh from open mud. For many centuries such new land has been reclaimed for agricultural use.

The most remarkable guardians of the coast are the mangroves, which colonise mudflats near the equator. For stability in the slushy mud they grow in, many develop stilt or prop roots. But because the mud is without the oxygen that is normally found dissolved in water and enabling most aquatic plants to prosper, these plants produce breathing roots, either finger-like or looped. Their role in protecting low-lying, sandy or soft-soiled coasts against the destructive pounding of the sea is vital.

Even the squalid deserts of modern industrial society – rubbish tips and land spoiled by pollution – can be reclaimed by plants. In the past, the only certain way of getting good cover on waste heaps was to top them with an expensive layer of inert material so that standard seed mixtures could be used. By trial and error a number of plants that grow in toxic sites have been found. Some are grasses, such as Brown Bent; there are members of the Pea family like Clover and Gorse; and trees such as Alder and Silver Birch. Better still is to find the plants that nature has crafted to deal with the problems; from them have been derived the Merlin variety of Red Fescue grass, for example, that is used on calcareous lead and zinc wastes, and the Parys Bent Grass for copper waste. Even the humblest grasses have their role of protector and provider.

Every part of ecosystem earth depends on the green life-support apparatus for its survival as a whole. Most valuable of all is the forest: in the words of the Buddha: "The forest is a peculiar organism of unlimited kindness and benevolence that makes no demands for its substance and extends generously the products of its life activity: it affords protection to all beings, offering shade even to the axeman who destroys it"

Rhizophora

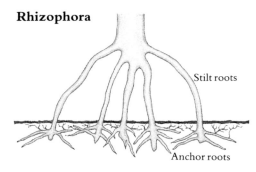

Stilt roots

Anchor roots

Avicenna

Breathing roots

Nutritive roots

Mangrove, or tidal forest, is the natural climax vegetation of estuaries and sheltered muddy inlets in the tropics. Several distinct genera have adopted similar life-styles to live in these muddy tidal places. Many like Avicenna (lower picture) have "breathing roots" or pneumatophores which are specialised mechanisms for dealing with the airless mud: their pores allow gases but not water to pass through; when the tide is out they absorb oxygen for a fast bout of respiration, providing energy for the controlled absorption of nutrients from the mud by the feeding roots below. Other mangroves, like Rhizophora (upper picture) have stilt roots which must exist primarily for support in the shifting, very fluid mudlands. The mud accumulates around the roots and slowly builds to soil. The intricate network of roots and stilts protects soft-soiled coasts from wave erosion and flooding. Mangroves produce fuel and timber and harbour many kinds of fish and shellfish, especially shrimp larvae.

Pollution, rubbish dumping and other uses of tropical tidal forests disrupt or destroy these fragile ecosystems, threatening the livelihoods of millions of people in developing countries who are directly or indirectly dependent on them.

Below *Coastal sand dunes form and stabilise through the agency of plants. Pioneer species such as Atriplex littoralis germinate on the drift line at the upper reach of spring tides (a). Wind-borne sand collects around them and an embryo dune forms (b). New species such as Marram grass (Ammophila arenaria) invade. As more sand is deposited the plants push up new shoots to counteract burial (c). As the sand accumulates on the seaward side, the Marram grass spreads through it, thus pushing the dune seawards. At same time the dune grows landwards as the onshore breeze carries sand up the windward face and deposits it in the lee (d). Vegetation binds the sand and covers the dune with a protective mat. But if this blanket is broken, by regular trampling from vacationers for example, the sand can easily blow away. More and more species colonise the dunes (e). As sand accretion lessens, the Ammophila is replaced by other species and eventually mosses and lichens become prominent. Different species are found in the depressions between the dunes which are often damper (f). Eventually the old dunes start to flatten, while a series of younger dunes forms to windward.*

Above *A mangrove swamp on Mahé, the principle island of the Seychelles in the Indian Ocean.*

Right and below *Marram Grass (Ammophila arenaria) is common on sand dunes out of range of the tide throughout western Europe. The root system is deep and wide spreading, and its long creeping stems root down at the nodes. Marram-stabilised dunes can reach over 30 metres high, and grow 30 metres laterally and 8 metres vertically over a ten year period.*

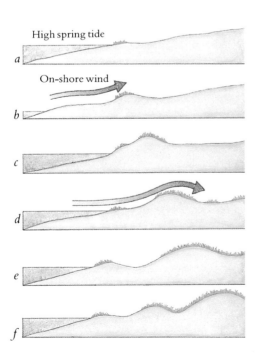

High spring tide

a

On-shore wind

b

c

d

e

f

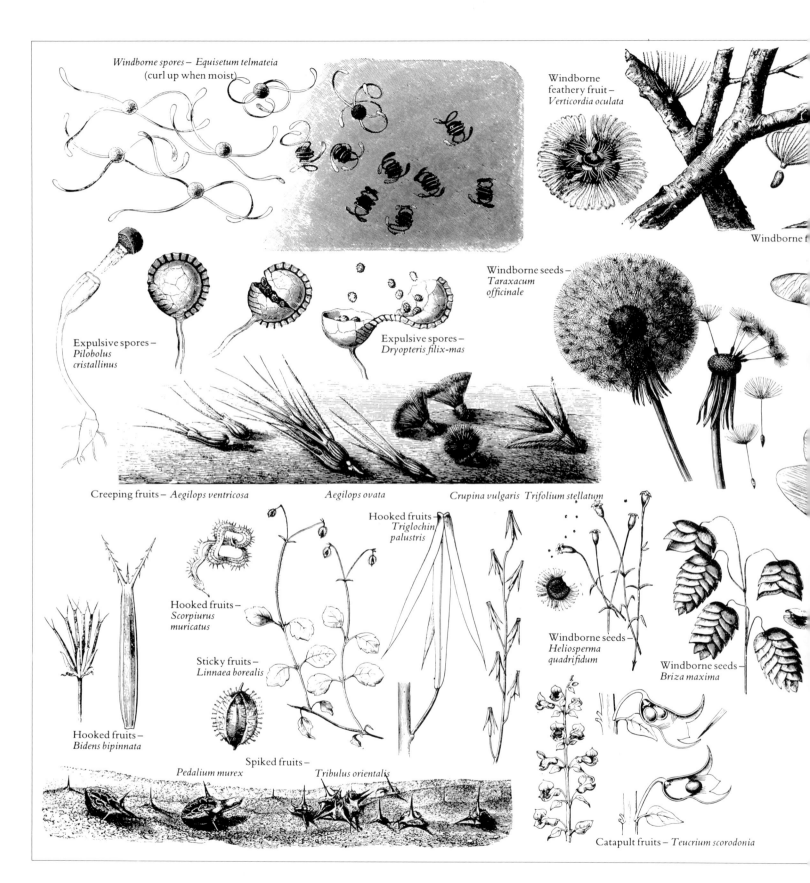

Windborne spores – *Equisetum telmateia*
(curl up when moist)

Windborne
feathery fruit –
Verticordia oculata

Windborne f

Expulsive spores –
*Pilobolus
cristallinus*

Expulsive spores –
Dryopteris filix-mas

Windborne seeds –
*Taraxacum
officinale*

Creeping fruits – *Aegilops ventricosa*   *Aegilops ovata*   *Crupina vulgaris* *Trifolium stellatum*

Hooked fruits –
*Triglochin
palustris*

Hooked fruits –
*Scorpiurus
muricatus*

Sticky fruits –
Linnaea borealis

Windborne seeds –
*Heliosperma
quadrifidum*

Windborne seeds –
Briza maxima

Hooked fruits –
Bidens bipinnata

Spiked fruits –
Pedalium murex   *Tribulus orientalis*

Catapult fruits – *Teucrium scorodonia*

42

...um nemorale (detaching and dropping)

Aerodynamic fruits –
Triopteris bifurca

Aerodynamic fruits –
Acer monspessulanus

Aerodynamic fruits –
Tilia europaea

Aerodynamic fruits –
Gyrocarpus asiaticus

Sling fruits – *Geranium palustre*

Green Travellers

Plants are easily distinguished from animals, even when they mimic their forms – the most obvious difference being, of course, that plants are generally static, whereas animals move around. Yet as every gardener knows this immobility of plants does not seem to be much of an impediment – they will arrive rapidly enough on any bare patch of soil! Plants have spread across the globe every bit as effectively as animals; indeed they managed to establish themselves on dry land well before animal life could do so, many millions of years ago.

The success of plants as colonisers depends on a remarkable characteristic: that small portions of a plant can survive away from the parent, to be moved by wind or water, insect, bird or mammal. Seeds and spores, of course, are the best known and most abundant of these "portions" – if they settle where conditions are favourable, they can grow into whole new plants. Their means of dispersal are varied and surprising; among the most remarkable cases, perhaps, being the "tumbleweeds" of the steppes – the whole plant becomes detached and is blown around by the wind, scattering the ripe seeds.

With the arrival of humanity, a new method of plant movement was added. At first, travellers carried plant material as food on their journeys, and discarded, dropped or deposited the seeds away from their native homes; later they carried many of the same seeds, plants and even trees around the world with the deliberate intention of extending their natural range. Modern world plant distribution is massively influenced by humans and many apparently "natural" landscapes are, in fact, humanized: the autumnal colours of New England woods are partly due to introduced species: suburban streets are lined with cherries from Japan or Ginkgo from China; crops are grown on alien continents; gardeners can take their pick of the world's flowering species. The rate of transfer is increasing – seeds and spores, for example, can now "hitchhike" on jets and liners, to spread around the world. Human-induced movement of plants is not necessarily a good thing. Just as over-enthusiasm for collecting plants threatens some habitats, the introduction of exotics can damage others, swamping the native flora and its dependent animal communities. Tragically, many thousands of plants species are now in danger of extinction through human irresponsibility.

Plant Origins

Magnolia campbellii

A hundred years ago, only a few eccentrics believed that the continents moved. Today, however, the concept of continental drift is a commonplace of science. The theory is that there was originally a single supercontinent – Pangea, or "all-earth" – which only began to break up about 190 million years ago, forming Laurasia to the north, and Gondwanaland to the south. The earliest land plants date from long before this. The extraordinary history of our moving continents thus underlies the present day distribution of many plants. Roughly 390 million years ago such primitive forms as liverworts, mosses, and horsetails had emerged, to be followed shortly by ferns. Conifers began to appear around 225 million years ago, and spread over much of the land surface. Charles Darwin called the origin of flowering plants "an abominable mystery" – the fossil record is almost blank as to how the evolutionary leap from ferns and conifers to true flowering species took place. Certainly they must have evolved and spread very rapidly indeed, on a geological time-scale. The earliest fossil pollen – of the waterlily, a primitive flowering plant – dates from about 140 million years ago; most is later. Yet present-day distribution suggests that flowering plants, or their immediate ancestors, must have colonised Pangea *before* it had completely broken up, when radiation could occur freely both within Laurasia and Gondwanaland, and between them, via landbridges which still existed some 125 million years ago.

While Rhododendrons show their Laurasian origin by a basic distribution in North America, Europe, Eurasia and South-east Asia, the Heaths (*Erica*), in the same family as Rhododendrons, have their centre in South Africa and only a few species in the Mediterranean and Europe: a distribution unrelated to the old supercontinent. The collision of the Australian and Asiatic land areas, at the most only 15 million years ago, gave rise to new migrations in which temperate Asiatic plants moved into Australia, and the mixing of plants – and animals – which had evolved separately in very distinct areas could occur.

The fact that seeds get moved around does not necessarily mean that plants can establish themselves everywhere. There are both physical and climatic obstacles. High mountain ranges are effective barriers: many plants found west of the Rocky Mountains of North America are not found east of the range and vice versa; the Magnolia, for example, is found east of the Rockies all the way round to China – but not on the west.

Climates have changed worldwide very considerably during measurable geological time and in that time-scale plants seem to have adapted to these changes relatively readily. Today many plants, adapted to one kind of climate, cannot transfer from one major climatic zone to another: plants from the tropics will not grow in temperate zones (though most of the west's popular houseplants are tropical), nor vice versa. Temperature, seasonal patterns and day-length (which can affect flower and hence seed production) are among the main controls. These problems are very plain to gardeners especially in North America where plants are designated to no less than ten zones according to what minimum temperature they will stand. Even in Britain, what can be cultivated in the Scilly Isles is vastly different from the possibilities of the Midlands, about 300 miles north-east.

Erica doliiformis

Erica infundibuliformis

Giant or King Protea *Protea cynaroides*

Laurasia

Gondwanaland

Magnoliaceae
Proteaceae
Erica

Pangea
200m years ago

135m years ago

65m years ago

Present day

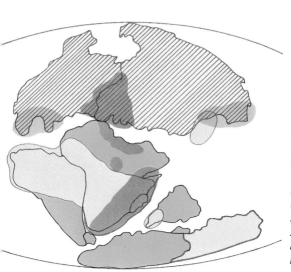

190 million years ago the supercontinent "Pangea" comprised Laurasia (now North America, Europe and Asia) and Gondwanaland (South America, Africa, Antarctica, India and Australia). At this time flowering plants were evolving and spreading: some current distributions are shown, left, overlaid on the ancient continents. Magnolias, primitive in floral terms, show a largely Laurasian distribution: eastern USA, Mexico, Japan, China and the Himalayas. A spectacular example of Gondwanaland spread is shown by the Protea family. Their multiflowered, brightly coloured heads vary from the bottlebrush shapes of Australian Banksias to the showy bracts of South Africa's King Protea. The Ericas evolved after the break-up of Pangea; their distribution reflects more recent continental evolution.

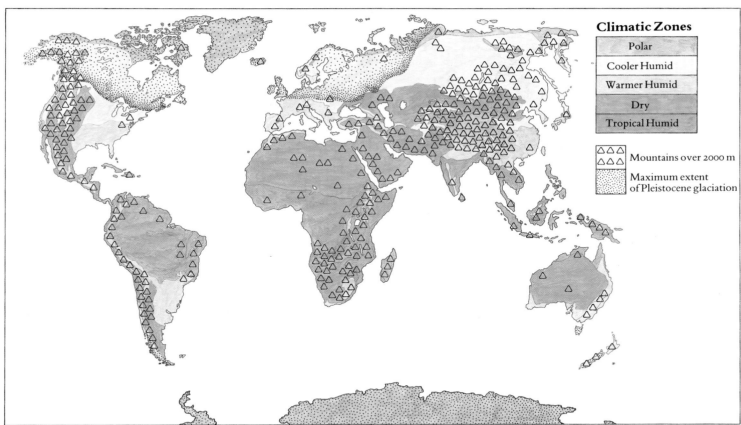

Climatic Zones

Polar
Cooler Humid
Warmer Humid
Dry
Tropical Humid

Mountains over 2000 m

Maximum extent of Pleistocene glaciation

Plants adapt to suit one particular environment and cannot transfer into another without changes, thus the climatic zones that band the earth have a major controlling influence. Mountains effectively compress the zones. Polar caps have been far more extensive, and during the Ice Ages fierce cold and grinding ice wiped the earth clean of plants across much of northern North America and northern Europe. In North America the Rocky Mountain chain running north-south worked to the plants' advantage as they could migrate along it at the appropriate height for the preferred climatic conditions. But in Europe, the Alps running east-west presented a barrier to travel and the survival of plants growing north of these mountains.

In comparatively recent times ice has been the great controller of plant life in what is now the temperate zone (parts were once tropical, including London). The Ice Ages started two and a half million years ago – ice spread southwards from the Arctic to recede by varying amounts in the interglacial periods. It last retreated 10,000 years ago. Re-colonisation of previously ice-bound terrain has taken place since – as well as during the interglacials. This fact explains why so few plants are found in northern Europe – they have had only 10,000 years to reestablish themselves. The present-day flora is also adapted to the now cooler climate.

The effects of the Ice Ages were not limited to the temperate zone; although temperature fluctuations were much smaller in the tropics, climate patterns were sometimes severely disrupted, particularly in Africa.

Colonisation of virgin habitats is spectacularly rapid in warm climates. It is best observed on volcanoes where ferns can germinate on the surface within six weeks of an eruption while it is still hot. But the most dramatic example of re-colonisation and demonstration of how plants can travel is that of Krakatoa, the island in the Sunda strait between Java and Sumatra which exploded most violently in 1883. After the cataclysm three islands of quite new outline were left, covered with ash and pumice 30 to 60 metres deep. As might have been expected the first arrivals were plants that required little or no soil and which were wind-borne over great distances. These included the very primitive blue-green algae, accompanied by lichens and mosses, and no less than 11 kinds of fern within the first three years. Soon there were also 17 kinds of flowering plant. Nine had arisen from seeds washed up on the beaches; of the remainder, four species were

The cactus Brachycereus nesioticus is restricted to the Galapagos Islands where it grows only in certain coastal regions on hard black lava flows. Lodging in crevices on the soil less rock, it makes wide-spreading clusters where virtually no other plant can survive.

Krakatoa provides a perfect example of tropical succession. In 1883 Krakatoa (pictured, above, six months before the explosion) exploded leaving Anak Krakatoa completely devoid of vegetation.

Botanical expeditions have charted the re-olonisation: the island was first dominated by algae, then by ferns, then by flowering plants and finally by trees, so that now part is clothed in dense jungle. More than 100

other plants did become established only to disappear in the interim. The diversity of the flora continues to increase, though it is still not as rich as the forests on nearby Java and Sumatra.

—— Coffee routes	▨ Coffee
—— Potato routes	▨ Potato
—— Breadfruit routes	▨ Breadfruit
—— Citrus routes	▨ Citrus

The Spread of Crop Plants

The map above shows how four crop plants spread around the world through human influence. Citrus (oranges etc), following the overland Silk Route from China, travelled to Europe in ancient times. Coffee from Africa, Potato from South America and Breadfruit from Tahiti travelled across the oceans to distant continents. Coffee and Potato have both had an extraordinary series of migrations, their spread largely related to the expansion of European colonial powers between the fifteenth and nineteenth centuries.

composites and two grasses, all with light airborne seeds. After four years the number of colonisers had risen to 61, most of the flowering plants being grasses; 23 years after the event there were 108 plant species, 22 years later the score was 276. Some plant arrivals were probably taken there by birds, the seeds either stuck on their feathers or feet, or in their stomachs. Today, much of the islands are covered with jungle.

Enter the Human Race

When international trade started is not all that clear, but a date around 2000 BC would probably not be far off the mark. Trade in vegetable products almost certainly took place quite early on.

The trade in spices, for example, enabled many colonists to acquire immense wealth up to quite recent times. One of the oldest records of plant collecting that we have is of frankincense trees being brought to Egypt from the land of Punt (Somalia), at the instigation of Queen Hatsepshut about 1495 BC. Dug up with large root balls and packed in wicker baskets, 31 out of 32 survived the journey to be planted at the Queen's great temple of Deir-el-Bahri.

Wherever the Greeks went they took the Olive tree with them, while the Romans would not go far without sowing Sweet Chestnuts. Although the gourmet Lucullus is said to have brought the Sweet Cherry to Rome from Armenia, where he was busy fighting in 73 and 72 BC, Theophrastus had

47

Above *The peach was cultivated in China before it was known any further west; it may have come to India, the Near East and, finally, Europe via the Silk Road, or it may have been brought by the Mongol hordes.*

Below *The wild carrot is found in much of Europe but it is only in Afghanistan that the roots are coloured. It is believed that carrots were first cultivated there, spreading to Asia Minor by the tenth century, Spain by the twelfth, north-west Europe by the fourteenth and England by the fifteenth. The familiar orange carrot was selected in the Netherlands by about 1600.*

mentioned it in his great *History of Plants* around 300 BC. What seems possible is that the cherry, which originated in Asia, had been domesticated in Asia Minor and Greece long centuries earlier, but that in Armenia larger and sweeter cherries had been selected and cultivated.

Ancient Armenia – now absorbed into eastern Turkey and neighbouring USSR – is near the centre of origin of many fruits and traditionally the home of much fruit development. It was overrun many times, so that its fruits travelled rapidly. The first apples are thought to have been bred there from wild crab apples and the Apricot *(Prunus armeniaca)* probably also got to Europe through Armenia.

Apart from invasion, there was deliberate colonisation, none more surprising than the great voyages of the Polynesians from AD 750. When they travelled vast distances by canoe – the Hawaiians to Samoa, 2500 miles, and the Tahitians to the Marquesas, 1000 miles, for example – they carried roots to plant. Among them, known from tuber remains in archaeological sites, were Taro and Sweet Potato. This is something of a mystery, because the Sweet Potato is known to originate in Mexico or northern South America. How did the Polynesians have it long before the Spanish invasions? In Peru Sweet Potato is called *kuma*: in New Zealand, *kumara*. Is this a proof of Thor Heyerdahl's theory that South Americans travelled to Easter Island – and thence into Polynesia? Or did the Polynesians visit South America and obtain the Sweet Potato there?

It seems that useful mutations among vegetables have been repeatedly lost. Pliny mentions an African Cabbage which sounds like the modern Brussels Sprout and then disappears from the records. In the fifteenth century there appeared the multi-headed cabbage which, judging from old illustrations, seems to have been halfway between the cabbage and the sprout, but it was not until the late eighteenth century that the Brussels Sprout as we know it today arrived.

Pliny's Lacuturnian Cabbage sounds like the first hearting cabbage, which did not then reappear until the thirteenth century. The Savoy Cabbage seems to have been grown in Spain by the Moors as early as the twelfth century; but this was lost. When the Spaniards reconquered Andalusia they must have neglected many of the vegetables grown by the Moors. It is fortunate for us that such mutations do recur periodically. People tend to be conservative with new vegetables. Cobbett was recommending American Maize or sweet corn in the 1820s, but it was only a century later that it became popular in Europe.

When colonisation of the New World began a number of Old World vegetables and fruits were introduced to the new plantations, while a number of New World vegetables were introduced first to Europe and subsequently to other continents. These included such crops as Maize, green beans, tomatoes, cucurbits, peppers and cocoa. An extremely important New World vegetable, the Potato, took time to become established since the original importation failed to produce sizeable tubers in northern Europe. It was not until at least a century after the original introduction that the Potato adapted to cropping in the new conditions and began to assume its pre-eminent position. Surprisingly enough, potatoes did not reach North America from the ancestral home, relatively close, but via the European settlers around 1621.

The Apple Story

The apple is certainly the most widely grown fruit in temperate countries, with an annual crop of over 20 million tonnes. The ancestral apple is thought to have originated in south-western Asia, around the conjunction of Russia, Iran and Turkey, where wild apples still grow in quantity.

There are about 25 species altogether, all inter-fertile. Of these about half a dozen, including Malus baccata, but especially the sweet apple, M. pumila, and the sour M. sylvestris, are among the many ancestors of the modern apple.

People migrating westwards from Asia must have taken apples with them among provisions and thus new colonies of wild trees, grown from pips, appeared all across Europe. Sizeable fruits were sliced and dried

for storing, as indicated by carbonised remains found on many European prehistoric sites.

The earliest records of deliberate cultivation are from the ancient Greeks and Romans, who by inventing the art of grafting – in which growths from a selected tree are "worked" upon wild rootstocks, as above – were able to multiply the most desirable of the otherwise one-off seedlings they found growing. The importance of rootstocks in determining the size and vigour of the tree was already appreciated and dwarf apple trees were grown.

The Romans carried favourites to settlements all over Europe and to Britain. After they withdrew, monasteries perpetuated some of their varieties. At least one of these, named "Court Pendu Plat" in the sixteenth century, is still in cultivation.

When Europeans colonised North America they grew their apples almost entirely from seeds. Although this inevitably resulted in a proportion of inferior forms, it meant that American orchards held much greater genetic diversity than those in Europe, where relatively few new seedlings were perpetuated. This has resulted in great differences in the apples grown on each side of the Atlantic.

Malus baccata

Malus sylvestris

Malus pumila

Capsicum annuum

Above *Capsicum peppers, all of them varieties of one very variable species, were introduced to Europe by the Spaniards and are the New World's main contribution to our array of spices.*

Coffee has been spread round the world, from its centres of origin in Ethiopia and central Africa to Brazil – which it reached via a highly circuitous route through Southeast Asia, Amsterdam, Paris and Martinique (see page 47).

Coffea arabica

The Rubber Tree *(Hevea brasiliensis)* was extracted from a local Brazilian governor by deception. Joseph Hooker at Kew wanted it to send to South-east Asia, but the Brazilians were trying to keep the monopoly; eventually it was on the pretext that the Rubber Tree seeds were to be a gift to Queen Victoria that permission was given to Henry Wickham to take them out of the country. Earlier importations of plants and seeds had not been successful. Wickham's seeds arrived at Kew in 1876, and germinated there. They were then preserved in Asia first in the Botanic Garden of Henaratgoda, Sri Lanka, and later at the Singapore Botanic Garden. But it was not until the end of the century that the setting up of plantations began in earnest. The great rubber boom of 1910, which made Malaya the greatest rubber producing country in the world at that time, might never have taken place but for a few dedicated scientists, in particular H.N. Ridley, who was then director of the Singapore Botanic Garden. His book *The Dispersal of Plants throughout the World* still remains the classic work on the subject.

Sir Joseph Banks (1743-1820), then *de facto* director of Kew Gardens, seems to have been the first to see botanic gardens as a means by which commercial crops could be distributed around the world. The encouragement of new economic crops is still one of the functions of botanic gardens.

It was comparatively easy to transport seeds from place to place: they usually had a high level of successful germination and provided the best method of propagation; even so some types were repeatedly lost. The real difficulties arose with cultivars. These do not breed true from seed: and with woody species it is necessary to graft a scion of the desired variety onto a root-stock to increase it. The invention of styptics made it possible to preserve scions in good condition, but distance, time and trans-equatorial change of season between, for example, Europe and Australia, made grafting hazardous. Although some cultivars were introduced from country to country in this way, it proved easier to import seeds and develop new cultivars from them.

Nowadays, with fast ships and aeroplanes this difficulty no longer exists, and one of the more popular modern apple varieties, 'Crispin', is a cultivar of Japanese breeding.

Food and medical crops are, not unnaturally, the most travelled members of the plant world, but ornamentals have become increasingly so as human life became less of a battle to survive. From the end of the seventeenth century onwards, the search for ornamentals accelerated and by the nineteenth century the trade had become so lucrative that nurserymen would pay well for foreign seeds, and those with sufficient capital would employ collectors on expeditions to all parts of the globe.

Sometimes these expeditions had more obvious commercial ends. The Oregon Association sent John Jeffreys in the 1850s to search the Rockies for new trees that might be suitable for forestry work. This followed on David Douglas's introductions of such plants as the Douglas Fir, the Monterey Pine and the Sitka Spruce, all of which have become major ingredients in forestry throughout the world. Even with Jeffreys, subscribers received the seeds of many ornamental trees as well as the conifers that it was hoped would prove profitable for forestry.

So far we have talked about the gathering of plant material by collectors as though there were no problems. In fact transport of young plants was extremely difficult. Imagine yourself several months out on a collecting expedition in the Amazon basin; you travel in canoes (there are no roads); it will be months before you get back to civilisation. Keeping growing plants alive takes incredible attention. Even the botanist, pressing specimens between sheets of paper, was hard put to it to keep these. On his great Amazon journey with the botanist Aimé Bonpland, between 1799 and 1804, the great Alexander von Humboldt wrote that, after travelling six thousand miles, a third of their specimens were found to be destroyed: "We are daily discovering new insects, destructive to paper and plants. Camphor, turpentine, tar, pitched boards, and other preservatives prove quite unavailing here."

Even on board ship for home, long sea journeys took their toll; apart from anything else plants needed water and it was lack of water for the crew which cost Captain Bligh his 1,000 Breadfruit plants and made him a castaway after the mutiny on the *Bounty*. One might think seed the simplest and lightest means of getting new plants into cultivation, but this was not always so. Seeds might lose their viability and become useless on long journeys (seeds of delphinium and Himalayan primulas, for instance, need to be sown very rapidly after collection, to germinate successfully); while in hot, moist climates they were often attacked by moulds and insects.

The attempt to bring Breadfruit from Tahiti to feed the slaves in the West Indies led to the famous mutiny on the Bounty (1787): the crew, incensed by thirst and harsh treatment, took over the ship when they saw their water reserved for the plants. In 1793, the vessel Providence accomplished the mission.

The need for conservation has been recognised only recently. One of the leading botanists of the last century was Sir Joseph Hooker, above. In his Himalayan Journals, *Hooker recommended the wholesale collection of the spectacular blue orchid Vanda coerulea, below, as a quick way of making money – without apparently expressing a twinge of concern for the species' survival.*

The great invention to protect plants was the glass enclosure, known as a Wardian case, invented independently by a Scot, Alan Maconochie, in 1825, and the London Doctor Nathaniel Ward in 1829. Within the sealed cases plants could survive for years if need be, safe from drying heat, wind and salt spray, in a climate of their own creation, and needing very little extra water since transpired moisture returned to the soil.

Like virtually everyone else, the plant collectors had no inkling of any need for conservation. Two of the worst offenders seems to have been Sir Joseph Hooker, in the Himalayas, and Benedict Roezl, who brought back 100,000 orchids from one region of Mexico alone. In comparatively recent times the Vesubie valley in southern France was denuded of *Lilium pomponium*, and northern Portugal of most of its wild narcissi.

Vegetable Carpet-baggers

Plants may always have travelled, but unfortunately, those that travel most today, with the aid of people, are what we call weeds. Although many seeds are adapted for transport by animals, once humans started moving the opportunities were even greater. Seeds travelled on clothing, blankets, covering, among imported seeds and roots, in mud on shoes, in the digestive tract; they moved on wheels and vehicles of every kind. Many plants, deliberately grown as crops or ornamentals, escaped into the surroundings with devasting results.

Sometimes humble garden nuisances can colonise very readily. The Dandelion, imported accidentally in grass seed from Europe to southern South America, now grows like a native on the pampas and is favourite food of the Rhea. The Plantain, brought by settlers from Europe into North America, spread so rapidly that the Indians called it Englishman's Foot.

Introduced plants, growing in isolation from their own finely-tuned ecological habitats, often get out of hand because there are no predators available to control them. An example of this is found on Mauritius, the one-time home of the Dodo – the very symbol of extinction. The indigenous vegetation is almost all irretrievably degraded by vigorous introduced species, encouraged by disturbance of the habitat due to alien animals such as pigs and Malaysian monkeys.

One of the saddest examples of invasion by exotics is in the Cape of South Africa, where a staggering 8,000 native species are crammed into an area made up of fragments totalling less than the area of the Kruger National Park! The Cape is so rich that it has been called the Cape Floristic Kingdom. There are only six such kingdoms in the world; the biggest, the Boreal Kingdom, covers most of the northern hemisphere north of the great deserts. Much of the Cape has been ploughed up for growing wheat, and countless hectares have been choked by invasive plants introduced by settlers from other countries.

These tales of opportunism could be multiplied many times. It looks as though these vegetable carpet-baggers, taking over not just areas where habitats have been destroyed by humans but full-blown plant communities where they find the conditions specially favourable, could one day be the inheritors of the earth's surface.

Prickly Pears, left, brought into Australia late last century as garden curiosities, found the conditions so perfect that by 1925 they occupied over 24 million hectares. They were eventually eradicated by a cactus-eating moth from Argentina. In the last few decades

Lantana, above, has taken over the habitats of many endemic species in Hawaii. The beautiful South American Water Hyacinth, top, has clogged tropical waterways worldwide, and invaded paddy fields in South-east Asia.

Rice — here being planted in an Indonesian paddy field — is one of the "big three" cereals that have become world staples.

CHAPTER FOUR

Our Daily Bread

The range of plants known to have been used by humans as food, drink or flavourings is astonishing – as many as 10,000 species including fungi and seaweeds have been recorded and we assume early peoples must have tried many more. It is hard for us today to conceive the human cost of identifying this wealth of natural resources. The great majority were probably first consumed by hunter-gatherer tribes, living off the land in isolated, local communities. Often these people must have died or suffered as they learned by trial and error not only which plants but which part of them – the fruit, flower, leaves, stem or root – were safe, poisonous or edible only after culinary treatment.

Many of these plants are still eaten from the wild but only about 3,000 seem ever to have achieved wide acceptance and only about 150 have been cultivated to any extent. During the long centuries of selection for the heaviest seed-head, the most useful food, the sturdiest plants, our modern crops have gradually evolved, and certain favoured staples have come to dominate the global menu. Today we rely on a mere 20 species to provide 90 percent of the world's food needs, and over half of our calorific intake is supplied by just three grasses: wheat, rice and maize.

Over the last fifty years, the process of specialization has accelerated, fuelled by genetic research, until an increasingly large share of our harvest rests on certain carefully bred, high-yield strains designed to feed a hungry world. The more highly bred and artificially cultivated a crop, the more prone it is to attack by new strains of disease or pest; one third of all food produced is destroyed by pests and diseases.

To keep one jump ahead in this leap-frog struggle, new resistant strains are constantly needed. The key to maintaining this improvement lies in the stock of three types of plant, all vital for the future. First are the very diverse traditional cultivars – land-races – which are being replaced by the modern, uniform new crops of the Green Revolution (p. 71). Second are those wild relatives of crops which are still to be found in their undisturbed natural habitat; recently wild crop relatives have played an increasingly significant and fascinating role in crop development, especially in breeding disease resistance into the modern strains. The third potential resource for the future, also threatened, is the unused potential of the other 10,000-plus species of which we have inherited knowledge. Never has the need for exploring new possibilities been greater; these plants may be valuable in cultivation, cross-breeding and genetic improvement, and also have potential as new staples or useful foods.

Virtually all the staple foods we know today have been cultivated since antiquity. It is surprising we have added so little to our ancestors' choices: a great innate conservatism seems to have been at work, since useful food plants will perform admirably away from their natural homes under cultivation when given the chance. Once people get used to a few kinds of food as major parts of their diet they stop experimenting.

The staple foods come from a small range of families: the 130 most important food plants fall into only 32 families out of a possible maximum of about 420. The most important are the Grass family, Gramineae – rice, wheat, maize, sorghum, barley and sugar cane; Solanaceae – potato; Convolvulaceae – sweet potato; Euphorbiaceae – cassava or manioc; Leguminosae – beans, pulses, soya bean and peanuts; Palmae – coconut; Musaceae – bananas; and Chenopodiaceae – sugar beet.

Wheat is the most important crop in the world: the principal food of 35 percent of the world's population, 350 million tonnes are produced annually on more than 200 million hectares of land, providing 20 percent of the world's calorie consumption as well as a large proportion of all our essential nutrients. Rice is the leading tropical crop – even more important than Wheat in terms of direct consumption – while Maize ("Corn" in North America) is staple in many tropical and subtropical regions.

Rice   Wheat

Of the worlds's 13,074 million hectares of land, about a third is used for producing food – some 10.6 percent is arable, 0.6 percent carries various permanent crops from orchards to plantations, and 23.3 percent is permanent pastureland, mostly for meat-yielding animals. 31.1 percent is designated as forest and woodland – some of it being rapidly destroyed – and 34.3 percent as "other", including towns, mountains, and deserts. As the map, right, shows, the southern continents, though large in area, have a lower percentage of good arable land for crops than some northern ones. Drought and poor soils also affect many southern croplands, and the effect on their production is evident from the second map, opposite. The world's cereal harvest is heavily dominated by the north. Moreover, increased yields – a gift of the new crop varieties, fertilizers, and technology of the Green Revolution (p.71), have barely touched Africa, and only moderately helped South America. In Africa, particularly, crop improvement is lagging.

World Land Use

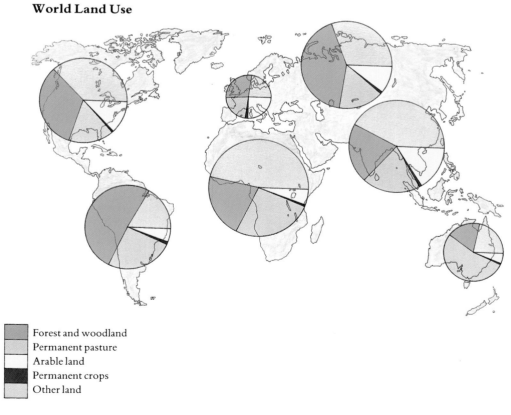

Forest and woodland
Permanent pasture
Arable land
Permanent crops
Other land

Maize　Sorghum　Millet　Barley

In virtually all undeveloped countries, winnowing chaff from grain is carried out by hand.

World Cereal Production

(million tonnes)

654.0

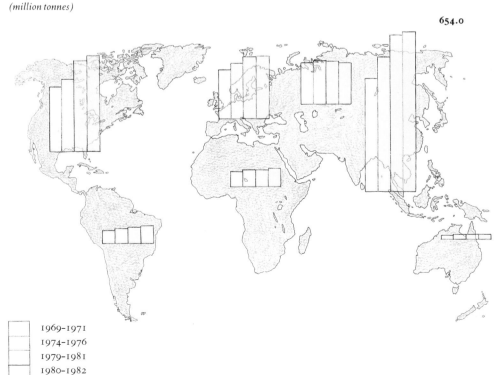

	1969–1971
	1974–1976
	1979–1981
	1980–1982

Cereal grains are the major source of concentrated carbohydrate for both food and fodder. After the "big three" – wheat, rice and maize – the most important are barley, sorghum, oats, millet and rye. Which cereal is dominant where is determined by climate, and influenced by local preference. Barley is tolerant of most conditions and can grow from the Arctic to the Andes, from the Himalayas to Ethiopia, including soils too saline for other cereals. Sorghum and millet are both staples in the drier regions of Africa and Asia. Sorghum is particularly hardy and drought-resistant: it is the predominant cereal in areas too hot and dry for maize. China and India are the major Millet-producing countries.

Other cereals of local importance include the Teff of Ethiopia, and Job's Tears or Adlay of India which has much as yet unrealised food potential (p.78).

A few plants not of the Grass family produce cereal-like grains: the Amaranth, widely grown in the Andes and South-east Asia; the Quinoa, a declining crop in the Americas, and Buckwheat, widely grown in Canada and the USSR.

Dioscorea alata

Yanomami Indians of the Amazon harvesting Cassava for a feast.

Apart from the almost ubiquitous Potato, world production of starchy roots and tubers divides approximately into temperate and tropical. Brazil is the major producer of cassava or manioc (Manihot esculenta), seen being gathered by Amazon Indians above right, while China dominates the sweet potato (Ipomoea batatas) league. The Greater Yam (Dioscorea alata), above, originated in South-east Asia and became the most widely distributed of all yams. Their importance, however, is gradually being eroded by the less nutritious cassava or by cocoyams in some areas.

The Potato (Solanum tuberosum) is the most important non-cereal world food plant; production accounts for over half the annual tonnage of all starchy roots and tubers. The USSR and Poland are world leaders in potato-growing; indeed the potato is the only root crop in those countries. It now grows world-wide except in the lowland humid tropics; but the very tasty, small tubers of the potato's Andean homeland are rapidly declining in availability.

Other temperate roots are comparatively unimportant though sugar beet, a very recent crop, now accounts for almost half the world's production of sugar.

World Root and Tuber Production
(million tonnes)

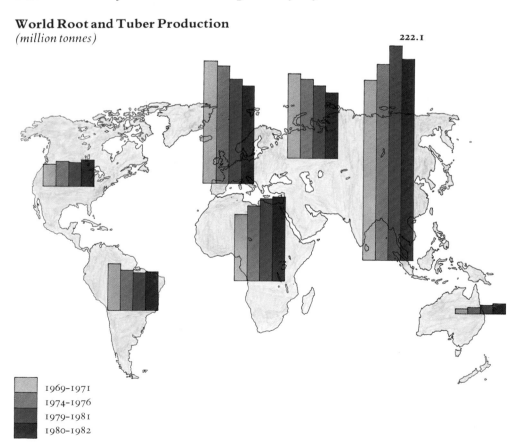

222.1

1969–1971
1974–1976
1979–1981
1980–1982

58

Lens esculenta

Fleshy roots, tubers and rhizomes, collectively known as root crops, are one of nature's ways of ensuring continuity for perennial plants over dry or cold seasons all over the world. This made them naturals for early people to exploit, particularly in tropical lands. They are vitally important providers of food energy for populations throughout the world – especially the potato and the tropical yams, cassavas, cocoyams and sweet potato. Carrots, parsnips, swedes and turnips also feature prominently.

Pulses are the hard, dried, edible seeds of the Pea family, Leguminosae, and a most important source of protein; in the tropics grain legumes are often the only source available to supplement the carbohydrate crops, while forage legumes such as Clover and Lucerne provide high protein diet for livestock. These useful plants have root nodules containing nitrogen-fixing bacteria and are therefore important in maintaining soil fertility, especially in tropical areas of nitrogen-deficient soil. Often deep-rooted, legumes are further valuable in aerating the soil and allowing rain to permeate.

Many plants produce oil reserves rather than starch, but only about 30 species have been used for oil extraction, and of them a dozen or so account for 90 percent of the vegetable oil supply. The Olive tree is characteristic of the Mediterranean region, where there are probably 500 million trees including some very old specimens. Numerous references in the Bible confirm that the Olive was one of the earliest trees to be grafted.

The soya bean (Glycine max) is not the most appetising of the pulses but it outstrips the others both in quantity produced and variety of uses including new "meat analogues". Its vast expansion as a western crop only occurred 50-odd years ago. It overtook wheat and maize as the most important US cash crop in 1973. However its future potential is threatened, in that many of its wild relatives are being destroyed.

The USA is world leader by a wide margin in the production of all grain legumes (chiefly soya), followed by China (likewise), India (groundnuts and chickpeas), Brazil (soya) and the USSR (dried peas).

India produces about a third of the world's lentils (Lens esculenta), above – one of the oldest and most popular of Old World crops. Tasty and nutritious, they contain 25 percent protein. Glass lenses were named for their resemblance to Lentils.

A minor leguminous crop is the carob (Ceratonia siliqua), a tree producing large pods rich in sugar and protein, eaten raw, made into alcoholic beverages and a "health-food" substitute for chocolate, or used as fodder: its seeds were the original carats or jewellers' weights.

World Pulse Production
(million tonnes)

21.4

1969–1971
1974–1976
1979–1981
1980–1982

The African Oil Palm, very widely cultivated in the tropics, gives a higher oil yield per hectare than any other oil plant. It produces two quite different types of oil, that from the palm kernels, used for making margarine and soap, and that from the fleshy part of the fruit used more widely for industrial processes. This is one of the most rapidly expanding plantation crops today.

The Sunflower is the world's second largest vegetable oil crop. Some seeds are eaten, but mostly oil is made from them, and the remaining seed cake is valuable as stockfeed. Enormous fields of bright Sunflowers, most of them in the USSR, are perhaps the most attractive crops of any.

Sesame has been claimed as the oil seed most anciently used; there are numerous records of its use in cooking, medicine, cosmetics and for ritual. It is a fast-maturing annual and its seeds can contain 60 percent very nutritious oil. Yields vary but more attention to breeding Sesame could greatly improve its standing among the world's oil supplies.

Coconuts are multi-purpose palms of humid tropics, capable of producing food from their fresh nut meat and "milk"; copra from the dried meat, used for stockfeed; oil pressed from the copra, mainly used for soap; and coir fibre from the husks.

Nuts, other than the leguminous Peanut, are minor crops, but nonetheless quite widely grown in some areas. They are borne on trees or shrubs: sweet chestnut, walnut, hazel and filbert, pecan, cashew, pistachio and macadamia nut – the last being one of the few useful native Australian food plants, now becoming widely grown and the subject of recent breeding.

Fruit must always have been among the items which people have added to basic diet to lend taste and interest and, in particular, to satisfy a desire for sweetness. Some fruits became important very early on. Among these are the Grape – largely because of its capacity to be made into wine – and the

Above Peanuts (Arachis hypogaea) are grown throughout the warmer parts of the world and, except for about 5 percent, all are consumed or processed locally. The high (30 percent) protein content of the Virginia type makes it a valuable source of energy in the diet, while the very high (47-50 percent) oil content of the Spanish-Valencia type is more suitable for oil production. The flowers grow above ground in the orthodox way, but after pollination the developing seeds – the groundnuts – are pushed under ground. This old illustration pre-dates the discovery of this fascinating self-sowing mechanism.

Right The Olive tree (Olea europaea) seems to have originated in the eastern Mediterranean but as early as the fourth millenium BC variable hybrids certainly existed, as kernels found at Byblos confirm, and the Olive ancestor is not known. From its eastern origin it has spread westwards to Greece, Italy, north Africa, and to Spain. Currently some one and a half million tonnes of oil are produced annually. Olive oil has been one of the great foods of this historic area but production is declining now since harvesting depends so much on manual labour: one can still see the olives being beaten down with poles onto sheets on the ground, just as ancient Greek vases depict, or fallen ones picked off the soil by hand.

Date, which was the staple of North Africa and the Middle East and now runs to a world population of nearly 100 million trees. More is said about these fruits in Chapter 9.

The most widely grown tropical fruit is the Banana, which arose in South-east Asia. Modern varieties are almost entirely seedless so new varieties are bred from semi-wild types and arise also by the numerous mutations which constantly appear. The Pineapple is another important tropical crop, mainly grown for canning. It is unusual among fruits in not growing on a tree or bush but from a spiny rosette – it is a bromeliad like the indoor Urn Plant – the fruit being an oval thickening of the floral axis, with the seeds embedded in the outside skin.

A fruit beloved of animals is the South and Central American Avocado, intriguing among tree fruits in being savoury rather than sweet. It contains much protein and is a favourite food of carnivores like jaguars. It was probably eaten by people as early as 7000 BC, and cultivated by 5000 BC. Widely grown, there are many distinct varieties, though these are seldom named to the consumer.

The Tomato is usually called a vegetable, though the parts we eat are fruits. In western countries it has become a very important crop and in the US its annual value is barely below that of potatoes. Tomatoes have a flavour different from that of any other vegetable and are rich in vitamins, notably vitamin C. The tomato tagged along as a weed in maize and bean fields for centuries. Like the potato, the tomato was introduced to Europe by the Spanish invaders of South and Central, though only a tiny proportion of the potential varieties were brought across the Atlantic, and only in this century have other species which have become important for pest and disease resistance been used for breeding.

Green leaves and sometimes shoots or stems are very important additions to diet, mostly in providing protein and a little fibre, but especially calcium and vitamins often lacking in other foods. Sadly the intake of leaves is far less in many poor tropical countries, where it is almost essential for well-being, than in richer temperate ones even though supplies, often plentiful, can be obtained from the "spare" parts of root crops like Cassava.

The Cabbage tribe, grown in temperate regions, deserves special mention because of its extraordinary variety. Cabbage began as a woody plant with a few loose leaves. In its current forms numerous tightly packed leaves surrounding a terminal bud give us cabbages, enlarged side buds of packed leaves on a long stem Brussels sprouts, flower buds enlarged into edible "curd" the cauliflowers and various broccoli, and thickened stems the kales and the turnip-like above-ground kohl rabi.

The Onion tribe have been recognised since very ancient times as providing a unique flavour; some like garlic and chives are more important as flavouring than as basic food. Their medicinal and tonic value was also appreciated early on. There are references to onions, garlic and leeks as early as the first Egyptian dynasty (3200 BC) and many in the Bible, while garlic features in early Chinese records. Besides the globular bulb onion and smaller shallot, and the elongated leek and green-leaved Egyptian Kurrat, eaten as vegetables, there are several kinds of bunching onion which are eaten green – in northern China one can see people gathering wild forms of these to liven up their meals

Citrus aurantium

Another important fruit group, Citrus, has many manifestations – from Oranges, sweet (above) and sour, Mandarins, Tangerines and their like, to Grapefruit, Lemons and Limes, and the less familiar Pummelo (p.78). Their wild relatives are in danger from destruction of Asian forests.

Below *The modern Cabbage, with its mass of tight-packed leaves, developed from wild ancestors with only a few tough leaves. Such tight-headed varieties were being cultivated in the twelfth century.*

This street stall in a western Chinese town offers a range of dried pulses with which people can vary their staple diet of rice – and help to offset the depleted nutrient value of the milled and polished rice normally eaten which, if used as the sole item of diet, could result in deficiency diseases. Cereals and pulses are a natural combination which enhances their individual protein values.

Differences in Diet

More than enough grain is grown annually to feed the whole world. The problem is not only one of its distribution but of the way in which we use it. Dietary habits lie at the root of many of our troubles. In the west a great deal of meat is consumed, and meat-producing animals need feeding. In the United States nearly 90 percent of the grain harvested is now fed to these animals, apart from vast areas of grass and other fodder crops. A westerner eats about 65 kg of grain a year, plus meat enough to account for over 900 kg of grain more. By comparison, the average Chinese eats 160 kg of grain products and under 20 kg of meat. Foods considered necessary to feed 200 million in the west would be adequate for 1500 million Chinese.

Big business creates associated problems. In Europe production from dairy farming for example exceeds demand so that the European Economic Community currently staggers under a "butter mountain" and is awash with a "milk lake" engendered by a price support system. The pastoral idyll of cattle grazing in a flower-filled meadow is often far from reality. The stock are pastured on near monocultures of ryegrass inimical to wildlife, or reared on feeds of cereal, Soya, Manioc, or even surplus milk products. Cattle in particular are often unhealthy and short-lived under these modern feeding regimes.

In the Far East where milk has not traditionally been part of the diet adults do not retain the ability to digest it, so dairy farming is hardly practised. For the majority of people in the tropics the amount of meat, eggs, milk and fish, as well as fat and sugar in the diet, is low. The staff of life is some cheap, stomach-filling plant food, like boiled rice, cassava or sweet potato, horrendously boring to prosperous tastes. Often few green vegetables are eaten.

Deficiency in vitamin A, which is provided ready-made in milk, eggs and liver, but which otherwise the body manufactures from the pigment carotene found in abundance in green leaves, causes among other things degeneration of the eye surfaces that can result in destruction of the cornea. The annual number of children newly blinded by this is estimated at 200,000 and many die of associated diseases. It is dreadful that they should so suffer when one leaf of taro is sufficient to cover the daily needs of three toddlers, and two teaspoons of cooked fresh greens a day could protect a child from a life of blindness.

Many greens could be gathered free to supply this requirement. In some European countries there is a widespread habit of collecting wild greens, often the tops of assorted meadow or roadside plants. Chickweed, white dead-nettle and stinging nettle are all prized by the initiated. Basic tropical crops, such as cassava and sweet potato, grown for their tuberous roots, pawpaw for its fruit and milky latex, and jute for its fibre, can supply the all-important green component and if leaves are picked in moderation this will not affect the main crop. The protein component of leaves is important where food intake is marginal, and fresh greens supply many other important components of diet, such as vitamin C, iron, folic acid and calcium. In China, this problem is recognised: every family in a commune grows its own plot of greens to add to their rice. This is just as well, for in their largely vegetarian diet well over 90 percent of calories are provided by cereals, and

Contrasts in cultures in the market place. Above, leaves strewn on the roadway are the main items on sale on this Calcutta riverside, seen at sunrise. Left, a greengrocer's stall at Iraklion, Crete, offers a wide range of fruit and vegetables, nicely presented – almost all grown in the comfortable climate of this mid-Mediterranean island.

What we eat

Comparisons of average food intake in different continents in three categories – fats, protein and calories – reveal some sharp divisions in the world. Despite producing more than enough to feed the world's peoples, we still have not eradicated hunger and malnutrition.

On each map, animal products are shown in red, those from vegetables in blue. Figures are 1975-77 averages. Such averages conceal sharper variations at local and regional levels. It is estimated that malnutrition affects ten percent of the world population – but in developing countries as a whole, the figure is nearer 20 percent, while in individual countries, it can be 30 percent or even more.

This is not so much a failure of production as of organisation: in Bangladesh, after the 1974 floods, 4 million tonnes of rice accumulated because the great majority were too poor to afford it. In Senegal development aid funds have been used to irrigate the desert in order to grow aubergines and mangoes for export while the hungry are unemployed. And in China visible hunger has been eliminated in 20 years while in India, with twice the cultivated acreage available, many still go hungry.

Top *The figure on each circle represents the total average calories per person per day. The contrast between developed nations and Third World countries in Africa and Asia is again particularly noticeable. South America shows a halfway situation. The world average is 2590 calories per day, 83 percent from vegetable products, 17 percent from animals.*

Centre *Proteins in grammes per person per day: world average is 69.3 grammes, with 35 percent from animal and 65 percent from vegetable products. The difference between developed nations and Africa and Asia is very pronounced, with Australasia heavily dependent on animals as a source of protein.*

Bottom *Total average fats eaten per person per day. World averages are 62.7 grammes per day with 54 percent from animal, 46 percent from vegetable products, Australasia again consuming an amazing 75 percent of fats in animal form, with USSR not far behind.*

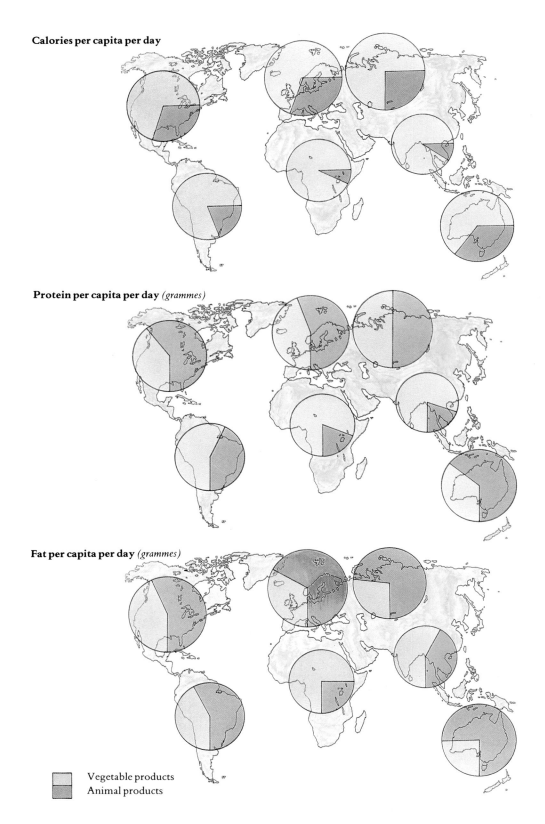

Calories per capita per day

Protein per capita per day *(grammes)*

Fat per capita per day *(grammes)*

Vegetable products
Animal products

Food Consumption *(kg per capita per year)*

Regional comparison of per capita consumption of cereals, tubers, pulses and meat show up differences both in diet and in total consumption. The high grain consumption in developed countries reflects their high meat diet – most of the grain reaching the table indirectly, via animal feeds. In the US, nearly 90 percent of grain is fed to meat animals – an extravagant use of a precious resource. Globally, the figure is nearer 40 percent. The greatest meat-eaters are the Australians, the lowest the Africans and South-east Asians. Their modest consumption of cereals and roots is doubly significant when one bears in mind that here these staples play a major role in the diet, providing most of daily calorific intake. Not all staples, of course, provide similar protein and nutritional value per kg, and consumption figures can be less important than calorie-intake comparisons, in this respect. The geographic reliance on various staples is shown below.

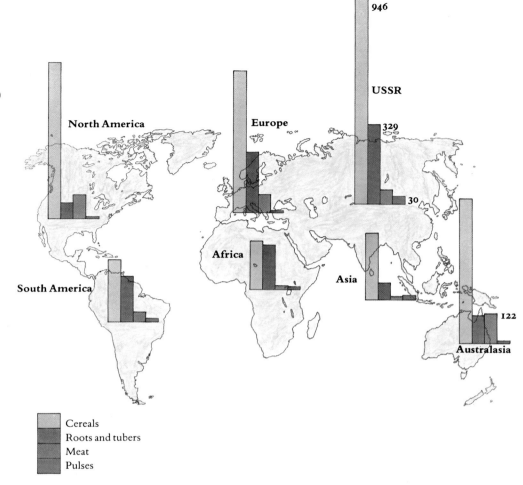

Cereals
Roots and tubers
Meat
Pulses

The Staple Crops

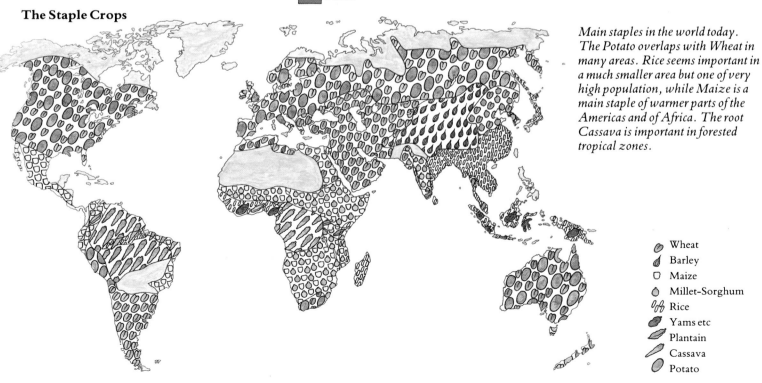

Main staples in the world today. The Potato overlaps with Wheat in many areas. Rice seems important in a much smaller area but one of very high population, while Maize is a main staple of warmer parts of the Americas and of Africa. The root Cassava is important in forested tropical zones.

Wheat
Barley
Maize
Millet-Sorghum
Rice
Yams etc
Plantain
Cassava
Potato

65

Despite the apparent barrenness of their homeland, Bushmen of the Kalahari desert find enough sustenance here. They are among the few surviving hunter-gatherers, following a lifestyle which began for emergent Homo sapiens around 20,000 years ago. Besides plants they eat insects and whatever other animals share their harsh environment.

most proteins from cereals and legumes; a great deal of the cereal is rice. In its unrefined state this is a good food source comparing well with wheat, but unmilled brown rice is often scarce or expensive. In China, as elsewhere in Asia, white rice, milled and polished, is preferred. All the nutritious coloured pericarp is removed as bran; the protein content decreases from ten to seven per cent in polishing, and washing and cooking methods deplete the nutrients further. A diet too heavily dependent on refined rice can result in deficiency diseases such as beri beri.

There is growing evidence, too, that western foods are very damaging to health. Some scientists say that the food we eat, especially so-called "junk food", is the main cause of death and disease, and that we should dramatically reduce our intake of sugar, salt, animal and dairy fats – the modern killers. Many rural Africans, like the Dogon tribe, are not prey to such problems as coronary heart disease or cancer of the bowel for instance, and the main difference between the diets is the amount of fibre in the food. Dietary fibre is the indigestible part of plants such as bran, which western food refiners remove so that, for example, bread is spongy, light and white, not a healthy, heavy, brown chew. Fibre aids digestion and the rapid passage of matter through the body; it thus prevents cancer of the bowel by quickly flushing the poisonous agents out of the gut. The low proportion of roughage that many of the elderly of Britain consume means that food may take *two weeks* to pass through the alimentary tract.

Properly used, plants can supply all our carbohydrates, protein, edible fats and oils, vitamins and minerals, and feed our animals. We need all these components of food and a mixed diet is absolutely essential.

The Beginnings of Cultivation

Primitive people operated as "hunter-gatherers" from perhaps 20000 to 8000 BC, killing wild animals for food, fishing, collecting molluscs, and gathering all manner of edible plant material. This way of life still exists in a small way: Australian Aborigines, Kalahari Bushmen and some central African tribes do not attempt any cultivation.

Gathering nature's gifts seems a carefree life, and one might wonder why ancient peoples turned to agriculture. In fact, hunter-gathering is not always very comfortable. The Aborigines, for instance, were always faced with a harsh environment with scanty resources.

As we saw in Chapter 3, hunter-gathering means keeping on the move. Settling down in one area was possible if small numbers of people inhabited rich food areas, especially if there was good fishing adjacent from sea or lake. And once one has settled, there is first of all the possibility of stockpiling food over cold winters or dry seasons.

The earliest record of settlement combined with such storage is of the Natufians of Palestine, who dug store pits which they lined with plaster and had grinding stones and sickle blades. Around 9000 BC they began to gather cereal seeds to augment their diet of wild gazelle and other game. Such a settled lifestyle is a prerequisite for agriculture to begin, the settlers becoming familiar with their plants at all seasons and, in due time, able to tend growing crops consistently.

Right *Barley and Wheat were both cultivated in ancient Egypt from the fifth millenium BC, Wheat becoming the more important of the two cereals. These tomb paintings from the Eighteenth Dynasty (1567-1320 BC) show how the ripening Wheat crop was sized up by inspectors with measuring lines, who set the government's tax quota. After harvesting the crop went to the granary for final tallying.*

Above *A coin of Cunobelin, king of the Belgic Catuvellauni, who invaded Britain in 75 BC, made his capital at Colchester and had an alliance with Rome. It shows an ear of cereal, probably Barley which was the most abundant grain in cultivation in Britain from Neolithic to Viking times.*

There is little doubt that crop cultivation developed independently in several places. For a long time the "cradle of agriculture" was thought to be sited in the "Fertile Crescent" of the Near East; this was largely because there were in that area accessible, well preserved archaeological remains of stone or mud, many of Biblical significance, which were among the earliest to be investigated.

In these dry conditions evidence of early agriculture has come from seed imprints on pottery, grains preserved in ancient caves and tombs, or carbonised near fires. Such grains have been radio-carbon-dated as 9,000 years old. Archaeological evidence equally·confirms that northern China was the centre for an agricultural system 7,000 years ago: it was based on Foxtail Millet, which by 2700 BC came to be held sacred.

Squashes, beans and maize were cultivated – in an ingenious self-balancing triple-crop system in the same patch of ground – in Central America at the same time; while a system based around potatoes, cultivated with digging sticks, started up independently in the South American Andes some 8,000 years back. In warmer areas of South America, Cassava was clearly being cultivated as early as the third millenium BC since there is good evidence of trade in Cassava flour.

Despite the liability of succulent fruits and roots to decay in hot moist areas, radio-carbon-dated remains in South-east Asia suggest that yams were part of a vege-cultural civilisation (Hoabinhian) in 8000 BC. Yams are a vital part of early agricultural history since different species exist in Asia,

From the wild Sunflower (Helianthus annuus) above, with its flimsy stems and relatively small flowers and few, small seeds, have been selected the massive forms now grown commercially for their oil-rich seeds, as in Provence, France, top.

Africa and tropical America, and formed the basis of early vege-culture in these areas (in America rather overshadowed by Cassava) and are still vital to subsistence agriculture in many areas. Yams are cultivated from small pieces of tubers or by stem cuttings, and their propensity for rapid rooting must have been noticed early on as people gathered them and left odd bits in the ground. Curiously enough cultivated yams seldom set seed, so that many varieties have been increased for thousands of years by vegetative propagation.

Hypotheses of the domestication of cereals are very different. Best known is the rubbish-heap hypothesis of how cultivation began. It describes a scenario of rubbish piled up beside the homesteads – fruit cores, seeds, bones, offal and excreta – all decayed into rich compost. Some of the seeds would germinate in the fertile ground, and the plants that the gleaners had trudged many weary miles to collect would suddenly be there on the doorstep, a gift from the gods. The gatherers would have collected proportionately more of the bigger and least fragile wild produce, so the plants on the heap would already be diverging genetically from the wild. The people gradually discovered that some examples of plants produced better seeds or fruits than others so were worth deliberately storing for later sowing and harvesting. And weed plants that could not survive in the fierce competition of the primeval woodlands beyond the settlement would luxuriate on the kitchen middens. Some, such as amaranthus, legumes, squashes and cucumbers had potential as food crops; others like Nightshade turned out to be deadly poisons – but even poisons have their uses.

Plums and their relatives have a complex ancestry and probably originated in central Asia. The delectable Greengage, Coe's Golden Drop, above, was raised in 1800. Like most plums today it probably derived from the Damson Plum (Prunus institia), the Cherry Plum (P. cerasifera), and the Sloe or Blackthorn (P. spinosa), below. The spininess of many ancestral forms is now lost in cultivated kinds. Cultivated plums have six sets of chromosomes; the wild plums two.

How Crops Develop

We can begin to see a pattern emerging from historical obscurity. All kinds of wild plants are tried out for food; some prove better than others. Then some ingratiate themselves with people and thus become prime candidates for cultivation, though they are not deliberately chosen.

If one places the wild species and the crop derivative together for comparison, one of the most noticeable things is that the crop plant is much bigger, and not always just in the character desired, such as the grain in Wheat, root in Carrot, or fruit in Apple, but in other parts as well. Thus the Sunflower is bigger flowered, bigger leaved and thicker stemmed than its wild relations. Crop plants may change proportions: the Peanut that splays its nut-bearing stems metres away from it, in the wild neatly burying them in the ground after flowering, gathers them round its centre when domesticated. The garden cabbage has a firm solid heart – its wild ancestor a few loose leaves. Wild wheat ears are brittle, shattering at a touch when mature to give the seeds a chance of being spread around. The pieces have long "beards", hard to remove from the seeds, which aid them to winkle their way into cracks in the soil, ready to germinate when rain comes. Primitive gatherers would have favoured any wheat which had mutated so as not to shatter when harvested.

How have these changes occurred? Early cultivators gradually realised that there were bigger grains of wheat than normal, and by and by non-brittle ears; larger yam tubers, more prolific peanuts, sweeter apples. The "better" forms were sown or replanted so that gradually there was an improvement in the crop by the process of selection.

During such early stages of selection natural breeding between closely related species could occur, say in the wheatfield, resulting effectively in quite new plants. Often there also occurred unpredictable internal changes in plant cells, known as mutations or sports, which give rise to new forms. One common change is the doubling of the number of chromosomes from the standard double set (diploid) to a quadruple set (tetraploid), which very often creates a larger and more vigorous plant. This was for instance very important in the development of wheat.

A cultivator with a sharp eye would pick out such novelties and grow them on separately. Until the very recent achievement of deliberate cross-breeding the only way that people improved their plants was selection of the best in a crop, with special reference to unusual, fortuitous seedlings or sports. In the same way unwanted characters, for instance natural plant defences like spininess in the wild plum and pear, or bitterness and toxicity in the wild potato tuber, were "selected out" early in the course of their gradual domestication.

Clearly, crops develop a wide range of physiological adaptations as they are grown in unnaturally cultivated and fertilised soil, and later in new habitats as people transport them. Many become able to survive in conditions quite different from those of their original homes. The progenitors of maize are plants which time their lives according to the sun's short-day regime in tropical climes; it has since been transformed into a plant that will grow in the long-day cycles of temperate climates. The same is true of the Potato from equatorial South America.

The process of adaptation means that many crop plants may become quite unfit to compete in the wild with their original congeners: they may lose their power of natural dispersal as in non-shattering wheat; the shortening of the peanut flower stems to convenient length for cultivation equally reduces its ability to spread successfully. Selection for rapid, even germination of seeds puts all the eggs into one basket: the wild plants hedge their bets by staggering germination.

Plant Breeding

Modern agriculture hinges on purposeful plant breeding. This has been carried out only during the last 200 years and was not possible on any scientific basis until the monk Gregor Mendel worked out the principles of inheritance in 1865 (and this work was neglected till the early 20th century). Certainly the more advanced methods of maintaining or improving soil fertility, and mechanisation, have had their effects; but without breeding, the high-yielding crops responsive to high fertility would not have been produced, nor would the thick-skinned cultivars that can put up with mechanical harvesting and transport to markets (even if this often makes them less palatable, as with tomatoes).

Plant breeders aim to improve yield and quality, and have various methods of achieving this. Given a crop with a fair amount of natural variation, a great deal can be done with a keen eye, a rabbit's tail for pollination and a prayer; but in this space age breeders have a new range of tactics – irradiation, chromosome doubling, tissue culture, and so on – to encourage "unwilling" plants to breed and then to sort the progeny.

One of the landmarks of plant breeding this century has been the development of Triticale – the first time a crop has been synthesised by hybridising species from different genera, *Triticum* (Wheat) and *Secale* (Rye). Natural hybrids of the two have frequently been reported but are usually sterile, and so are non-starters as cereal crops. It was only with the improvement of embryo culture and chromosome doubling techniques in the 1930s that work began in earnest, aiming to combine the winter-hardiness of Rye with the high-yielding properties of Wheat. The result resembles Wheat in appearance, but it is hardier, and in poor, parched soils will out-yield Wheat. It is better nutritionally with higher content of protein and essential amino-acids. More than half a million hectares are planted each year with Triticale. At present it is used mostly as animal feed, and experimentally certain lines of it have produced higher growth rates in rats than other cereal grains. But hopes are high that it will prove its worth as human food, not only because of its nutritional quality, but because it grows better than Wheat on marginal land.

Rice is a spectacular example of breeding for high yields. It was being hybridised as early as 1906. Breeding in Japan and the United States and, finally, in combination, steadily improved the cropping capacity of rice until, in the late 1960s, several "semi-dwarfs" appeared – compact, stiff and erect, with plenty of side shoots, early maturity, no sensitivity to day-length, and responsive to high amounts of nitrogen fertiliser. Breeding initially achieved considerable resistance to major pests and diseases, but now these are out-pacing the breeders' efforts. The new Rice varieties replaced long-strawed ones, traditional in Asia, adapted to grow above the weeds and floods (breeding to increase the weight of grain on such plants would have caused them to keel over).

The use of these new high-yielding Rice and also Wheat varieties in Asia has given rise to what is called the "Green Revolution". This, alas, has shown that plant breeding for higher yields is not always a success, at any rate in human terms. The amount of Wheat and Rice produced in developing countries has certainly been greatly increased but at high social cost, and also loss of genetic resources.

The revolution has become like a pyramid of cards with the high-yielding crops balanced precariously on top. Remove the fertiliser, or the irrigation water, and the stack collapses. Further inputs are needed, and also herbicides to suppress the weeds, fungicides to quell disease epidemics that attack the vast acreages, and machinery to apply the pest-killers and fertilisers as well as to plant and harvest.

The high-yielding wheats were produced by the International Wheat and Maize Improvement Centre in Mexico. This was founded on money from the Rockefeller Foundation which teamed up with Ford to found the International Rice Research Institute in the Philippines which produced the miracle rice. Multinational corporations were in on the start of the Green Revolution and, by supplying the chemicals, seeds and machinery have continued to profit from it since. An example of the social consequences of such activity is Bangladesh where the introduction of combine harvesters has taken work and income from a great many pairs of ill-fed hands.

Ancient cereal grasses had heads which shattered readily so that the seeds would scatter widely, and long "beards" which, caught by the wind, helped the seeds force their way into the soil. Accidental hybridisation and, in particular, mutations produced some varieties with non-shattering heads and more easily removed beards; it was these which primitive people selected, first for harvesting from the wild and later for deliberate cultivation. Once their natural mechanism for seed dispersal is lost, the plants become dependant on their cultivators for survival. Among the earliest domesticated wheats were Einkorn (Triticum monococcum), near right, a diploid (with two sets of chromosomes) once grown in Turkey and Europe; and Emmer (T. dicoccum), centre, a natural tetraploid (four sets of chromosomes) once grown in the Near East, Africa and Europe, together with another wheat, T. timopheevii. Today's bread wheat (T. aestivum), far right, is a hexaploid hybrid between Emmer and species of closely-related Goat Grass (Aegilops).

T. monococcum   *T. dicoccum*   *T. aestivum*

Teosinte

Maize

Often the rural peasant does not benefit at all. Such technology is unafford-able. The tenant farmer and sharecropper get into the hands of money-lenders or are thrown off the land their families have farmed for generations so that the landlords can increase their acreage. The mechanised agribusi-ness does not require the peasants' labour, so they are not only dispossessed but unemployed. India has witnessed some particularly ugly scenes.

It is of particular concern to botanists and plant breeders that the wide adoption of the new high-yielding varieties of Rice and Wheat has caused tremendous change to the genetic resource. The new, uniform varieties are fast replacing the diverse but less productive land-races developed over thousands of years. In Pakistan, for example, all the areas to which access is easy, by road or path, have been planted up with the new cultivars. Yet the variation in the land-races was an essential ingredient in breeding the new crops and will be needed again to improve them and keep up with rapidly evolving pests and diseases. Breeders will have to work fast to collect the surviving range of types before they are exterminated. This problem is dealt with at greater length in Chapter 11.

Maize

The story of Maize reflects, in microcosm, the story of agriculture. It nourished the great civilizations of ancient America and today is the prin-cipal food plant of the western world, with more than 300 million tonnes produced annually. Yet it is a monster which cannot live without people. The cob, gift-wrapped in papery layers of husks, does not shatter at maturity and kernels are clamped tightly to the central core. If the cob is not harvested it eventually drops to earth and the seeds, all germinating at once, will choke each other in mass fratricide. Quite possibly not one of the 1,000 or so seedlings would survive to mature and breed, unless people or machines shucked the kernels from the core and sowed them apart.

There are many different varieties of Maize, each having its own qualities tailoring it for its environment and end purpose. Most commercial Maize today is yellow or white "flint" or "dent". The flint corns are hard, sometimes with a small amount of opaque floury tissue near the centre of

Maize, left, is believed to be derived from the wild grass Teosinte, above left, its familiar heavy cob being equivalent to Teosinte's relatively miniscule ear, see facing page. Modern Maize, or Corn, is a biological monstrosity, created by human cultivation, and quite unable to survive natural conditions. Teosinte can interbreed quite easily with Maize; indeed, it has apparently swapped genes with it naturally from ancient times, though breeders have not made use of it. The explorer C. Lumholz travelling in Mexico at the turn of the century discovered that Teosinte was known to be good for the corn. Traditionally seed was saved from one crop for the next year's plantings, and where there was any distance between one cultivation and the next, the isolation could well have led to inbreeding and the associated depression in yield. A dose of strange genes from Teosinte would without doubt have injected a healthy spurt of hybrid vigour into the offspring and rejuvenated the line. The name itself, Teosinte, comes from Aztec "teocentli", meaning God's ear of corn. Maybe this reveals the cultural memory of the wild grass being taken into domestication; in many parts of Mexico Teosinte is known as madre de maiz (mother of maize).

the kernel; dent types have a central core of soft starch which shrinks on drying, causing the surface to dent.

Maize arrives at our table as butter-drenched golden cylinders of corn-on-the-cob, sweet corn out of a tin enlivening many a dreary rice salad, or that party favourite, popcorn. We fry in maize oil and use cornflour to thicken gravies and make puddings; we might even take a little as breakfast cereal or drink it as whisky. A huge proportion goes to feed livestock so we eat it eventually, transmitted into meat, eggs and dairy products.

In less wealthy parts of the earth, as in Latin America, Maize is a vital element of diet, often coarsely ground and made into a paste or gruel. But it is not an ideal food for humans, as it is low in protein. Only recently have plant breeders incorporated mutant genes to improve the nutritional value, and one day these could be of great benefit in preventing malnutrition.

No-one knows for sure when or where Maize was born, nor its exact ancestry. Very small cobs, only about 20 mm long, found at St Marco's Cave, Tehuacan, Mexico, have been carbon-dated to about 7,000 years old. They bear the hallmark of cultivation; the grains are arranged in several rows on a rachis that does not break up at maturity. Scientists have discovered a two-metre deep accumulation of rubbish and subsequent excavations at this site have revealed a sequence of cobs showing the evolution of Maize. Bat Cave in New Mexico concealed an ear of primitive pod popcorn for 5,000 years; complete ears dated at 500 BC are similar to races found in Andean Peru and Bolivia today (though these are distinct from both current or archaeological Mexican Maize).

The Indian peoples grew their crops mostly in slash-and-burn clearings in the forest. After three or four years of cultivation the clearings were abandoned for ten years or so until fertility was restored. The Colombian Indians of the Choco region still practice a primitive form of this "swidden" cultivation; they scatter seeds in a freshly cleared plot, only returning to the crop at harvest time. Open grasslands like those of the southern USA and the Argentinian pampas, now major crop producing areas, were not used by early inhabitants because their crude implements could not break the mat of roots. However, in arid areas Maize could be grown in sunken fields. In northern Chile, for example, sand was cleared down to a level at which soil moisture was present, then planted. A similar form of agriculture is carried out to this day by the Hopi Indians who dig a series of widely spaced pits, planting about ten kernels in each. They add soil gradually round the plants as they grow.

The centres of Maize variability seem linked to the ancient civilisations. The Mexican and lowland Central American dents are associated with the Mayan culture; the variability of Maize found in the central Andes is linked with the Incas; the Guatemalan and north Andean flints with the Chibchans. The conical corns of central highland Mexico were the power behind the Aztecs, and Montezuma, the last Emperor, demanded a tribute of some 3,000 bushels each year from his 20 provinces. It is possible that these diverse centres indicate independent origins of Maize agriculture.

When Columbus landed on Cuba in 1492, he found Maize agriculture in full swing. Indeed Maize was being grown right from the mouth of the St Lawrence River in Canada in the north down to central Chile in South America, with some 200 to 300 local varieties. Since then, Maize has spread

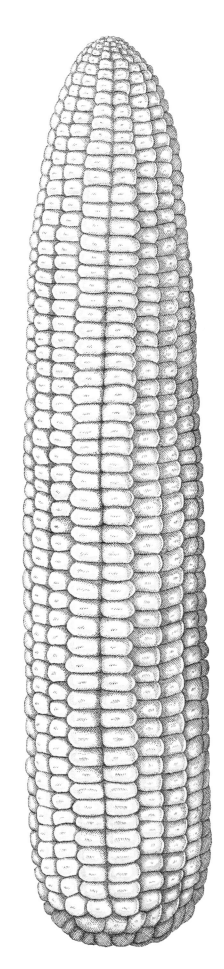

the world over. Cuban and Argentine flint corn gave rise to the true flints used throughout the tropics and sub-tropics. The flints of temperate zones are often traceable to the northern flints and flour corns of the USA. Dents of Mexican and lowland central America have also spread around the tropics. Some of the Mexican dent corn was taken into the southern USA where in the mid 1800s it crossed naturally with flint types. This north-south fusion gave rise to the dents now of prime commercial importance in the US Corn Belt and which grow so well in southern Europe too.

The early European settlers of the Americas adopted the local varieties of Maize with no attempts at breeding better strains until the mid-1800s. Then they started to produce prize corn for exhibition at agricultural fairs, where a standard idealised corn was required. The emphasis was on large cylindrical ears of dent maize produced on single-stem plants with no sideshoots. The craze led unfortunately to the elimination of much variety, and the industry is now based on only two of 200-plus primitive varieties.

Repeatedly crossing one type of Maize with itself quickly produces a pathetically weak strain. However, crossing two distinct inbred varieties produces plants far out-yielding the parent types: this is the phenomenon known as heterosis or hybrid vigour, and is important in no crop more than Maize. The hybrids are uniform in appearance and all other qualities, which is virtually essential in modern crop production and use. To get a really bumper yield, seed resulting from the cross of two pure parent lines must be planted every time, and cannot be saved from the previous crop, so a specialist producer of hybrid seed is required who maintains the pure lines and produces hybrids for the farmer to sow.

To perform these precise crosses it is essential to ensure that a plant does not fertilise itself. This used to involve a great deal of manual labour in removing the tassels (male flowers) from the plants which were to produce the seed, so that female flowers could be fertilised with pollen only from specified male parent plants. Then in the late 1940s a special form of male-sterility which prevented pollen formation was found in some Texas Maize. A plant with this factor was suitable for the seed-producing parent of the hybrid and did not require de-tasseling. Its progeny, pollinated by a fertile male line, were self-fertile and had full hybrid vigour.

The Texas male-sterile factor was a rare and lucky find, and thus very widely used. However, this sterility was activated in the cytoplasm of the cells rather than controlled by genes on the chromosomes in the cell nucleus, as such factors usually are.

At one time virtually all commercial Maize had the same cytoplasm so, though appearing varied, the vast acreages of the crop grown in the USA were identical in this one important feature. The inevitable happened and disease struck in 1970. The fungus *Helminthosporium maydis*, revelling in a warm damp spring, spread like wildfire across the Corn Belt, travelling as much as 150 km a day. At harvest dark clouds of spores billowed around the combines. It was very lucky that this outbreak of Southern Leaf Blight caused no more than 15 percent loss overall, though in some of the southern states more than half of the crop was lost. Consider the consequences if the outbreaks had occurred in a country where Maize is the primary human staple. In Kenya, for example, where it constitutes more than half of all food consumed, there would have been a tragedy.

Many of the primitive Maizes show an astonishing range of colour, with the greatest variety of all being found in the central Andes. Various parts of the kernel are white, yellow, lemon, orange, red, purple, brown or pink, and these may also be speckled, spotted, striped or streaked – as illustrated by the assortment, top right, hanging in the house of an Otavalo Indian ready for next year's sowing. These Maizes are maintained on innumerable small plots, each with its locally adapted varieties, such as the one illustrated, bottom near right, in Narino Province, Colombia – a far cry from the huge areas of monoculture in Maryland, USA, bottom far right. As modern "super-Maize" takes over, the genetic diversity preserved in traditional cultivation is all too easily lost.

An early depiction of the Potato (Solanum tuberosum) clearly shows the five-petalled flowers typical of the family Solanaceae. The fruits, too, are typical, resembling those of its relative the Tomato (though in the Potato's case they are poisonous). Most Andean ancestors of the Potato have rather small tubers, but this painting shows quite large ones, though far more irregular than is considered desirable in commercial terms today. Our modern potatoes, conveniently shaped and of lavish size, are nonetheless rather dull vegetables – and will grow only in temperate climates. In Peru, however, many varieties, each with a different flavour, are known, while in the Potato's Andean homeland many wild varieties grow, offering hope for cultivation in the tropical lowlands.

Nearly all Maize improvement has been achieved by using the genetic resources of the variety within the crop itself. There are just two cultivars into which breeders have introduced genes from *Tripsacum*, a related wild grass, which can be crossed with maize only with difficulty. For years one of the wild maize species, *Zea perennis*, was believed extinct in the wild, kept alive only in botanical gardens. Then in 1977 Rafael Guzman, searching in the remote mountains of southern Mexico, came across a stand of it. Not content with discovering the Holy Grail of maize botanists he then, not far away, came across a stand of a totally new plant, *Zea diploperennis*. Some experts believe it is the true ancestor of Maize, and so great is the excitement concerning this wild grass that it has widely been called the botanical find of the century.

Maize is an annual, these two grasses perennial. This conjures dreams of amazing labour-saving fields cropping year after year without resowing. However, making perennials annual is a common feature of domestication because then the plants put an all-out effort into filling the fruits, not wasting food and energy on (to humans) useless vegetative organs and over-wintering devices, so making Maize perennial is not likely to be a major triumph of Guzman's discoveries.

Zea diploperennis crosses freely with Maize, and has many useful features, especially immunity to many of the major virus diseases that ravage corn. It has been estimated that as much as $250 million a year could be saved if only one percent of the US crop were protected.

Yet the tragedy is that these two new Maizes – merely a few corn stalks – only grow in a tiny area, a few hectares only, now threatened by forest cutting and squatter agriculture.

Present Problems

Advanced agriculture often causes greed where it should create plenty, and starvation in the wake of apparent munificence. Worse still, it produces new problems as fast as it solves the old. Nature responds with evermore pests and diseases, vastly encouraged by our huge monocultures; mutating as rapidly as the pesticides and fungicides to control them are changed, these attackers are often one jump ahead.

Probably the most notorious crop failure was that of the Potato in 1845 and 1846 which caused famine in Ireland and a surge of emigration to the New World. Cultivated for thousands of years in its native Andes, the Potato was first brought to Europe around 1570. It did not catch on immediately in its new environment because the early introduction did not prosper in the long-day seasons of temperate regions. But satisfactory clones eventually arose and by the early nineteenth century the Potato had become the major item of diet of the Irish poor, and also of their pigs.

Here was a recipe for disaster: large acreages of one crop built on the slenderest genetic foundation, and the whole peasantry entirely dependent on it. In mid-August 1845 a blight struck the crop on the Isle of Wight and in the course of few weeks spread throughout the British Isles. Contemporary accounts state that it destroyed between quarter and half the crop. The following year the epidemic began earlier and was even more destructive.

The Potato Famine of 1846 was caused by the fungus disease Late Blight, which swept through the Potato fields of Britain, all planted with the same crop variety, in successive waves of destruction. The collapse of the Potato harvest produced an enormous social upheaval in the British Isles. In Ireland nine-tenths of the crop rotted; with no produce the peasants were unable to pay their landlords, who went bankrupt. The people either stayed and starved, or emigrated; many went to the New World, such as the Irish immigrants, shown above, disembarking at New York.

It was some time before the nature of the disease was properly understood. In damp conditions the green parts are attacked by the fungus *Phytophthora infestans* so the tubers do not fill out, or if they become infected they are weakened and are rotted by secondary pathogens. By 1926 resistance from related wild species had been bred into the commercial crop and scientists thought they had late blight conquered. Then in 1932 a race of *Phytophthora infestans* arose which overcame the resistance in the new varieties. Eventually a new resistant cultivar was created, which also in due course fell foul of a new race of the disease. This cat and mouse game between breeders and the blight has been going on ever since. Furthermore, this fungus is just one of the many organisms that appear to enjoy the potato as much as we do, and each of which the farmer has to fight tooth and nail.

This example can be repeated with almost every crop plant that has been much altered from its ancestors and is grown on any scale.

Pests are even more difficult to control than fungus diseases and are on the whole a worse problem. At least one in ten of the world's million-plus insects is a crop pest, and mice, rats, birds and other large creatures are also serious pests. Between them these probably cause the loss of at least a third of world crops. It has been calculated that in India's biggest state, Uttar Pradesh, there are more than 600 million rats, which consume food produced enough to support 100 million people. Breeding can be undertaken to give appreciable resistance to attack by small pests like aphids and eelworms, but not to the larger ones.

The attentions of these worlds rival to our own call for new methods of control, and the pesticides and fungicides mainly used add to the energy deficit of the world in a horrific way. This is the other sting in the tail of modern agriculture; it is dependent on a vast energy consumption to produce pest and disease controls, fertilisers and weedkillers. High dependence on chemicals seems continually to increase; and in the USA it has been calculated that the proportion of energy expended on these, compared with that on machinery for cultivation and harvesting (itself no mean quantity) is in the region of 8 or 9 to one.

There is therefore a need for greater use of natural pest controls where these can be encouraged, and of new crop plants that will, at least in the less favoured areas of the earth, crop heavily without the need for such vast inputs of energy.

The Future

There is no reason to suggest that our present balance of food crops is the best possible for the future. It clearly places vast strains on the world's economy which may be impossible to maintain. Yet world population increases and needs to be fed.

In the long term one may foresee a world in which the West's present eating habits, concentrated so much on meat, may be changed so that less energy and space are expended on feeding the animals concerned. Equally needing change are the social structures in many third world countries which, especially under repressive regimes, keep the peasants half-starved and often in debt.

The Pummelo (Citrus maxima) is still an unfamiliar fruit in Western eyes. A native of tropical South-east Asia, it is a large-fruited, sweet-flavoured species which has often been used in hybridisation with Sweet Oranges and Mandarins. The resulting offspring have been large and of good flavour, but unfortunately most have large numbers of seeds. Recently it has been found that some varieties of Pummelo are salt-tolerant, opening up possibilities of cultivating citrus fruits on saline soils. The forests of South-east Asia have many hundreds of wild fruit-tree species, and around 125 are locally cultivated. Some offer potentially wider markets, such as the Mangosteen, the Rambutan, or even the Durian – with its delightful taste but infamous smell (eating it is described as being like consuming almond custard in a public lavatory!).

But this book is not a forum for these problems. It can only point to other avenues for crop plant development. The scope for change and improvement in present staple crops is still great, and will remain so as long as the variety of types, which are the raw ingredients for modification, survive, as explained in chapter 11.

Quite a number of other food crops also have scope for improvement. Improvement of Cassava and the various Yams has barely begun for instance, and both have great possibilities.

Job's Tears, *Coix lachryma-jobi*, a grass, is sometimes grown for ornament – the grains being large enough to make beads from. It is a very nutritious cereal which could possibly replace Wheat and Rice in disease-prone areas. A few local strains exist but no big effort has ever been made to develop it. The Australian grass *Echinochloa turnerana*, too, has potential; it can yield crops of good grain after one thorough initial watering, but has never been domesticated.

The Breadfruit, from a tree, has a very high starch content and is made into flour for bread, or the fermented pulp into dough cakes. Many varieties, as in Bananas, are seedless. The related Jackfruit, weighing 20 kg or sometimes much more, is boiled and roasted, or eaten fresh for dessert when ripe; and a less important relation, the Champedak, likewise. These *Artocarpus* species originated between India and Malaysia, but Breadfruit and Jackfruit are quite widely grown in the tropics as subsistence crops. They are permanent plants rather than annual ones so, once established, need little attention; they have considerable potential as food plants.

Most agriculturalists will be reluctant to change the overall pattern of cultivation in the world's fertile areas at present, though there would seem to be advantages in using other crops than the big three cereals in some circumstances, which may be desirable especially where pests and diseases overtake breeders' achievements. Where we can most profitably develop seems to be in using land which has been considered basically unusable for food crops – not, one hopes, by eradicating existing wild plants where these are desirable, but in dry semi-desert and possibly eroded areas.

Most particularly new possibilities exist for saline soils, which in some areas are unfortunately the result of over-salinisation by irrigation schemes. At least a quarter of once-used crop land has been ruined in this way. Across the globe nearly 4 million square miles of land are useless to agriculture because they are dominated by salt. Compare this with the 6 million square miles of cropland and the value of drawing such deserts into the agricultural sphere can be appreciated. In many places underground water reserves which are saline could be pumped up to irrigate suitable crops.

There are some edible wild plants which grow naturally on salt and could certainly be grown as crops, having good yields and food value: these include pickleweeds, saltworts, saltbushes and saltgrasses. The latter have been tried in an alkaline, dried out lakebed in Mexico which now supports livestock. One of the few flowering plants that grow in the sea, Eel Grass, is harvested by the Seri Indians of coastal Mexico who grind the grain into flour. This marine grass offers the surprising prospect of using the seas to grow our bread!

Then there are wild relatives of numerous currently grown crops which tolerate salt and could be bred with existing strains to create new varieties

The Yeheb Nut (Cordeauxia edulis), a bush growing to 2m high on the savanna soils of Ethiopia and Somalia, is on the edge of extinction in the wild through chronic overgrazing. The nutritious seeds have a pleasant sweet flavour and were formerly of importance in the local diet. The Yeheb is now being cultivated in Kenya and Somalia and is suitable for introduction in other regions of low rainfall. The Yeheb is only one of several locally known staples with drought-resistance, many of which have been much neglected. There is the Amaranth, once a very important grain crop in Central America, with a history of 7000 years of cultivation, and still grown for its grain in Andean regions and South-east Asia. Also from the Andes comes the Tarwi, with an equally ancient lineage. The plant is grown for its beanlike seeds, more nutritious even than Soya or Peanuts. However, the seeds need treatment before eating to remove bitter, toxic alkaloids. If plant breeders can solve this problem, the Tarwi may join the ranks of valuable new foods.

for saline soils. Among these are a sugar beet and several cereals – barley, millets, sorghum, rice and wheat. A form of garden beet is known to grow in 75 percent seawater, and there are tolerant forms of date palm, pistachio and pummelo. New hybrid Tomatoes have been bred which can grow in 70 percent sea water, derived from garden varieties crossed with a small-fruited species found on the shores of the Galapagos Islands.

Plants with potential in really arid areas include several yams from the Australian deserts: used by the Aborigines, they have scarcely been investigated. The Aborigines' intimate knowledge of food plants in drylands remains a largely untapped resource. Another intriguing root is the Buffalo Gourd from the most arid places in Mexico and the south-western United States. Its vast starch-filled tuber – 3-4 metres long – can weight 145 kg in old specimens, and up to 30 kg after only two seasons. On top of this it produces round fruits whose seeds contain 30-35 percent protein and up to 34 percent of oil. A hectare of this plant could produce 2 tonnes of seed, yielding nearly a tonne of vegetable oil. Once established, care needed is minimal; the potential crop value approaches 700 dollars per hectare. Wild populations of the Buffalo Gourd show considerable genetic variation – some plants are prolific, some have larger fruits, some are barren – so there is much scope for the plant breeder to select new strains from the wild.

The Somalian Yeheb nut, recently on the verge of extinction, is now being cultivated in east Africa for its nutritious and tasty nuts, while its foliage can provide animal fodder in its arid haunts.

Another dry-loving plant is the Morama Bean of the Kalahari desert, where some Bushmen live for months on end on little else. Old plants produce bean-bearing runners in a 25 metre radius, though 6 metres is more normal; the beans, high in both protein and oil content, are usually toasted, or pounded into a flour from which a soup or porridge is made. As well as the nutritious beans it has tuberous roots which make a good vegetable when eaten young, at 1 or 2 kg. Old roots can reach 100 kg or more. When watered under cultivation, the Morama Bean grows very quickly and produces a phenomenal crop.

Under more normal humid, hot conditions the Wax Gourd grows more easily than its relations the squashes, pumpkins and melons, and so fast that three or four crops could be raised in a year. The gourds are 2 metres long and up to 35 kg in weight, and their crisp and juicy white flesh can be eaten at any stage of growth, in various ways. It has a mild flavour, and is prepared as a cooked vegetable, in soups, or as a sweet mixed with syrup. Their thick waxy skin allows the gourds to be stored for up to a year without refrigeration.

A final example of a number of barely appreciated possibilities is the Winged Bean. Like the Morama Bean it has multiple uses – it is really a dream of a crop, producing edible leaves, flowers, seedpods, seeds and tubers. Food researchers have dubbed the plant "a supermarket on a stalk". The leaves taste like spinach, the sautéed flowers like mushrooms; the young pods are like green beans, the young seeds like peas; the tubers, richer in protein than potato, yam or cassava, can be boiled, fried, baked or roasted. The mature seeds are like Soya Beans, and also yield oil. Like most legumes it harbours nitrogen-fixing bacteria in root nodules, so improves the soil in which it grows. This powerfully climbing bean originated in

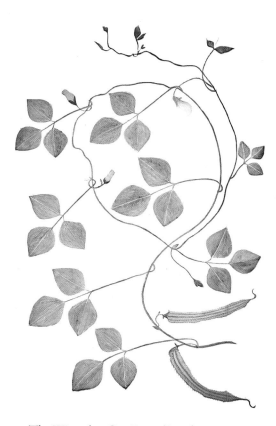

The Winged or Goa Bean (Psophocarpus tetragonolobus) has been grown for many generations as a "poor man's crop" in South-east Asia and Papua New Guinea, but only recently has the remarkable versatility and nutrition-value of this food attracted international attention. Every part of the plant can be eaten. The immature pod, considered a delicacy, is the plant's most popular part. But it is the dried seed which offers hope against malnutrition from protein and vitamin deficiency in the tropics. It provides high-quality protein, and substantial quantities of oil. In many respects it is a rival to the Soya Bean, which is difficult to cultivate in the humid tropics. The Winged Bean is now being grown in more than 70 countries, and is a strong contender for further development.

South-east Asia and is already an important garden plant in several tropical countries. Many hundreds of wild varieties in South-east Asia are now being studied; researchers hope to find short-stemmed, sturdy characters suitable for extensive cultivation. Perhaps the most extraordinary aspect of the Winged Bean story is that this important food plant should have been ignored so long.

Seaweeds were quite widely eaten in Europe and north America within this century, though seldom today. The Hawaiians, Indonesians and other Pacific dwellers eat them in some quantity, but it is in China and notably Japan that they are most prized. Hundreds of thousands of tonnes are collected in Japanese waters annually for home consumption and export to China. Improved methods of collection – by cutting rather than grappling – will indeed be needed if the seaweeds are not to be eradicated here. In both countries there is some cultivation of seaweeds, especially kelps.

Seaweeds are rich in sugars and starches, have some protein, and many contain vitamins A and C. They also contain iodine and this results in the iodine-deficiency disease goitre being almost unknown in Japan.

An even less expected food has been made from the primitive blue-green alga *Spirulina*, found on Lake Texcoco, Mexico, and the small lakes surrounding Lake Chad in Africa. These are very salt and have high alkalinity content, in the region of pH 11, and virtually nothing but *Spirulina* will tolerate these conditions.

The pre-conquest Aztecs collected the algal mats that drifted in the wind to the lake edges, and made sun-dried biscuits of them, as the shore dwellers of Lake Chad do today. These biscuits have the phenomenal food value of 70 percent protein dry weight; they contain vitamins, especially B12, and are readily digestible. The health food market was not slow on the uptake and *Spirulina* pills are now on sale, while the alga is being produced commercially in Mexico as a high-protein, high-carotene additive to chicken-feed. It is this carotene which gives the African flamingoes their glorious pinkness. Wider use of the alga as a human protein supplement, maybe a meat substitute like the Soya Bean analogues, is within the bounds of possibility, though at the present time its production cost is high.

This blue-green alga, an example of the very first organisms on earth to contain chlorophyll and hence with the ability to produce food from solar energy, consists of single cells, sometimes arranged in chains or groups. There are other micro-organisms which are rather similar, though without chlorophyll, which are being developed more extensively, and these are described in Chapter 11. The great advantages of these is that they can be made in factories in relatively small areas rather than cultivated in vast fields like the staple cereals. As such they may help us to save further areas of natural vegetation.

To recapitulate, we have seen how vulnerable our crops are. Over the years we have come to depend on a smaller and smaller number of crops. Today, less than 20 crops supply more than 90 percent of the world's needs; three (Wheat, Rice and Maize) provide more than half. And within each of these crops, the variation is diminishing: more than half Canada's prairie wheatland is planted with a single variety. Their uniformity has made them far more vulnerable to epidemics of pest and disease which, because each cultivar is planted over such enormous areas, can be catastrophic. In 1970 the US Maize crop was devastated by Southern Leaf Blight because 80 percent of the plants were susceptible to the disease.

Plant breeders fight a constant battle to keep one step ahead of pests and diseases. Resistant races of insects, fungi and bacteria rapidly develop to overcome resistance in uniform crop species. For every Barley variety marketed in Britain in the last 20 years, resistance to Mildew has been lost within three years.

The answer is, as so often, to be found in the wild. Recent exploration in the Himalayan foothills of north-eastern India has yielded many primitive Rice cultivars resistant to major diseases and pests, including Blast, Bacterial Blight, Tungro Virus, Gall Midge and Stem Borer. A single population of Wild Rice (*Oryza nivara*) from central India is the only known source of resistance to Grassy Stunt Virus, which was once a serious disease. Resistance from this rare wild plant was bred into a cultivar, IR36, whic has since become the most widely grown variety of Rice – but for how long?

Plant breeders are able to transfer favourable characteristics from one species or cultivar to another. They find these characteristics from among the diversity of the crop itself as well as from the species related to it. Yet it is the advanced cultivars which, by their very success, are wiping out the variable and diverse plants on which future breeding will rely: the success of the agricultural revolution is destroying these resources essential to the future of good farming. This must surely be one of the most worrying trends in the world today and one which demands the attention of every politician and policy-maker.

There is no need that the plant kingdom cannot supply. There is no challenge to which it cannot rise. All that is required is a measure of human ingenuity, intelligence and the political will to care for it.

Twists of the blue-green alga Spirulina, above left, each just a quarter of a millimetre long, are potentially of great importance in feeding a hungry world. Spirulina is suitable for industrial production in open ponds or closed polythene tubes, and out-performs all of the major crops with yields ten times higher than Wheat. A mat of Spirulina is shown, above, on a conveyor belt at a processing plant in Mexico.

Foraging for the famous Perigord Truffle, an unusual underground fungus, one of life's great gourmet delights.

The Spice of Life

There are a few things in life we cannot do without: sufficient plain food, good water, and protection from cold. Then there are those luxuries that – for the fortunate – add to the joy of living: a scented bath, a gourmet meal, a fine old malt whisky.

Luxuries are, by definition, rarities. They are also subject to the whim of fashion. A local product, gathered from the wild, or casually cultivated by an indigenous community, suddenly becomes a craze in another culture, often halfway across the world – who had heard of Jojoba oil cosmetics a few years ago? The initial burst of enthusiasm is the danger point for a wild plant, when collection is heavy but before it becomes profitable to cultivate the species. The sandalwood craze of the seventeenth century nearly wiped out the species. Today wild palm-hearts are a delicacy that threatens other trees with extinction.

Every country has its larder of wild produce, a cornucopia for the initiated. Pre-agricultural people exploited hundreds of plants for food, but with the adoption of agriculture there was less time for gathering wild plants, and less need, so much knowledge faded. However, when the maize crop failed in Tanzania in 1952, some people managed to support themselves in the famine conditions on wild produce. Their relative health surprised governments officers since only Baobab fruit had been officially recognised as a wild food. Subsequent research identified 40 bush foods, with an additional ten roots eaten in times of dire emergency.

In places like Britain hardly any people rely on what they can glean from the hedgerows. Wild foods are regarded as luxuries – a few fashionable restaurants serve nettle soup in season. In much of Europe, however, especially the south, country people use native plants for food and medicine as an important part of their life. For many other peoples, the knowledge of the hunter-gatherer is still a necessity. The aborigines of the Kalahari desert, Australia, the Philippines, India and South America all have complex diets in which plant foods are of critical importance.

Of all the plants gathered from the wild, fungi are among the most fascinating: the autumnal fungus foray is a special event in northern Europe and Russia, with the extraordinary exception of Britain. One of the most luxurious food items in the western world is an underground fungus, the Perigord Truffle, which currently retails at about £1 a gramme. It resembles

Fragaria chiloensis

The modern cultivated strawberry, Fragaria
ananassa, is the offspring of a union between
two American species brought independently
to Europe: F. virginiana (native to Eastern
N. America) and F. chiloensis, above
(native to Chile, and locally cultivated in
Western N. America). The first hybrid
seems to have been an accident, arising in a
garden near Amsterdam around 1750. The
European Strawberry, Fragaria vesca,
below, was probably the species cultivated
by the Romans in 200 BC.

Fragaria vesca

a piece of coke – blackish, warty and up to 7 cm across. This esteemed vegetable is gathered with the help of pigs or specially trained dogs which rootle around the forest floors near Perigueux in France to find it by its smell. Other fungus species, such as the Italian White Truffle or the Morel, Cepe and Chanterelle, not quite so highly prized, are widespread.

Luxury Fruit and Vegetables

In terms of luxury some fruits are classier than others. For instance in Britain the Pawpaw, Persimmon, Lychee and Loquat are regarded as something out of the ordinary, a distinction they lack in their countries of origin. The luxury value thus appears to be based on "foreignness" and unavailability, especially as the very weight and perishability of fruit make them expensive to transport and handle, while the opening up of export markets may shift the price of fruits such as mangoes beyond the reach of the average local pocket.

A few fruits transcend the requirement for foreignness, the strawberry being an obvious example. There are about 35 different species of strawberry plants found wild in northern temperate areas, into the subtropics and in South America. All bear edible fruit and were probably items of fare in the hunter-gatherer's diet. Certainly the Romans cultivated a strawberry, probably the European one, way back in 200 BC, and this species was also grown in medieval Europe. Today's strawberries are our most important soft fruit crops, with well over a million tons produced each year, sometimes in poor countries as cash crops for export.

Vegetable luxuries are fewer. With the admonitions of nutritionists ringing in our ears we eat up greens because they are good for us. Only a few are regarded as delicacies – the tender tips of Asparagus shoots and the thistle-like heads of Artichokes, for instance, are dignified as luxuries by their usual position of appetizers at meals. Indeed, Artichokes were the most esteemed vegetable in England during the seventeenth century.

Asparagus developed from wild European species. Grown in beds of rich soil supplied annually with manure, it is an extravagant vegetable since it takes several years to become fully established, only crops over about six weeks in the year, yet remains in place for long periods.

As for the Artichoke, only the fleshy bases of the bracts and the base of the flower are eaten, while the aptly named choke – the immature flower – is discarded: a sophisticated approach indeed! The tender central leaf stalks are also edible. (Cardoon, a close relative of Artichoke, is occasionally cultivated for the leaf stalks which are blanched.)

It is remarkable that anyone discovered you could eat true thistles. (One is reminded of Tigger, the parvenu tiger, in A. A. Milne's *House at Pooh Corner*, who found that thistles are not what Tiggers liked best only after having eaten a mouthful of Eeyore the donkey's favourite clump.) Yet they can be delicious – not the initial taste on biting, but the meltingly sweet after-taste. Even the heavily armed Marsh Thistle has an edible central core, and stalks or young shoots of many other species have been eaten as a delicacy since hunter-gatherer times, wherever they are found growing in the northern hemisphere.

Palm hearts are an increasingly popular luxury vegetable – crisp, succulent and delicately flavoured. Much eaten locally for centuries, they are now being canned and exported. However, their popularity is of special concern to conservationists because in harvesting the single heart – the cabbage-like bud which is the only growing point – the tree is killed. One canful of only a dozen segments requires the death of a tree at least 8 years old and up to 20 metres high. The major sources are wild Brazilian trees of various species including *Acrocomia, Euterpe, Prestoea, Roystonea* and *Sabal*. Only recently have plantations been established to replace wild sources, reputedly in part of Brazil's nature reserves.

Food Flavourings – Herbs and Spices

A way of creating a good meal, if one cannot afford to start with expensive ingredients, is to enliven humble fare with flavourings. Herbs and spices are widely used today to add variety and interest to the diet. But in medieval times, an era before refrigeration, their principle function was to disguise the flavour of rotting food.

There is a strong link between herbs as food flavourings and herbs as medicines, and this is not coincidental. Often the medically active substances are precisely the flavourings the cook will wish to incorporate into a dish. Chopped Garlic releases a sulphur-containing volatile oil which has antibiotic activity, is an expectorant, a weak vermifuge and also helps to lower blood pressure. Spearmint contains the volatile oil carvone which

Far left The Artichoke (Cynara scolymus), is an ancient crop native to the Mediterranean and Canary Isles. It was cultivated by both the Greeks and the Romans.

Left The Milk Thistle (Silybum marianum), a wild plant of the Mediterranean, is generally edible, including the leaves when trimmed of their prickles. In Turkey people crunch the stems raw in the street, though the delicate-flavoured young shoots are more usually boiled.

85

stimulates gastric secretions, so is useful for stomach disturbances. Thyme contains thymos, a good antiseptic; and so on. In his *English Hus-Wife* of 1615, Gervase Markham recommends a mixture of pennyroyal, coriander seeds, aniseed, sweet fennel seeds, caraway seeds and brandy as a cure for digestive problems.

These herbs are all of European (mainly Mediterranean) origin, and were doubtless found in the domestic herb gardens of seventeenth century England. But even at this time, trade in exotic spices from the Orient was significant too (it had, of course, been in progress for several thousand years). There was a great deal of money involved. The Mediterranean cities of Alexandria, Genoa and Venice owed their prosperity to the spice trade, and its history is woven into that of the peoples and powers along the great trading lines. The caravan routes led westward from China, India, Sri Lanka and Indonesia, crossing the River Indus at Attock, on through Peshawar and over the Khyber Pass, through Afghanistan and Iran to Babylon, then onward to Europe. Most Europeans thought of spices as "Arabian" – an ignorance encouraged by the traders.

One of the most important spices was Black Pepper. It was known to the Romans, and in medieval times rents were sometimes paid with it – hence the term peppercorn rent. This now means a nominal sum; but in times past pepper was a scarce luxury, and it was sometimes preferred tender. Botanically unrelated are the New World peppers; Jamaican Pepper *(Pimenta dioica*, also known as pimento or allspice) belongs to the Myrtle family.

The capsicums are related to the Potato. *Capsicum annuum* takes many forms, from the sweet Bell Pepper which is delicious as a major part of a meal (or, when powdered, is paprika) to hot Chili Pepper which must be used sparingly. Chili peppers range in size from the Bell, big as a fist, to the fiery little Chiltepin, no bigger than a pea. Most of the ornamental peppers grown for their colourful fruits and sold as houseplants also belong to this species. The Mexicans were using peppers, probably similar to the Chiltepin, as early as 7000 BC.

Some families are particularly rich in flavourings. The Umbelliferae (Carrot family) provides angelica, anise, caraway, celery, chervil, coriander, cumin, dill, fennel, lovage, parsley, rock samphire and sweet cicely. The Labiatae (Mint family) include balm, basil, marjoram, the various mints, rosemary, sage, savories, thyme. From the Compositae (Daisy family) we have alecost, chamomile, southernwood, tansy, tarragon and wormwood. Others – bay, capers, cardamoms, chives, cinnamon, citrus, cloves, fenugreek, garlic, ginger, horse-radish, mustard, nutmeg, mace, saffron and turmeric – are scattered through the plant kingdom and represent almost every part of a plant. The most expensive spices are saffron (Iris family), vanilla (Orchid family) and cardamom (Ginger family).

A few spices are still gathered from the wild. Melegueta Pepper *(Aframomum melegueta)*, which is a substitute for the expensive cardamom, is generally collected wild in West Africa. Allspice is collected wild in central America. Wild-collected herbs and spices are often regarded as inferior since their flavouring is not so intense. Unlike the other food plants in which breeding has generally reduced the strength of flavours, these plants when cultivated often have increased volatile oil contents, and are generally preferred to wild sources.

Spice Plants

Right *Saffron comes from Crocus sativus, an attractive flower native to Greece, but now grown widely in warmer non-tropical regions. The part used is the three-branched orange-red style which must be hand-picked from the newly opened flowers. Up to a quarter of a million flowers are necessary to produce a pound, but only a tiny amount is needed to impart the flavour and yellow colour to a dish.*

Below right *Vanilla is the product of an American orchid Vanilla planifolia. The Aztecs used it to flavour chocolate. The long, yellow seed pods are picked unripe and have to be cured before the flavour develops.*

Below *Cardamom (Elettaria cardamomum), is related to Ginger. Before 1800 all cardamoms were wild-collected from the jungles of southern India, but since then plantations have been established. Once again care is needed in gathering, as the little seeds must be retained within the capsules if the flavour is to be maintained; thus they are hand cut with scissors before they are fully ripe, and carefully dried.*

Black Pepper *is provided by the berries of the Indian jungle vine Piper nigrum. Always an important spice, pepper was a luxury in medieval times; but like salt, it is now an almost universal condiment. The plant was originally called Poivrea, in honour of Pierre Poivre, the adventurous eighteenth-century French spice hunter.*

Crocus sativus

Piper nigrum

Elettaria cardamomum

Vanilla planifolia

87

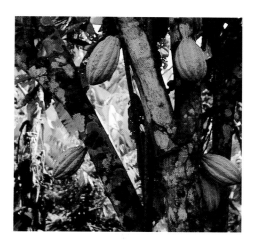

Chocolate comes from the Cacao tree (Theobroma cacao), which originates in north-eastern South America. Its centre of diversity is north-east Peru and adjacent Ecuador, areas where much of the forest is threatened.

Tea is made from the young leaves of the bushy Camellia sinensis. It varies in flavour immensely depending on the variety of plant, and method of production: China tea contrasts with the stronger tannic brews of Indian brands.

Chocolate, Coffee and Tea

In the America of the pre-Aztecs, chocolate was the "Food of the Gods". The Aztecs too valued cocoa, not only as a drink but also as a means of paying taxes. In fact cocoa beans were used as currency until 1887.

It was not until the sixteenth century that cocoa and its products became known in Europe. The Aztec emperor Montezuma is thought to have entertained the Spanish conquistador Hernando Cortez by offering him "xocoatl" – a drink prepared from cocoa beans and flavoured with capsicum peppers. The result must have been rather bitter. It was apparently Spanish nuns who first mixed chocolate with vanilla and sugar, making it palatable to European taste. Today, two-thirds of the world's cocoa is grown in Africa; most of these plantations are descended from one chance introduction by a West African farmer who took some pods home from a trip to Fernando Po.

Coffee, in contrast, comes from a plant that grows wild in the forests of the Ethiopian massif, *Coffea arabica*. Red coffee berries develop from beautiful white jasmine-scented flowers on laurel-like bushes. The berries, much loved by monkeys which raid the plantations given the chance, each contain two seeds generally known as beans. In the fifteenth century it was discovered that chewing coffee leaves and beans helped to relieve pain, hunger and fatigue – uses long known to the indigenous people. Even today, dried coffee berries are eaten by East Africans, or fermented to produce an alcoholic drink. As a hot beverage coffee only became popular after its introduction to Europe; by 1675 there were already 3,000 coffee houses in London, and by the 1960s coffee had become the largest single item (in value) imported by the United States. Today it is widely grown in the tropics, and is the most important crop in many Latin American countries.

Tea, another beverage containing the stimulant caffeine, originated from a different continent – maybe in Tibet, or possibly further north in central Asia. It has been cultivated for more than 2,000 years in China, where its earliest uses were probably medicinal. Commercial tea did not reach Europe until after coffee drinking had become well established. Habits too vary from place to place: delicate teas are often drunk without milk or sugar, sometimes with lemon; in Russia tea is taken with jam, while in Tibet rancid yak butter is always added.

Many other teas or tisanes are made by infusing dried leaves, like maté made from *Ilex paraguariensis*, a Paraguayan holly. Some people prefer this to tea or coffee since it contains almost no tannin. Mint tea is favoured in North Africa and the Middle East, and many herbs like chamomile are made into herbal teas. One is endangered even: in the Sierra Nevada of Spain, tea fanatics search for the elusive and endemic *Artemisia granatensis*. Not content just to make tea from its leaves and flowers, they also use it for an alcoholic drink.

Today most commercial production of cocoa, coffee and tea is in places far removed from the plants' original home. Yet these places may contain wild relatives vital to plant breeders. For example, wild and semi-wild Cacao trees from the upper Amazon Basin have already increased yields and provided resistance against several diseases. The genetic base of the world's cocoa crop is still very narrow and today new sources of disease resistance

The grape vine Vitis vinifera: most European grapes are grown on rootstocks from a combination of three North American wild vines, because virtually all the European grape vines were destroyed between 1870 and 1900 by Phylloxera, an insect pest. Resistant American plants saved the industry.

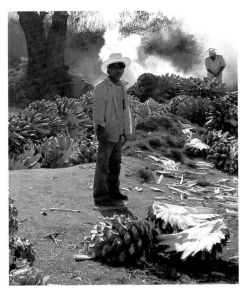

The popular Mexican drink mescal, and the more refined tequila, result from distilling the juice of Agave tequilana. The centres of the plants are first chopped up and baked in stone-lined pits, then crushed in donkey-powered circular roller presses, before distillation. Another popular Agave drink is pulque, made from the sap that fills the plant's centre after the flower-bud has been cut out.

are badly needed. However, these forests, especially in Peru and Ecuador, are fast coming under threat from resettlement schemes, logging and drilling for oil.

The danger of relying on a small gene pool is also illustrated by coffee. (Most of the Brazil's 'typica' coffee originates from the progeny of just one tree, introduced from East Africa via the Caribbean.) In the 1870s Coffee Rust (*Hemileia vastatrix*) devastated the Sri Lankan crop, and the disease has since spread to South America. Finding resistance to this disease is a top priority. However the wild and semi-wild coffee, from Ethiopia, is in critical danger as the last forests where it grows come under the axe, a fate that is all too common in the poverty-striken and crisis-ridden Horn of Africa. If the wild coffees do survive, they may offer significant benefits to this important and ever-expanding crop.

Booze and Tipples

Virtually any carbohydrate can provide a food from which yeasts can create alcohol – the process of fermentation. The sugars in grapes produce wine, the starches in barley, Scotch whisky; apples, rice, bananas, cherries, pototoes – any good sugar or starch source will do. Even the sap of some palms can be used, such as the rare Chilean Wine Palm (*Jubaea chilensis*).

The flavour depends on the type of plant used. It is the female flowers of Hops (*Humulus lupulus*) which give beer its distinctive bitter flavour. Three wild American ancestors of modern Hops are the essential basis of the crop grown in almost half the world's hoplands. In England alone it is reckoned that these wild plants have contributed some £8 million a year. Of course, the flavour of a good beer does not just depend on the Hops and other ingredients: the ageing process and the way the beer is stored are important too, as real ale enthusiasts know.

Making beer or wine sounds very simple, but it is actually rather difficult to make a good alcoholic drink with a pleasant flavour. It is important that only the desired organism is introduced; villains such as *Mycoderma aceti*, the Vinegar Bug, are ever ready to take advantage of unsterile conditions.

One of the less enticing alcoholic potions is surely chicha. (There are also non-alcoholic versions.) This is made in South America by fermentation of maize, manioc, palm fruits, plantains, potatoes and so on. The starting material is chewed and spat out so that the enzymes in saliva catalyse the conversion. Kava is the Polynesian equivalent, made from chewed roots of *Piper methysticum* or *Macropiper latifolium*.

For those who like a stronger tipple, spirits are distilled from the products of fermentation. They can have up to 50 percent alcohol content. Plants are again used as the starting point. Whiskies are made from barley or rye, gin from juniper berries, and rum from molasses (a product of sugar cane). Vodka originated during the fourteenth century in Russia, where potatoes are frequently used as the raw material for fermentation.

Even some of the plants used for making wine and spirits may come under threat: it may be too late to save one plant that was extensively used in wine making – *Pseudophoenix ekmanii*, a palm from the Dominican Republic. Sadly it is now endangered or possibly extinct.

Hallucinogenic Plants

About 60 species of plants worldwide, from South and Central America especially, have hallucinatory properties, allowing participants to have visions and mystical experiences, and shamans to commune with spirits, heal, and direct people in rituals.

Amanita muscaria

Many Morning Glory relatives are hallucinatory – the seeds contain lysergic acid derivatives, and were used by the Aztecs in divine rites. Seeds of garden Morning Glories (Ipomoea tricolor, shown above) have been sampled by modern "hippies"; however, they produce very nasty hangovers including nausea, constipation and vertigo.

Psilocybe semilanceata

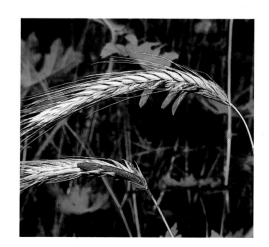

Cannabis sativa, above, has been known to the Chinese for over 4,000 years, and probably almost as long to the Indians. Marijuana, kif, grass, hemp – it has many names – was used to produce euphoria, hallucinations and, in Africa, for communal ritual. Cannabis resin, or hashish, taken in large quantities increases aggressiveness and courage – the Persian word "ashishin" gives rise to both "assassin" and "hashish". Cannabis is now very widely taken by westerners and is widely, if dubiously, regarded as no more harmful than alcohol, though there is obvious evidence of the damage caused by both.

The Fly Agaric (Amanita muscaria, the "fairy" toadstool) was taken communally by tribesmen in Siberia to produce euphoria, a desire to dance, and happy visual hallucinations. Poorer Tartars waited till participants in the ritual needed to pass water, and drank their urine with equally satisfactory effects. It was used, too, in priestly ritual in India, where the fungus was worshipped. Smaller mushrooms such as the Psilocybes were ritually used in Central America and now often supplement Christian rituals.

Peyote – the "mescal button" (a spherical, spineless cactus, Lophophora williamsii, above) – and several other cacti of Mexico and southern USA are ritually consumed to provoke kaleidoscopic coloured visions, either wonderful or horrible, and ritual dancing. (Eating them must take some willpower as they are nauseating.) Shamans contact the spirit world under their influence and the peyote cult is often involved with Christian ritual. The ease with which dried "buttons" can be kept, and the vivid picture of their effects given in books such as Carlos Castaneda's "Teachings of Don Juan", has caused the cult to spread widely in North America.

Left Dark projecting grains in cereal heads are infections of the fungus ergot. In the Middle Ages those who ate bread contaminated with ergot were seized with "St Anthony's Fire", suffering gangrene and possible loss of limbs, convulsions and sometimes violent hallucinations either of being pursued by wild beasts, or of a religious nature. Chemical extraction of lysergic acid, a constituent of ergot, led to the creation of the drug LSD which psychiatrists have used in therapy, while individuals use it for "instant Zen". But it is a very dangerous hallucinatory, leading for instance to an often fatal belief that one can fly, and/or to permanent psychosis.

Drugs and Stimulants

More important than the hallucinatory drugs illustrated opposite are opium derived from the Opium Poppy and cocaine derived from Coca; because of their value in medicine they are described in Chapter 7. The effect of potentially hallucinogenic plants depends on the amount of the active ingredient taken, though it is often impossible to administer precise doses because of the natural variations from plant to plant. The state of mind of the recipient and what they expect to happen are very influential as well. A timid person who dared to take cannabis in sufficient quantity, whether smoked in a cigarette or eaten in a sweetmeat, may end up paralysed with fear; yet it emboldened Al-Hasan's infamous hashashins to become the holy terrorists of Islam in the twelfth century. Furthermore, the critical dose will vary between individuals; the amount that will leave one person unmoved may pole-axe another.

Inebriants, and the less potent caffeine-containing stimulants (tea, coffee and cocoa), are all drunk; the daily stimulant in the Far East and Southern Asia, used by millions of people, is however chewed. This is betel, which contains the mild alkaloid arecoline. The betel nut, part of the fruit of the Betel Palm *(Areca catechu)*, is grated, mixed with lime and spices and wrapped in a leaf of *Piper betel*, a relative of Black Pepper. The nut can be used fresh or cured, though cured it contains less tannin, therefore tastes better. The alkaloid is used medically to cure tapeworm infections, and chewing betel has this useful side-effect. Countering this benefit, it encourages heavy spitting, while long-term use discolours the teeth (in some islands of the Pacific, black teeth are a mark of high social standing); and recently it has been suspected that the lime encourages cancer.

Tobacco is one of the most controversial and widely used drugs. There are huge campaigns to stop people smoking on the grounds of individual health as well as a sweeter atmosphere for everyone else. These are countered by the devotees who claim their health is their own business and that the do-gooders ought to set about removing pollution from other sources such as car exhausts before interfering with personal freedom. Ironically revenues derived from taxes on tobacco are an important part of the national budget in some countries.

The two cultivated species are very variable, and there are a number of different categories of tobacco, which can be affected as to quality by both cultivation and climate. The most important are flue-cured tobacco (named after the metal flues that distribute heat in the curing barns); a thin-leaved, light coloured tobacco known as "burley"; oriental tobacco; and air-cured tobacco. These have specific uses in cigars, cigarettes, pipe and chewing tobacco, and snuff, though they are sometimes blended.

The chief active ingredient is the alkaloid nicotine which tranquilizes the nervous system. It is manufactured in the roots and transported to the leaves, the part harvested. Tobacco is now grown throughout the world except in Arctic and near-Arctic regions. In 1980 world production was estimated at 5,386 million kilograms, over 2 million in Asia alone. Most of this ends up smoked for human enjoyment, but nicotine's other important use is as an insecticide: it is lethal to most insects and, although in principle it is toxic to mammals, in low concentrations is reasonably safe.

There are two species of Tobacco Plant in domestication, Nicotiana tabacum shown above and N. rustica, both South American members of the Potato family. The earliest record of use is a bas-relief from a temple at Palenque in Mexico, which has been dated to AD 432. It shows a Mayan priest blowing smoke through a tubular pipe during a ceremony. The smoking habit was taken up enthusiastically by the Spanish settlers early in the sixteenth century, and rapidly spread across Europe and into many parts of Asia. Even today many peoples are newly adopting tobacco, as the tranquil backwaters of the world fall under western influence.

Flowers are used extensively in perfumery. Unlike the other essential oils produced by plants, flower perfumes are designed to attract pollinating insects. They are derived from, and replace, pigments akin to chlorophyll. Thus brightly coloured flowers tend to lack perfume, whereas highly scented flowers, such as Ylang Ylang (Cananga odorata), and Tuberose (Polyanthes tuberosa, shown above) are pale.

Lily of the Valley (Convallaria, shown above), is an important scent in perfumery; it has thick, fleshy petals which hold the strong perfume. In this it resembles Honeysuckle (Lonicera) which is pollinated by night-flying moths and is particularly heavily scented. Night-pollinated blooms are typically pale-coloured, glowing like soft beacon lights at dusk.

Perfumes and Cosmetics

As a means of survival, the human sense of smell is relatively unimportant. We do not sniff out our mates, proclaim territory, or find our way home with it. We can just about locate where dinner is being cooked, or a dead mouse under the floorboards, or tell if the house is on fire. Yet, for all its uselessness, few luxuries compare with the sheer hedonistic pleasure of a beautiful perfume.

Just as medicine and cookery have a lot in common, so do cookery and perfumery. The same kinds of substances are active in all three fields. Subtleties of taste in food are virtually all smell. The taste buds just below the surface of the tongue are merely sensitive to saltiness, sourness, sweetness and bitterness; all flavours are actually detected by the olfactory cells in the mucous membrane of the nose.

Perfumes have a long history. Part of the mummification of rich Egyptians involved filling the body cavity with myrrh, cassia and other perfumes after the intestines had been removed. The Queen of Sheba visited King Solomon to negotiate sole rights for the overland trade in frankincense and other goods between southern Arabia and the rich markets of the north. In these times, as early as 3,000 years ago, all people in the Fertile Crescent – even labourers – used cosmetics and perfumes, the latter usually based on sesame oil or on wine. The Romans learned about cosmetics from the Egyptians and used them widely.

Emphasis on scent was again strong in Europe from the Dark Ages onwards. This may have been in part due to the generally malodorous conditions that prevailed, especially in town houses. Pestilence often resulted, in which posies of fragrant flowers were carried to ward off disease. The nursery rhyme Ring a Roses recounts the course of bubonic plague in gruesome detail; the pocket full of posies was sadly ineffectual.

Hygiene seems to have been practically non-existent in western Europe at least until the sixteenth century. Scent must have been highly valued, and indeed for many generations the strewing of aromatic herbs was practised. Plants such as Sweet Woodruff, Sweet Rush, Hyssop, various mints, Germander and Chamomile were spread on the floors to release their fragrance when trodden on, periodically to be swept up and renewed.

Queen Elizabeth I had a female retainer who had to provide perfumed plants for the household. Apart from alleviating stink, these plants deterred fleas, lice and other vermin. They were also placed among clothing for both fragrance and vermicidal qualities. (The present-day visitor to Nepal will find pungent artemisias still being used for this purpose.) The court of Louis XV of France was known as "la Cour Parfumée" because of the extravagant use of scent. Napoleon Bonaparte is said to have had 60 bottles of double-extract jasmine delivered every month, and two quarts of violet cologne were supplied to him each week.

The perfume industry has been revolutionised this century by the creations of organic chemists, but even now expensive perfumes rely on natural products, with the synthetics adding new notes and tones to the perfumer's repertoire. The most important natural oils in perfumery are absolutes derived from the flowers of rose, jasmine, and orange. Oil of orange is pressed from orange peel, and lemon and bergamot oil also come from

Very different plants may release similar odours. The popular perfume of Sweet Violet, (Viola odorata, shown above) is closely resembled by scents from the roots of Costus, (Aucklandia costus), the grass Vetivert or "Khus-khus" (Vetiveria zizanioides), and Orris (Iris pallida). Roots of Vetivert are woven into sun-blinds in India and Malaya, to be moistened in the heat of the day and so they both cool and scent rooms.

The perfume of Sandalwood is characteristic of the heavy scents of the Orient. Attar of Sandalwood (from chips of the wood) is used extensively, and vast quantities of scented Red Sandalwood timber are used to build temples and houses, and in religious caskets and ornaments. This has led to the severe decline of several Santalum species, including Santalum album, above. One species, from Juan Fernandez, the Robinson Crusoe island, is now extinct.

citrus fruit peels. Labdanum and patchouli are derived from leaves; cinnamon bark is used in perfumery as well as in cookery; the lichen oakmoss contributes earthy notes; cedarwood a refreshing resinous scent.

The current trend in cosmetics, too, is to emphasise their herbal origins, thus we have apple shampoos and avocado face packs, but the ingredients have changed little over millenia. Such poisonous excesses as ceruse (white lead) and belladonna are no longer in use, but the basic oils, gums, starches, lampblack and colourings keep on turning up with fanfares of advertising in bright new disguises.

Even so, many women today follow a similar make-up routine to that of Egyptians 3,000 or more years ago. In the time of Tutankhamun a lady of consequence would prepare her face for the day by first applying a cleansing cream and natron (a sort of natural washing soda, similar to bath crystals), then pluck her eyebrows. She would outline her eyes with bold green sweeps of powdered malachite in oil, and touch up her eyebrows with lampblack. Red ochre was rubbed into the lips and cheeks. Henna was used on the nails, the palms of the hands and soles of the feet to tint them a delicate pink.

Where clothes are few or lacking, body paint becomes necessary as a mark of caste or tribe. Africans use mineral colourings such as red or yellow ochre mixed with oils. Ancient British warriors stained themselves with woad and North American Indians used natural plant dyes such as madder and indigo, which were semi-permanent and did not smudge. Sometimes the plant dyes were made even more fast with aluminium and iron salts, mordants well known in the dyeing industry.

The ancient craft of dyeing is based on plant lore. The wrappings from mummies have revealed that the Egyptians were familiar with the dye indigo 6,000 years ago. Indigo was produced from a number of plants including European Woad *(Isatis tinctoria)*, the Chinese Indigo (Polygonum tinctorium), and – chief source of supply before synthetics – the shrub *Indigofera tinctoria*. Madder, produced by several plants, was also known to the Egyptians and remained an important plant dye until the Second World War. The colouring principle, alizarin, gives reds and oranges on mordanting. This industrial use of plants was suspended when, in 1856, an 18-year old chemist, W. H. Perkin, created mauveine by the oxidation of crude aniline, thus producing the first synthetic dyestuff. Others followed rapidly; in this industry, as in others, chemists took naturally occurring substances for their pattern. Notably, alizarin was manufactured in 1869 from the coal-tar product anthracene, the first vegetable dyestuff to be made artificially, and artificial indigo was created in 1878 although natural indigoes are still widely used in non-industrial situations.

Among other plants, dyes can be obtained from Weld, Saffron, Fustic, onion skins, logwood chips and lichens. Craft-minded people nowadays like to use these natural dyes to colour hand-spun, hand-woven cloth. Thus luxuries come full-circle; the brilliant dyes of industrial origin are rejected by those who prefer a return to nature. Will this resurgent interest in wild products, from herb teas to plant dyes, from flower-based soaps and make-up to rare spices and food, be converted into yet another threat to our harassed wild environments – whether or not we, as consumers, intended this? There are signs that this may be happening.

US grasslands, seen here at Teton Rouge, feed the world – wheat production is big business, organised on a monolithic scale.

CHAPTER SIX

Green Wealth

If money makes the world go around, then plants are the engine. Fortunes are made and lost by people dealing in commodities they never see, from timber to rattan, from soya to coffee, from oil seeds to resin, rubber, and latex. They buy and sell as prices rise and fall, gambling not only on this year's produce, but on "futures" too. In every field of human enterprise, plants are the primary producers: energy, industry, clothing, housing, crafts and fine arts – all depend on plants.

Food crops are big money, whether bought and sold within their countries of origin, or entering international trade. Many foods – from peanuts to luxury strawberries or artichokes – are grown entirely for overseas sale; they are "cash crops" designed for export earnings. This is fine where the country growing them has also enough capacity to grow its own staple needs; or where, like Israel, it can import staples in exchange for high-value cash exports. But in poor countries the cash crop market, which encourages farmers to plant non-essential foods, can lead to disaster: if the buyer switches to another source, the market drops, or disease strikes, the farmers have no money to buy the food they could have grown.

The greatest "green wealth" is the wild itself. Perhaps if its unexplored potential were assigned a dollar value in practical terms we would be less hasty to clear it for short-sighted reasons. Perhaps if the industries which stand to benefit from new plant discoveries paid "royalties" on the plants they borrow, the countries concerned would have adequate funds to conserve their heritage.

Today is a particularly exciting and challenging period for botanists. As oil becomes dearer and the end of the oil era comes into sight, possibly only 30 to 50 years away, industry is turning to our inheritance of plant capabilities for new solutions – plants to replace fossil fuels and all their derivations: plastics and oils, insecticides, chemicals, waxes, gums, pectins and resins. Their source lies in the wild, particularly the tropical jungles, and in the knowledge of wild plants and cultivars held by local peoples. The marine flora, too, has secrets of immense value.

Nowhere is the disaster of wilderness destruction, deforestation, and pollution more evident than in this: that potential benefactors, still awaiting our attention, may be gone before we can test and cultivate them. Fortunes are stillborn, industries of the future denied.

Energy from Plants

Petroleum, coal and natural gas are all fossil fuels – solar energy stored by photosynthesising plants laid down in the Carboniferous Era, nearly 300 million years ago. These are not renewable reserves: we now consume more coal every year than accumulated in 10,000 years. The hideous irony is that we are using the products of this primeval sunshine to destroy today's green wealth – it drives the tractors, chainsaws, water pumps, mining machinery and so on that are so swiftly eradicating natural habitats.

Replacement energy supplies are under urgent investigation: nuclear fission, wind and water power – and plants. Many countries are now considering, or even implementing, "biomass" production programmes: fermenting and distilling the energy-rich products of present-day photosynthesis, to obtain fuel alcohol or "gasohol". The Third World countries, in particular, hope to achieve a degree of self-sufficiency in energy production. However, there is concern over growing crops for fuel, rather than food, where malnutrition is so widespread.

The raw material for biomass production varies from country to country. Maize is the major distillery feedstock in the USA. Sweet Sorghum is also being considered as are wastes from cheese making, citrus and food processing industries. Beets are favoured in New Zealand. In South-east Asia, Sweet Potato seems the best crop since it matures more quickly than Sugar Cane or Cassava, the other main contenders.

In India, Pakistan, Sudan and various African nations, molasses has potential. In the past, it has been regarded as a waste product of the Sugar Cane industry (because of lack of storage and transport facilities), and returned to the land. Now it is seen as the major feedstock for alcohol production programmes.

Energy from the Forests

In the long term, the most economic form of plant life for fuel alcohol production is wood. Yields per hectare are very high; there is more total biomass available from trees than from any other source; and agricultural inputs needed are much lower than for many crops. The biggest disadvantages are that trees take a long time to start producing; and that lignocellulose, their major component, is not so easily processed as starch or sugars. Nonetheless, many people now envisage *Eucalyptus* on a five year coppice rotation as the "oil well" of the future. There are plans to grow it in Florida on old mining sites. Canada too has a policy of taking energy from the forest, using its native softwoods.

Wood has, of course, been our primary fuel source throughout most of history. In large parts of the world, this is still the case: more than a third of the human race depend on wood alone for cooking and heating; half the timber cut every year is for fuel, most of it used in developing nations. Worldwide, wood still provides 14 percent of all energy. In 1974 the USA produced more energy from wood than from nuclear power stations. New Zealand's largest dairy company has reportedly cut its fuel bills by 80 percent as a result of replacing oil power with sawdust and wood waste.

Brazil is growing Sugar Cane to convert by fermentation into alcohol for fuel; its National Alcohol Programme is being scrutinized the world over. Begun in 1975, it aimed at making 10.7 billion litres of "gasohol" a year by 1985 and substituting this for perhaps 40 percent of petrol consumption. Already, huge tracts of Amazon forest are being destroyed for the gasohol farms, like the one above.

Eventually Brazil intends that Cassava should replace Sugar Cane as the main gasohol feedstock.

Brazilian "Alcool" stations offer the motorist a choice of fuel grades, right. Standard car engines run on a blend of up to 15 percent alcohol with little or no tuning, and can be modified to use up to 40 percent; new cars have been designed that will run on alcohol alone.

The main by-product of gasohol production is a very rich organic soup which could be useful in fertilizer, biogas, or cattle feed manufacture. Instead it is dumped in rivers. It is a serious water pollutant and has wiped out many fish stocks.

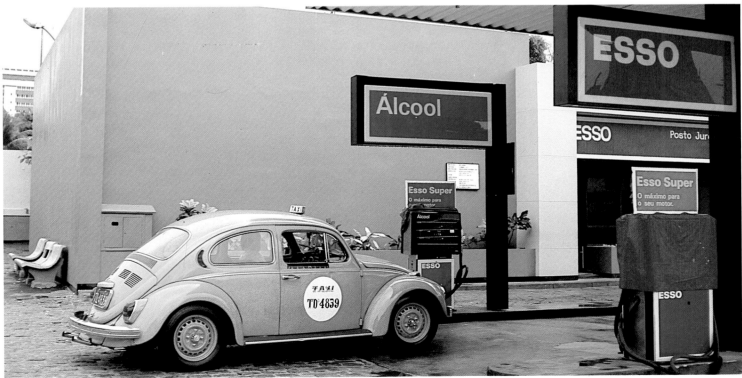

Large energy plantations are planned, or already operational, in many parts of the world, especially in the developing countries where the firewood is vital. For millions of people, meeting everyday needs is increasingly difficult as the forests disappear: in parts of Africa so many trees have gone in the last two decades that women and children have to walk many miles a day for firewood; the landscape is reduced to semi-barrenness. Where fuelwood is so scarce that it must be bought, heating the supper pot can cost as much as filling it.

One answer is to plant woodlots in gardens, market places, along road-sides, as shelter belts, as counter-erosion measures, even seeded from the air on to wastelands. Improving the efficiency of fuel use is important too. An open fire, the traditional way of cooking in many countries, wastes 90 percent of heat. Even fairly basic stoves can improve on this; providing energy-efficient stoves cheaply can help a great deal.

About three-quarters of tropical land is not really suited to conventional agriculture (though 35 percent of the tropical population lives on it); here the best possible agricultural use of land may be tree production. It is conservative of resources, guards against erosion and flooding, and can even improve the soil.

There are already some heartening success stories of firewood production. The beautiful flowering shrub *Calliandra calothyrsus*, transported to Indonesia from Guatemala in 1936, has been adopted as a firewood crop. Plantations now cover 30,000 hectares in Java. The dense wood burns well and is a good size for domestic cooking, though too small for lumber. In South Korea the leguminous shrubs *Lespedeza bicolor* and *L. thunbergii* bind and enrich the bare soil, provide fuelwood and foliage for livestock, and act as a nurse crop around pine seedlings to protect the tender shoots. The Indian Neem tree, introduced to the Accra plains of Ghana early this century, keeps up with the local demand for wood, and is reseeded by bats which eat the fruit. Above all, the fast-growing Australian Eucalypts are very promising, producing a hard, resinous, fiercely burning wood which grows well in many parts of the world.

Fuelwood is also an important source of income. Kenya exports charcoal to the Arabian Gulf, and Surinam ships charcoal to northern Europe. On a local scale too the production and sale of wood can be an important component of the economy: for instance it has been estimated that 6,000 families support themselves by supplying essential fuelwood to the city of Maputo in Mozambique.

Green Oil

Another way of using plants for fuel is to extract the oils they produce and use these as a direct replacement for petroleum. At present the 50 percent extra expense rules out widespread use, but a 3:1 mixture of Sunflower oil and diesel is similar in efficiency to straight diesel. This would come as no surprise to Rudolph Diesel, the inventor, who wrote as long ago as 1911, "The diesel engine can be fed with vegetable oils and would help considerably in the development of agriculture of the countries which will use it". Plant oils can also be used as "extenders" to make petroleum based fuels go

The obvious way to provide an adequate supply of firewood is to plant trees specifically for fuel, especially in areas now denuded. In planning fuelwood plantations, several important questions must be answered. How quickly do the trees grow (species that quickly produce branches of one or two centimetres diameter may be ideal for small cooking stoves)? Is it a good dense wood that burns well? Will it grow on poor soils or steep slopes? Is it a firewood acceptable under local customs? Those trees most likely to prove useful in fuelwood plantations are pioneer species which naturally colonise deforested areas. They withstand poor soil conditions and many are legumes with nitrogen-fixing root nodules.

This stand of fast-growing Leucaena leucocephala, left, planted for fuel near Poona, India, is only 3-4 years old. Already it is supplying local people with firewood, for domestic use above.

Wood is not the only fuel fit for burning. In eastern central Africa, the tall marsh plant Papyrus (Cyperus papyrus, above) from which the Egyptians once made paper, is now a fuel candidate. Able to produce an impressive biomass of 32 tonnes per hectare per year, Papyrus is one of the most productive plants in the world. It is not dense enough to burn well on its own, but machinery used for making briquettes from waste straw and wood chippings has been modified to turn out compressed papyrus logs which burn well.

To make paper, Papyrus pith was cut into thin slices which were laid down both vertically and horizontally, pressed, dried in the sun, and finally smoothed. This craft was certainly practised as early as 1500 BC in Egypt.

further. And plant oils in industry could become increasingly important as raw materials for the chemical industry. One consideration, however, is whether land is best used in this way: if more fuel is used (in tractors, sprays, extracting equipment etc.) to produce these oil crops than they finally yield, there would clearly be no point at all in growing them. The energy ratio (comparing the amount produced with the amount used) tends to be favourable, however: values of between 3:1 and 10:1 have been estimated.

The crops that can produce fuel oil include olives, sunflower, peanuts, soya beans, palms, rape, sesame, castor oil and eucalyptus, and some exotic species now being investigated for potential production in less favoured areas. This variety of possibilities is fortunate, since it means that a species can be chosen to suit its environment, not pressed into service in conditions where it cannot thrive. The Brazilian Babassu Palm for instance could be grown on impoverished savannahs worldwide. It can produce 60 tonnes of nuts per hectare; on dry distillation these would yield nine tonnes of methyl alcohol, nine tonnes of high grade charcoal, plus edible oil and cattle cake from the kernels and pigfood from the pulp.

Black Quince grows in the semi arid regions of north-eastern Brazil, where it is considered an invasive weed, producing 15 to 45 tonnes of dry plant matter per hectare. Steam distillation yields about one percent essential oil, which works reasonably well in unmodified diesel engines. The Petroleum Nut comes from the Philippines; its nuts yield a petroleum-like oil which, even when green, burns brightly when lighted. The Gopher Plant produces a latex which can be broken down into petroleum derivatives. This biennial needs very little water so can occupy desert areas where food crops cannot be grown. Copaiba is an Amazonian tree which the locals tap for oil. It is used medicinally, and in varnish manufacture, and the oil can be substituted for diesel.

Leading the new oil hopes is Jojoba (*Simmondsia chinensis*), the oil of which has recently gained renown as an ingredient of shampoos; it comes from the fruit of a bush that grows wild in the Sonoran Desert of Mexico and part of south-western USA. Its seeds contain up to 60 percent of a light yellow, odourless, liquid wax. Though nuts have long been collected from the wild, it was only recognised as being of potential importance in the late 1960s and first planted out on a field scale in the mid 1970s. Cultivation has now spread to arid lands in many places including the USA and Mexico, Israel, Sudan, the Middle East, parts of South-east Asia and Australia. Jojoba oil has a clinging quality which makes it an essential engine lubricant; it is even as good as Sperm Whale oil for nourishing high-quality leather goods; and it is an ideal cosmetic foundation.

In 1982 Jojoba was the latest way to get rich quick: British investors were invited to provide a minimum of £3,000 for half an acre in Australia. The oil was worth $20 a pound, and with possible yields of 3,000 pounds an acre this represented a fantastic gain. Prices are expected to fall as production increases and the bush becomes a proper domesticate but few doubt that its large scale production is a competitive economic proposition. It needs limited irrigation in its first year and very little thereafter because a tap root may penetrate 30 metres. It tolerates alkaline and saline soils and is claimed to stop desert land degradation. Jojoba starts bearing seeds at three years old and reaches maximum productivity at around 10 years.

Drought-tolerant Jojoba helps the greening of the desert in California, top, while providing a valuable crop for the farmer, above. No oil but Jojoba has been found to fill the vacuum left by Sperm Whale oil, banned by the USA in 1970; animal conservationists and industrialists alike are delighted that an acceptable substitute has been found for this endangered mammal's precious oil.

Paints, Polishes and Perfection

The civilised arts – whether it be paintings, luxury confections, or fashion – owe much to plant gums. The finer grades are used in clarifying liqueurs, finishing silk, and preparing artists' water-colours; lesser grades in pharmaceuticals, confectionery, printing inks, dyeing, and as a size for fibres; and the poorest in inks, emulsions and matches. Gums are also used extensively in cosmetics. Famous among these natural gums are gum arabic, gum tragacanth, manila copal and kauri copal. But the most astonishing is Guar, grown in Pakistan and the southern USA – it has applications in the food, paper, cosmetics, pharmaceutical and tobacco industries and is also used in the oil industry as a stabiliser for drilling lines. Frankincense and myrrh, of Biblical fame, are still used in incense and perfumes.

Resins have an extraordinary number of uses: in varnishes, polishes, and floor coverings; printing inks, sizes and waterproofing compounds; soap and cement. From resin is made oil or spirit of turpentine, an important solvent; distillations of resin go into medicines and ointments. The Southern Pine is a notable source of resin; it even flavours wine.

One of the finest plant waxes is secreted from the young leaves of the Brazilian Wax Palm. Though expensive, it is the main ingredient of car and furniture polishes, and also goes into varnishes and cosmetics. Another promising wax plant is the tall herb *Calathea lutea,* known as Cauassú. A common riverside plant and coloniser of waste ground, it could readily be developed into a valuable cottage industry in its native Amazonia.

Above *Guayule (Parthenium argentatum)
is a latex-bearing plant from the deserts of
Mexico and Texas. Its importance as a
major supplier of natural rubber fluctuates
with market forces, but it is of special interest
because it can be grown on desert land.*

Below *A wild rubber tree is tapped for
"caucho" in traditional manner in the
rainforest of Madre de Dios, Peru.
European explorers of Brazil and Peru
recognized the economic potential of rubber
when they learned of its water-proofing
qualities from forest Indians.*

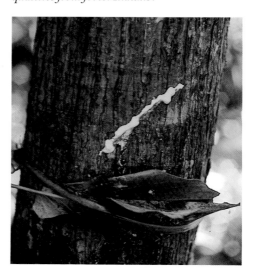

The World on Wheels

Rubber is another vital substance for humanity. Synthetics cannot match its qualities; ordinary motor tyres need at least 20 percent natural rubber, and tyres for heavy equipment and aircraft virtually 100 percent. The most familiar source is *Hevea brasiliensis*. This tropical tree from the Amazon jungles has latex vessels just under the bark which yield a milky fluid when cut. The tree is ready for its first tapping at five years old and should be productive for at least 30 years. The best selected clones produce two tonnes of dry rubber per hectare each year.

The Brazilian plantations once created fortunes, but fell foul of South American leaf blight and never recovered properly. It was a great piece of luck that the seeds smuggled out of Brazil to Kew in 1876 (p. 50) were not carrying this destructive disease, and that the Old World plantations which resulted have remained free of it.

Latex is in fact found in many plants. The Belgians conquered the Congo in 1883 with the aim of producing rubber from the inferior *Landolphia* vines. During the Second World War a dandelion, *Taraxacum koksaghyz*, supplied some of Russia's rubber needs. Latex from species of *Castilla*, *Manihot*, *Hancornia*, *Cryptostegia* and others has also been exploited commercially on a local scale and some of these might replace *Hevea* if the Far Eastern plantations ever become subject to serious disease. Wild stands of Guayule have been exploited for latex since the early twentieth century: in 1910 Guayule supplied ten percent of the world's natural rubber – 50 percent of the USA's. When, during the Second World War supplies of rubber from South-east Asia were cut off, the government invested $30 million in an emergency programme to revive Guayule, and it was grown on 11,000 hectares of prime land in California. When trade ways were reopened, these fields were burnt; but seeds of the 25 varieties that had been selected were stored in the gene bank of Fort Collins in Colorado. The World Bank has now forecast that demand for rubber will outstrip supply within the next 10 years, so attention is again focussed on Guayule.

Pest Control the Natural Way

Plants, being unable to move, have evolved many ways of deterring animal predators. Perhaps the most fascinating – and potentially useful – are the many chemicals they contain that are distasteful or poisonous to insects and can thus be used as insecticides. For example pyrethrin, extracted from *Chrysanthemum cinerariifolium*, is a poison more deadly to insects than DDT, yet hardly toxic to mammals or plants; it is non-persistent too, and so environmentally safe. Pyrethrin can be safely used as an insecticide in the house where food is processed and stored. Unlike the synthetic DDT, a wonder-worker in its time – especially against the malaria-carrying mosquitoes – it does not get into the animal food chain. The plants are now grown widely in uplands in Rwanda, Kenya, Tanzania, Ecuador and Japan.

Nicotine and derris are also killers of insect pests. *Derris*, a genus of tropical woody climbers, kills beetles and weevils as well, but unlike nicotine, has the advantage of being harmless to mammals.

Some plants offer alternatives to immediate death in controlling insect pests. *Ajuga remota*, a member of the Mint family, suppresses their appetites; while tannins from plants like Sugar Maple cause stomach-ache, thus rendering the insects vulnerable to predators.

Certain species of *Tagetes*, ancestors of French and African marigolds, release into the soil a sulphur compound that can destroy nematode worms (eelworms) within a radius of a metre. Early South American farmers kept eelworms at bay from their potatoes by interplanting tagetes.

Other plants disturb insect life cycles by producing "chromenes" – chemicals which interfere with the hormones of juvenile or larval forms and so prevent the insect going through the life-stages which lead to a breeding adult. Such are the Indian Neem Tree, a useful fuelwood, and its relation the Persian Lilac. Their extract is distasteful to insects in the first place and, if they persist with it, prevents regular moults and kills them. One of the advantages of the often-planted Neem is that its pest deterrent extract can be made by local farmers.

An astonishing adaptation occurs in a wild potato from Bolivia, *Solanum berthaultii*: the plant is covered with tiny sticky hairs which entrap the sap-sucking aphids that try to attack it, and the leaves give off a warning odour or "pheromone" which is identical to that produced by the aphids themselves if alarmed. A few cultivated varieties also produce the pheromone alarm signal, but in inadequate quantities. It should be possible to breed this character (and possibly also the hairiness) into cultivars in adequate aphid-repellant amounts, thus making a great deal of insecticide redundant. About 5.9 percent of the US potato crop, worth $1.8 billion per year, is lost to insects and about 22 percent to diseases, many of them transmitted by insect pests. The percentage is probably greater elsewhere. So the "Scary Hairy Wild Potato" (as it has become known), could be one of the botanical finds of the century.

Feeding the Soil

There are numerous ways of improving soil fertility without using artificial fertilisers. One of the best is digging in farmyard manure – faeces and urine from stock mixed with soiled straw or some other form of litter. This not only adds nutrients, especially the three most important – nitrogen, potash and phosphorus – but improves soil quality, opening up heavy soils and giving body to light ones.

Since herbivorous animals feed off plants, their excreta is a plant product, and their droppings should be a means of enriching soil the world over. Alas, in many countries, fuelwood is so scarce that animal droppings are dried and burned. As one travels in poorer parts of Turkey, India, and other eastern lands in summer one will see girls fashioning cow dung into "cakes" which are laid out in the sun to dry for fuel. In India alone, between 60 and 80 million tons (300–400 million tonnes fresh weight) are burnt every year. In richer countries, too, less animal manure is used as mixed farming gives way to monoculture.

Dead or uprooted plants can be composted to form a valuable soil improver, as many gardeners and small farmers know. The advantage of

*The Hyacinth Bean (Dolichos lablab) is a
legume with considerable future potential.
The young pods have many culinary uses,
while the foliage can provide hay and silage.
Some medicinal applications are recorded
too. Probably native to Asia, the Hyacinth
Bean or "Lablab", as it is sometimes called,
is now grown widely in India as green
manure, it has been introduced to Africa, and
spread generally in the tropics where it
readily becomes naturalised. Several
varieties are known, including a Caribbean
climbing form in Trinidad.*

composting is that the unwanted remains of crop plants are not wasted.
Cereal stubbles used to be ploughed back into the soil, but now they are
usually burned in the interests of "efficiency" – an extraordinary waste of
resources in an energy-hungry age.

Another way of improving soil fertility with plants is green manuring. A
green manure is a crop that is grown only to be ploughed back into the soil
without harvesting. It is usually planted between major crops and conserves soil nutrients. Various plants are used. In Britain, mustard is grown
on chalk, lupins on sandy soils, tares on heavy soils, and Italian ryegrass in
various circumstances.

Of these, tares and lupins are leguminous, that is, they are members of
the Pea family that form root nodules in which nitrogen-fixing bacteria
dwell, to the mutual advantage of both organisms.

By interplanting with a legume it is possible to improve soil fertility even
for a growing crop. Beans and maize can be interplanted to considerable
benefit, as farmers discovered very early. The arrangement cuts down
weeds, and slows the spread of insects and disease; the beans fix nitrogen,
which improves soil fertility, and the maize provides support for the beans.
Maize yields are unaltered, and bean yields are only slightly lower, so in
effect you get the beans for free.

Fixation of atmospheric nitrogen is extremely important in flooded rice
paddies. The floating aquatic fern *Azolla* is one prime source: the blue-
green nitrogen-fixing alga *Anabaena azolla* lives in association with it, and
can fix as much as three kilogrammes of atmospheric nitrogen per hectare
per day, which is released into the soil when the fern dies. This is particularly important in China and Vietnam – in Vietnam there is a temple dedicated
to *Azolla*. Lastly, in the soil and in and among the roots and basal shoots are
various nitrogen-fixing bacteria. It is only the presence of these organisms
that has kept rice yields traditionally as high as one or two tonnes per
hectare, without added fertiliser.

Wood – for Almost Everything

Wood's uses are legion, its potential almost inexhaustible. For all our new
technology, it is still the most extensively traded wild product in the world.
The vast evergreen forests of the north – both natural and planted – provide
us with softwoods – conifers such as pines, spruces, larches, fir and cedar.
Often having just one species covering a wide area, they are relatively easy
to exploit. The natural vegetation of many warmer regions, by contrast, is
hardwood forest – trees that are flowering plants such as poplar, sycamore,
ash, eucalyptus, teak and mahogany. These are very mixed communities,
which makes extraction that much more difficult and expensive. In tropical
rainforest there may be only a few species of commercial importance per
hectare. Conifers are preferred by most large-scale wood-using industries
because they are light, easy to handle and work, and generally speaking are
rather similar – so that one species can be substituted for another without
problem. The tropical hardwoods, on the other hand, have long been
prized for their beauty and durability; like the temperate hardwoods,
especially beech, they are valued for furniture, veneers, and luxury goods.

Export of timber from developing countries is on the increase. South-east Asia now accounts for three-quarters of international trade in tropical hardwoods. Japan is the prime consumer, followed by the US which receives most of its imports via Japan, as processed plywood and veneers. The bulk of timber exports from developing countries are as logs, sawn wood and panels; only about 8 percent is paper and pulp.

Paper is an essential civilised commodity, as vital to hygiene as to literacy, and places one of the major demands on the forest. The main source of paper fibre today is wood pulp; demand could not be met by the old materials – fibres of grasses like Esparto and Bamboo, of Kenaf, or the most famous source, from which paper gets its name, the Papyrus rush of Egypt. In basic paper-making the wood is ground under water, in such a way as to separate the fibres without damaging them. The watery mass is then drained on a moving wire mesh belt, leaving the fibres meshed together in a thin sheet. This is dried and smoothed over heated rollers, to emerge as a continuous roll. For better quality paper, a chemical and pressurised digestion process is used; if this is taken further, the cellulose in the wood dissolves entirely to produce viscose, from which the very fine thread rayon is made.

Virtually every part of a tree can be used for paper and board making – trunk, branches, leaves, roots, even charred wood after forest fires – as has been demonstrated by tree-growers turned arsonists in Portugal, eager to pick up guaranteed prices for charred wood.

The world uses an enormous amount of paper, cardboard and allied packaging materials. In Britain, 90 million trees are cut annually. A single issue of the National Geographical Society's Journal requires about 22,000 kilometres of paper nearly 2 metres wide. American newspapers are notoriously large, and one bumper issue of the *New York Times* is the end product of 400 hectares of forest.

Much of this forest, of course, is grown specially for making paper; in northern countries, particularly, it accounts for a formidable area of unnaturally covered land. However, an increasing amount of paper pulp is now obtained from natural forest, by giant machines designed to remove every tree and shrub. Some of the devastated, eroded land in Java for example has been created in this manner from virgin rainforest, and the process is well under way in Papua New Guinea.

We need paper, but there are alternatives to woodpulp which must be worth pursuing, if only to stop destruction of natural forest. Recycling of waste paper could be done on a far greater scale than at present; straw and sugarcane residues (bagasse) can be used to make paper too, and annual crops could be taken off esparto grass, reeds, bamboos, fibrous hibiscus species (already being used in the southern US), and residues from hemp fibre making. 4,000 hectares devoted to raising hemp could have a pulp-producing capacity equal to 16,000 hectares of pulpwood forest.

Another solution is to grow different kinds of tree, either very quick-growing ones like aspens and birches, or trees like poplars which will resprout when cut. Experiments with hybrid poplars have shown that eight crops can be taken from plantations of 9,000 trees per hectare. Alternatives to trees are, however, preferable because wood-pulp processing effluents cause much more serious pollution than other fibrous sources.

Wood is capable of being cut, turned, shaped, or drilled into almost any form. It provides the spears, harpoons, bow and arrows of the hunter; bowls, dishes, eating utensils, and boxes for domestic use; children's toys, cricket and baseball bats, hockey and polo sticks, tennis racquets, oars and paddles, grand pianos, violins, and nearly all our furniture.

All man's transport was originally wooden. The first vehicles were sledges, used as much on land as on snow. Wheels were first fitted to such sledges, and from these the two- and four-wheeled carts and wagons developed. Until the last century every kind of boat was of wood, too, from Neolithic dugout canoes to the huge warships and transports of the sixteenth and seventeenth centuries. In Britain oak forests were planted and cut down to maintain the Navy. The sea travel which resulted in the early movement of plants around the world was all by wooden ship.

Early aircraft were based on wooden frameworks, and the Mosquito, formed of balsa, was one of the most successful fighters of World War II. Balsa (*Ochroma*) is the lightest important commercial wood, with a specific gravity of 0.12. It is a favourite material for model-makers as it is so easily cut. (The heaviest wood is probably South American ironwood, *Krugiodendron ferreum*, with a specific gravity of 1.3, which sinks in water.)

Wood is one of our most basic building materials, the obvious choice wherever trees grow – peat and turf houses are still built in bleak areas, and still with wooden frameworks, if wood is available. In primitive and less developed communities branches form the support for coverings of hides, cloth, palm fronds, bark slabs or woven matting, from small shelters and teepees to the great communal houses of South America, New Guinea and so on. Some New Guinea houses were based on huge mangrove trees fixed upside down so that their spreading roots formed the support for the roofing material.

As tools and craft developed, shaped timber formed the structural basis of most buildings, even those as big as the Cretan Palace of Knossos. In dwelling houses, the timber structure might support wooden planking for walls, daub and wattle (itself a wood product), or bricks and mortar. (Bricks, incidentally, traditionally included straw to improve strength; straw of Teff, *Eragrostis teff*, still the most important crop in Ethiopia, went into making bricks for a pyramid over 5,000 years ago.) Wooden shingles, usually of cedar, went on the roof as tiles. Many present-day houses are still wholly or partly of wood.

Mahogany is one of the finest timbers in the world, with a long and colourful history. The original Mahogany was used by the people of Hispaniola to build canoes, and so was chosen by Spanish explorers to repair their sailing vessels in the West Indies. True Mahogany is ideal for everything from pianos to ships – there are 23 species involved, some of which are not even closely related. In the late seventeenth century a similar wood entered trade, originating this time from West Africa. It came from *Khaya* species which are close relatives of the Swietenias, both in the family Meliaceae. Trade in both American and African mahogany continued to expand into the latter half of the twentieth century. In 1966 British traders imported 79,000 cubic metres at £38 a cubic metre, which rose to 196,000 cubic metres at £230 a cubic metre by 1979. Dwindling supply of these mahoganies had forced prices up. Tragically, true Mahogany will probably be commercially extinct by 1990. Already the trade is looking elsewhere, to ravage another set of species. The timber of Dipterocarps (such as *Shorea* species), traded as Philippine mahogany, is currently being used for products at the cheaper end of the mahogany market. Some of the species involved were unknown in international trade before the 1950s. One wonders how long they will last.

Mahogany plantations have been established in Trinidad, Honduras and India, but a semi-mature plantation of Swietenia in Fiji was devastated by shoot-boring insects and had to be pulped. This is always a risk with monocultures, especially when clonal propagation of a high-quality original means that all the plants are genetically identical.

Fashions and Fastenings

Every tree and flowering plant contains fibres, which give it strength to stand and resilience to bend with the wind. Primitive peoples soon took advantage of this, twining sturdy ropes out of climbing stems, bunches of grass, and roots. The fact that their strength came from internal fibres was probably discovered when foliage or stems rotting in water were observed to leave a skeleton of tough threads. The idea of strengthening these fibres by twining them together to form yarn then led naturally to making this yarn into ropes and cords, interlacing strands to form baskets or, by weaving, into mats and cloth.

Weaving is surprisingly ancient: there is evidence of it from about 5000 BC. An Egyptian predynastic dish of about 4400 BC depicts a horizontal loom, the type that can be fixed to legs on the ground, or even between a tree or pole and the weaver's waist. You can still see such looms in Mexico today; they are ideal for nomadic people, who can simply roll up the weaving on its two end struts when they move on.

The original Mahogany (Swietenia mahogani, above) discovered by Spanish explorers when they visited the island now called Hispaniola, where they found the wood in use for canoe-building. Quantities of it were taken back as a gift for King Philip II, and it was used for furniture and fittings in the Escorial Palace, right, starting around 1584. Thus the trade to Europe began.

Then in the late seventeenth century a virtually indistinguishable wood was discovered, originating this time from Khaya species from West Africa. Trade in both American and African mahogany continued to expand into the latter half of the twentieth century. But supplies dwindled; the true Mahogany now faces commercial extinction.

Flax (Linum usitatissimum, above) was woven into linen in Babylonia and Egypt around 3000 BC. This dual-purpose plant also yields linseed oil. The strong fibres, up to a metre long, have special qualities of water absorption, drying and gloss. Knowledge and use of plant fibres is still strong in many cultures; this Machiquenqa Indian woman of Peru, left, is weaving "cushma" to a traditional design.

Although all plants contain them, only a few natural fibres have proved really useful to us. Wood fibres are so tough that they can only be separated by powerful machinery and are then too short for anything beyond the microscopic meshing which makes paper products. Flax, hemp, jute, cotton and sisal, on the other hand, have great importance.

Hemp (*Cannabis sativa*) appears to have been grown in China at least 4,500 years ago; several millenia later the original Levi-Strauss jeans were also made of it. However, not much goes into cloth today; in fact, in many countries, production is now so strictly controlled as to be virtually banned, because *Cannabis* is also the source of the drug THC, the active principle in marijuana. Although the varieties grown for fibre have low THC content, control of the marijuana market has hastened the decline of the hemp industry. The chief producing country today is the USSR.

The only important leaf fibre is sisal, which comes from *Agave sisalana*, a plant of Mexican arid lands. Its long harsh leaves are cut from the base of the rosette over several years, until the plant flowers and dies. The leaves are crushed and cleansed of pulp by machine. Sisal fibres are a metre long, very strong, but too coarse for clothing; they go into cord and binder twine.

It is the versatile cotton plant (p.20) which leads the field in clothing fibres. Very different from other plant fibres, cotton is produced on hairy seeds of species of *Gossypium*, relations of hibiscus and hollyhock. Each cotton fibre is a single cell, 3000 times longer than thick, and a kilo of cotton contains roughly 200 million seed hairs up to 5 cm long. With cotton, the tedious processing of leaf and stem fibres is unnecessary: it has simply to be spun into thread.

A similar seed fibre is that of kapok or silk-cotton, *Ceiba pentandra*. Though not suitable for spinning, it is used to fill jackets and other cold-resistant clothes, mattresses, quilts, and sleeping bags; buoyant and impermeable to water, kapok is an essential ingredient of life-jackets.

In industrialised countries, synthetics have taken over from many natural fibres, often being cheaper, harder wearing, and able to resist insect and bacterial attack. They are not always so comfortable, however: the label "100 percent pure cotton" is still proudly carried by some expensive garments. In many more basic cultures, natural fibres are still depended on for both cloth and cordage.

One remarkable plant still used in cloth manufacture has remained a step ahead of any technological equivalent – the Fuller's Teasel, with its egg-shaped flower head, each floret surrounded by long, fine, spiny bracts. Mounted on frames or boards, these heads are still used to raise the nap on some cloths; for most fabrics wire substitutes will do, but for top-quality dressed cloths nothing surpasses the elegant teasel.

The Renewable and the Irreplaceable

Plants, in their infinite variety, provide wealth to large sectors of humanity. But we seldom distinguish between short-term and long-term gain. Domesticated crops, occupying land irrevocably transformed from its original plant cover, can be considered renewable assets – insofar as we manage the croplands well. But fortunes today are made from wild plants –

An important stem fibre is Jute (Corchorus capsularis) a cultivated plant about 3 metres tall, mainly grown in the Ganges delta of India. Too coarse for clothing, Jute fibre goes into burlap or hessian, and is used for sacks and as backing for linoleum and other flooring. Jute only became established as a commercial crop in the mid nineteenth century, after the Dundee spinners had learned how to use the fibre.

and these are often irreplaceable. Used as we are using them today, wild species and the vegetation they comprise – particularly tropical forests and savannas – are, in fact, non-renewable resources.

But wealth from the wild *can* be renewable, with proper management. Rattans are a marvellous example: these multipurpose tropical climbing palms can be sustainably culled from managed forest, and are the second most important item of trade from the rainforests of South-east Asia. The stems are used to make ropes, baskets, matting and furniture; the spiny leaves are made into fish traps and anti-theft devices. Once the spines are removed, the leaves are split and woven to make window blinds and thatching. Rattan production tends to be a village-based industry chiefly during slack agricultural periods, so local people can benefit from it more than from commercial timber operations. Since rattan extraction does almost no damage to the forest structure, the cottage industry can operate within forest reserve areas; and, since it provides an income, it may be a useful bargaining piece for conservation – for naturally, if the forests disappear, so do the rattans.

This type of sustainable forest exploitation can include a huge variety of commercially valuable substances – Indian forest plants, for instance, yield medicines, spices, foods and beverages, forage, gums, oils, resins, tanning and dyeing materials, pesticides, honey and other animal products.

Another type of wild vegetation offers great potential for renewable use – the ocean flora. Seaweeds provide ingredients for a huge range of products in industry – from fertiliser to food stabilisers, emulsifiers and gels; from microbiology to shampoo; from paints and dyes to deodorants, even building materials. Giant kelp is now being tested for alcohol production, offering a vast biomass resource. As for medical uses, research is only just beginning. Seaweed has been largely a wild harvest – but Chile, the Philippines and China now practice "mariculture" – they are farming the wild plants of the sea.

This concept of a sustainably managed ocean harvest is a very far cry from the senseless gobbling up of every vestige of green growth in a forest by pulping machines, leaving nothing behind. In terms of wealth, it makes no sense at all to continue using up the irreplaceable. It makes very good sense to concentrate instead on exploiting all possible uses of plants we already cultivate. And for the wealth of the future, there is a deep necessity to resuscitate land which has been over-cropped, or ruinously denuded of its original cover.

The modern Brazilian entrepreneur, intent on opening up the country for ranching, alcohol factories, oil and mineral exploitation, says of the irreplaceable tropical jungle he is cutting down, "Here there is nothing". But conversely the Indian will say, "The forest has everything. It supplies all our needs, the food we eat, timber and thatch, wood for bows and arrows, fruit and medicine". The forest is either *nada* or everything. It depends who you are.

Such knowledge was until recently common to people who lived in the forests, all too few of whom remain. A Peruvian tribe, for instance, has been recorded as familiar with the characters and uses of 50 species of palm tree alone. Before it is too late, "civilised" man needs very urgently to record this knowledge for his posterity.

Seaweeds manage to subsist on rocky tidal coastlines, perhaps the most changeable environments in the world; beyond the range of tides there are forests of kelp, as on the Falkland Islands, seen above. Individual plants may be over 50 metres long – the Giant Kelp (Macrocystis pyrifera) is reputed to reach 200 metres on occasion. The greatest value of marine plants to humanity is as the foundation of food webs which support fish, the wild harvest of the oceans. But they have many direct uses too. Cast-up seaweed is applied as a manure in coastal regions, and seaweed products – alginic acid, agar, carrageenin and gelans – are widely employed in the food industry. In textiles, seaweed products are used to size cloth; and they have numerous uses in medicine and cosmetics. Agar is probably best known as a microbiological culture medium for growing fungi and bacteria and for tissue culture. Kelp harvesting provides coastal peoples with an income in many areas, whether as a cottage industry or as a commercial venture, using modern cutter boats, left.

The chart shows the long history of medicinal plants as recorded. The oldest traditions come from China, Sumeria, Egypt and India. In Europe, the Dark Ages produced a long period of ignorance from which modern western medicine slowly emerged. Today Eastern and Western traditions are converging – producing a dynamic interaction of ideas out of which a new medicine may be born.

China Around 3000-2730 BC the legendary Emperor Shen Nung composed the Pen T'sao Ching, with 365 herbal remedies. Ginseng was prescribed from at least this time together with opium and ephedra.

Near East Sumerian ideograms of 2500 BC list several medicines based on plants. Circa 2200 BC tablets record 1,000 medicinal plants.

Around 2500 BC the Assyrians listed 250 medicinal species.
Hammurabi of Babylon, who ruled 1728 to 1686 BC, listed many healing plants.

Hammurabi receives scroll from a god

Egypt Dating from 1550 BC, the Ebers Papyrus gives details of Egyptian medicine, with material going back five to twenty centuries before. It has 877 prescriptions and recipes. Most are medicinal.

Egyptian papyrus with charm for women's diseases

India Dating back more than 3,500 years, India's medicine has an ancient history. The knowledge was formalised in sacred poems or vedas. Ayurveda, as this system is known, is still practiced in over 14,000 dispensaries. It contains over 8,000 herbal remedies, and has spread across South-east Asia.

From 1563, the Coloquios of Garcia da Orta (who was Portuguese) present first-hand knowledge of the medicines of India.

Greece and Rome
Born in 460 BC on Kos, Hippocrates was the most distinguished physician of antiquity. He travelled abroad researching and practising medicine, leaving a legacy of some 400 remedies.

In 332 BC the medical school at Alexandria was founded. It attracted the foremost Greek scholars. Scientists travelled with the armies of Alexander the Great from Greece to India. The learning of these conquered countries was set

down in 700,000 or more books. All were destroyed by a mob of Christian fanatics in AD 391.

Circa 120 BC Crateuas was physician to King Mithridates of Pontus. Only fragments of his work remain.

Born in AD 23 in Verona, Pliny the Elder was a Roman bookworm. His life's work was 37 books, eight of which dealt with medical botany.

In the first century AD, Dioscorides wrote De Materia Medica. This described some 500 plants and was the standard source book for 1500 years. He was an army surgeon.

Born around AD 131 at Pergamon, Galen travelled extensively, studying medicine at Alexandria. The allopathic and homoeopathic systems of medicine are based on his doctrines. His books were much copied during the Middle Ages.

A little known Roman of the fourth or fifth century, Apuleuis wrote an Herbarium of which Saxon and later translations exist.

Hippocrates the Greek physician, founder of medicine

Arabia Beheaded in AD 303, St Cosmos and St Damian are the patron saints of surgery. They were Arab physicians who travelled extensively preaching Christianity and healing. Plant-based medicines were important in Arab culture from the earliest times.

Born near Bokhara in AD 980, Avicenna was one of the most famous Arab doctors. His greatest work, the Canon of Medicine, refers frequently to Galen and Aristotle.

Arab physicians continued the tradition of medicine after the decline of Rome, translating the Greek books and adding their own observations. The culture ended with the Mongol invasion which took place in the thirteenth century.

from an Arabic copy of Dioscorides circa AD 1222

Europe Written between AD 900 and 950, the Saxon Leech Book of Bald (a friend of King Arthur) was the first English herbal written in the native language.

Founded during the ninth century AD, the first organised medical school in Europe was at Salerno. It gradually declined in the twelfth century.

During the fourteenth and fifteenth centuries, Montpellier had the foremost medical school in Europe. Others arose at Bologna, Padua and Paris.

PARACELS 9.

Paracelsus (1490-1541), a Swiss alchemist, developed the Doctrine of Signatures.

Born in 1501 in Siena, Mattioli tried to reconcile the teachings of Dioscorides with the innovations of the Arabs and the new herbal remedies that were flooding in from across the world.

In his New Herball of 1551-1568, William Turner was the first Englishman to study plants scientifically.

In 1585 the Herbario Nuovo of Castore Durante was first published in Rome. It presented all the known medical knowledge of plants of Europe and the East and West Indies.

The first large-scale British herbal is that of Gerard, published in 1597 in two large, heavily illustrated volumes. It was largely based on the work of the Dutchman Dodoens.

Even more popular than Gerard was Culpeper, whose herbal of 1652, first entitled The English Physician was condemned by contemporary medicos for his heavy reliance on astrological botany.

"Le Propriétaire des Choses", Paris 1500

South American figurine chewing coca

Born circa 1514, Francisco Hernandes was dubbed First Physician of the Indies by Philip II of Spain. He wrote Rerum Medicarum Novae Hispanae Thesaurus concerning Aztec medicine.

In 1552 the Badianus Manuscript was compiled by two Mexican physicians at Santa Cruz describing and illustrating healing plants used by Aztecs.

In Chronica del Peru of 1553, Pedro de Cieza de Leon mentions Coca among other plants.

South America *In the fourteenth century AD, the well-developed medical knowledge of the Aztecs was set down in pictograms. Most were destroyed by Spanish invaders.*

First printed in 1569, the Dos Libros of Nicholas Monardes, are concerned with the medicinal materials of the West Indies and New Spain as reported to Monardes in Spain.

North America *Seventeenth century settlers imported European plants. They used Culpeper's English herbal extensively. They also experimented with herbs well known to the native Indians, some of* which they exported back to Europe.

In 1718 the Canadian Jesuits started to export native Ginseng to the Orient to supplement the scarce Chinese supply.

North American Indian medicine man

Australia *Written herbal history dates from the first British settlements in the late eighteenth century. Only a few aboriginal herbs have entered mainstream herbalism.*

Africa *There are no written records so one can only surmise the antiquity of African herbal learning. The oral tradition is still extensive, but its value is only now appreciated.*

Green Medicine

Green medicine is very old. Five thousand years ago, the civilisations of antiquity knew plants such as Ephedra and the Opium Poppy, still used for the drugs ephedrine, morphine and codeine. It is also very young: scientific investigation into the medical properties of plants, from cancer cures to contraceptives, is today sparking off a revolution in our understanding. Interest in eastern drugs such as ginseng, and in the disappearing plant lore of indigenous cultures, is matched by concern for the unexplored potential of tropical species now threatened by forest clearance. The gap between western and traditional medicine is closing at last.

Only recently some scientists believed that medicinal plants were a thing of the past. Since some drugs originally derived from plants can be synthesised directly far more cheaply and easily, it was felt that once the secrets of their chemical composition had been discovered, medicinal plants would become redundant. But in the early 1970s attitudes started to change. On the one hand many people in developed countries, especially America and Britain, became curious about herbal medicine and welcomed it as part of a "back to nature" philosophy as well as for its lack of side-effects – a disadvantage of many powerful pharmaceuticals. And in many developing countries, policy-makers started to encourage a revival of traditional medicine using local herbs, because it was cheap, available and a part of their culture. Furthermore it reduced dependence on imported drugs.

Magic to Medicine

Early peoples must have shown an insatiable curiosity in sampling and testing plants, for they acquired over the millennia of prehistory an intimate knowledge of many thousands of species. Besides food plants, there were those that could dull pain, heal wounds, cure fever, or give energy and strength. Others could create hallucinations, induce sleep, or calm the spirit. And some were potent weapons – poisons which killed instantly. Since certain plants could kill, create visions, or cure depending on the amount taken or the part used, their powers were seen as magical or divine: thus magic and medicine became inextricably linked, as the preserve of witch doctors. These knowledgeable specialists were immensely powerful

Meadow Saffron (Colchicum autumnale) is the main source of colchicine. This poisonous painkiller is remarkably specific: excess causes diarrhoea or even death but in small doses it relieves the pain of gout. Unfortunately though, it does not reduce the high level of uric acid which causes the affliction. Various species of Colchicum have been used for over 2500 years. The resemblance of the root of Meadow Saffron to a gouty foot earned it a long folk reputation.

in their communities, and since they were more often interested in the spiritual cause of illness than in diagnosis, the nature of plant medicines long remained obscured by ritual and superstition.

Over the centuries, knowledge grew and was passed on orally from generation to generation; in Africa and South America the oral tradition is still strong; in Asia and Eastern Europe written records – the great "pharmacopoeia" – began very early. In western Europe, plant medicine remained as folklore until the birth of organic chemistry in the nineteenth century. Only then did the curative properties of plants, the compounds involved and their modes of action, begin at last to be unravelled, as the scientific tradition emerged.

A curious example of how modern knowledge is born of apparent quackery is given by the Doctrine of Signatures. Widely invoked by societies from the ancient Chinese and North American Indians to the Europe of the Middle Ages, it taught that like cures like: a heart-shaped leaf must be good for heart disorders, kidney-shaped for kidneys, a yellow juice for the treatment of jaundice. Most of these "cures" are unsubstantiated; but some plants have been found to be useful in other ways, while one or two actually deserve their reputation. The trembling leaves of White Willow resemble the shaking of a fever patient; a derivation from its bark, long since used in the treatment of fevers, now has its place in the blueprint for aspirin. And the Meadow Saffron, with a foot-like projection on its bulbous root, proves to be effective against the pain suffered by the gouty.

Modern medicine, with its thriving pharmaceuticals industry and bright technology, tends to make us forget that the average medicine off the shelf was probably first made, not by a chemist, but by a green plant. The current British Pharmacopoeia contains no less than 80 plant genera – about 30 percent of modern prepacked medicines are based on plant products while 80 percent or more were plant-based at some time. But this is small compared to the range of healing plants known to traditional medicine.

The Healing Potential

Plants are extraordinary chemical factories. Their storage of sunlight energy, their daily growth, their flowering and seeding, are complex enough, involving the syntheses of a huge range of organic molecules. These primary activities are common to all plants. However, individual plant species produce many other specialised substances, called secondary compounds, which differ from plant to plant depending on their circumstances. Plants do not flourish in isolation, but in intimate relationships with many species, from those that feed off them or attack them to those that help their pollination or seed dispersal. Some of these chemicals are therefore defensive, some advertise the plant's presence or play a role in symbiosis, some are waste products or toxin neutralizers. Many are of great value to man – for instance as hormones and antibiotics, narcotics and antihistamines, pesticides and poisons.

Certain plant families are strong in one or more types of secondary compound. Within a group of closely related species, some small changes in genetic instructions will cause slight differences in the chemistry so that the chemicals produced may have dramatically different effects. Such changes are of immense interest to the pharmacist.

Three very important groups of secondary compounds are the alkaloids, glycosides, and saponins. Alkaloids, nitrogenous compounds such as caffeine, morphine, quinine and strychnine, many of which affect the central nervous system, can be lethal if large amounts are taken. Deadly Nightshade and the Opium Poppy are alkaloid-bearing plants.

Glycosides are a type of secondary compound in which a physiologically active molecule is linked to a sugar molecule. Such compounds include the cardiac glycosides valuable in heart treatment extracted from Foxglove; purges like Cascara, Senna and Rhubarb; and the saponins, which foam or froth in water like soap – Soapwort can literally be used to wash the hands.

Plant compounds are big business: in 1973 natural products accounted for 41.2 percent of the total prescriptions dispensed in community pharmacies in the USA, with 25.2 percent derived from higher plants; a UN study estimates world trade of medicinal plants in 1980 at $550 million and identifies 400 botanicals (plant drugs) used commercially. Some plant compounds are isolated by laboratory techniques and made up into medicines; some are completely synthesised in the laboratory. But we still have much to learn. Some compounds – the cardiac glycoside from Foxglove is one – have so far resisted attempts at synthesis and it is still necessary to use plant material as the basis of every dose administered; others, as in the case of curare (see p. 116) are more effective than their synthetic derivatives. The drug in aspirin, on the other hand, probably the most widely taken medicine in the world, is now entirely synthetic.

The strange story of aspirin is typical of plant research and discovery. Since Dioscorides, it was known that the bark of the White Willow (Salix alba, below) could kill pain. Decoctions or infusions of it were used against fevers, rheumatic pains, gout, toothache, earache and headache. The active ingredient was first isolated from willows in the nineteenth century and named salicin. A similar compound, salicylic acid, was isolated from Meadowsweet, Filipendula ulmaria (then called Spiraea ulmaria, below right). In 1899 it was found that the combination of salicylic acid and acetic acid – the chemical acetylsalicylic acid – was more effective. This substance was then, confusingly, named "aspirin" after Spiraea. Salicylic acid is still in use today against athlete's foot and skin diseases like acne.

White Willow
Salix alba

female

male

Meadowsweet
Spiraea ulmaria

The Mandrake's remarkable career started with the resemblance of its forked tuberous roots to a human body. Barren women in its native Near East hung the roots up in their houses. Rachel's barrenness was ended with the birth of Joseph after she had begged her sister "Give me, I pray thee, of thy son's mandrakes" (Genesis 30). From preventer of barrenness to aphrodisiac: the Romans reputedly used Mandrake in orgies.

The magic that came to surround Mandrake is extraordinary: in the first century Josephus wrote "He who would take up a plant therefore, must tie a dog thereunto, to pull it up, otherwise if a man should do it, he should surely die in a short space after".

The narcotic properties of Mandrake were more real: Dioscorides wrote that it was given "to such as shall be cut, or cauterized... For they do not apprehend the pain, because they are overborn with dead sleep..." Greek, Roman and Arabian doctors used it as anaesthetic and to calm maniacs. In Palestine when the Romans started to crucify criminals, relations offered a sponge soaked in Mandrake juice and placed on a pole for the men to drink, so that they became unconscious and were mistaken for dead.

Mandrake was long an important herbal plant but its basic alkaloid, mandragorine, is not now used medicinally.

Poisons and Panaceas

However they are prepared, our powerful modern plant-based drugs have usually reached our notice by one of two routes: either their reputation as healers in folk medicine provoked scientific investigation; or they were originally known as dangerous poisons, and then tested for remedial possibilities because plants with the capacity to kill can often cure. Knowledge that a plant contains strong toxins is today a spur to investigation, working on the principle that what can destroy or paralyse in large quantities may also have a useful action in small concentrations.

A striking example is the Calabar Bean, once used for the ritualistic practice of trial by ordeal, in which the accused had to imbibe a poisonous liquid; death meant guilt. (Those who knew the ropes gulped the liquid down and promptly vomited; the fearful sipped it slowly and died quickly of asphyxiation from paralysis of the respiratory muscles.) Synthetics derived from its alkaloid, physostigmine, are now used to build up muscle strength in the disease myasthemia gravis and, especially, to treat eye disorders. In these respects it is similar to an even more valuable eye medicine, pilocarpine, derived from the Jaborandi tree, considered by the World Health Organisation to be one of the most important plant-based drugs in the treatment of glaucoma.

Toxins used for hunting or warfare have also yielded some powerful medicines. South American Indians made one such poison, curare, from several plants including a species of *Strychnos* and various Chondrodendrons, and used it both for war and to kill game. Not until 1939 was the active principle of curare isolated – a muscle relaxant now widely used in abdominal surgery to facilitate cutting by relaxing striated muscle. The early Europeans tended to kill their enemies with poisons from the great Solanaceae family, with its roll-call of sinister names – Mandrake, Deadly Nightshade and Henbane. Every part of the last two is poisonous; they have a long record of use by professional poisoners. The chief symptoms were flushing, a dry mouth, dilated pupils, and delirium with death from respiratory failure. Interestingly enough, this family also includes the Potato and Tomato, both thought to be wholly poisonous when they were first brought to Europe from the Americas.

Today, the Solanaceae rank high in the list of potent healers. Extremely valuable alkaloids are found in Deadly Nightshade, Henbane, Thornapple and other daturas, and the Australian *Duboisia*. Medically these are active against a large number of complaints, being useful in asthma, and for treating diseases of the central nervous system such as Parkinson's Disease. Atropine and hyoscine are used in ophthalmology to dilate the pupil and against stomach and duodenal ulcers. Hyoscine allays colic and other internal gripings, and is used in mania and alcoholic delirium and as pre-anaesthetic medication. Its most familiar use is for travel sickness.

To produce these important drugs, Nightshade and Henbane are now grown commercially in North America and the Balkans, as are species of *Duboisia* in Australia. A good deal of atropine still comes from the Egyptian Henbane *Hyoscyamus muticus* in the wild. Although atropine can be synthesized, all the drugs are still made from the starting point of the dried leaf, flowering tops, and roots of the various plants.

Kill or Cure...

Hyoscyamus niger

Atropa belladonna

Datura stramonium

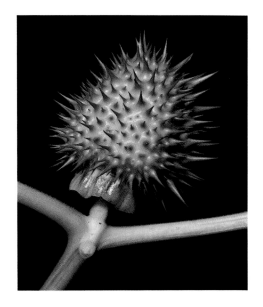

Deadly Nightshade is named *Atropa belladonna*, *Atropos* being one of the Fates who severed the thread of life and belladonna meaning "beautiful lady" – women used to place a little dilute juice in their eyes to expand the pupil and give themselves a bright, wide-eyed look. This capacity is today valued by ophthalmologists, who need to dilate the pupil for examination. Deadly Nightshade is especially dangerous because its bell-shaped flowers are followed by glistening black berries, sweet to taste, and tempting to children – to whom two or three are lethal. The Roman poisoner Locusta is reputed to have killed the Emperor Claudius with belladonna. Its effects start with hallucinations and delirium, then paralysis before death.

Henbane (*Hyoscyamus niger*, above) is a tall, thoroughly evil-looking, evil-smelling plant with large open bell flowers – veined with purple on lurid yellow in the north European species. Dioscorides recommended the milder white-flowered Henbane of the Mediterranean (*H. albus*) as an "easer of pain" with many uses. In Europe later on, criminals used it to render victims unconscious.

Thornapple (*Datura stramonium*, above right) an American native now widespread in many countries, has an attractive white trumpet flower succeeded by large, thorny seed capsules, right. Its American name, Jimsonweed, comes from Jamestown where sailors once nearly killed themselves eating what they believed to be spinach. Indian prostitutes doped clients with it then robbed them, and it played a part in the white slave traffic.

Opium Poppies

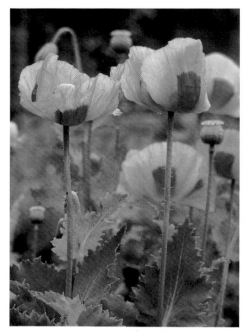

The two-edged sword of healing and destruction common to all these poisonous medicinal plants is wielded most strongly by the Opium Poppy (Papaver somniferum). It is the source of the painkiller morphine, which still cannot be synthesised chemically. The dreadfully addictive heroin is made from morphine.

In its crude state opium has been known for several millenia in the west for its sleep-inducing and pain-killing qualities. Among the medicines made from it were paregoric, given to babies to calm them and make them sleep (still available) and laudanum (now called tincture of opium), widely prescribed as a painkiller in the last century. Coleridge wrote Kubla Khan under the influence of laudanum; Elizabeth Barrett Browning became an addict while under medical attention; and in this century Cocteau's hallucinatory drawings and writings are a reflection of its influence.

Opium is a mixture of some 25 alkaloids, including morphine. Named after Morpheus the Greek god of dreams, this is the greatest natural painkiller of all and its medicinal value in extreme cases has been considerable. Unfortunately its side-effects can be most harmful and for this reason its use is now prohibited in the USA. It relieves pain and resulting sleeplessness, calms anxiety, and reduces all disagreeable sensations apart from skin irritation. It is also a mental stimulant, and it is this impression of self-alertness without inhibition or doubt that attracts the user in the first place. Those addicted who try to give it up suffer appalling symptoms, both physical and mental, stomach spasms sometimes leading to rupture and death.

Codeine is a household painkiller used in cough medicines, cold remedies and for a host of diseases; about one-fifth as strong a painkiller as morphine, it is very much less addictive. Another important alkaloid of opium is the non-addictive moscapine, which relieves coughs, especially in bronchitis and whooping cough.

Native to south-eastern Europe and western Asia, the Opium Poppy is now widely cultivated from Turkey eastwards, especially in India, Burma and Thailand. Some governments are trying to encourage the cultivation of alternative crops to supplant their peoples' economic dependence on harvesting this deadly crop.

The Greeks celebrated the Opium Poppy and its calming powers in literature, art and religion from earliest times. The Cretan Poppy Goddess, left, dates from the later Minoan period, 1700-1400 BC. The Greek culture regarded sleep as the greatest healer, hence the frequency with which poppy heads are found on figurines, vases, utensils, jewellery and coins. The Greeks also called opium "nepenthe", and in Homer's Odyssey Helen offers Telemachus a philtre of this to "lull pain and bring forgetfulness of sorrow".

Many other plants as poisonous as these were once harnessed as medicines, but are now considered too dangerous to use – for instance the Buttercup family, which includes such popular garden plants as hellebore, delphinium, columbine, and monkshood or "wolfsbane" – a name in keeping with its lethal character. Ironically the peony, named after Paeon, a favourite physician of the Greek gods, has also dropped out of use in the West despite a long tradition; but it remains in Chinese herbalism.

Quinine – the "Bark of Barks"

After painkillers, the plant cures which have probably done most to relieve human suffering are the febrifuges, and the greatest of these is quinine, which acts against malaria.

This widespread fever – "the ague" – has had an extraordinarily harmful effect in human history. It regularly ravaged Rome, which Cicero called "a pestilential city"; the fall of Rome and of ancient Greece have both been attributed to malaria. Alexander the Great died from it. Africa repelled European settlers for centuries because of its prevalence. Until quinine became widely available, malaria probably killed two million people a year, half of them in India, and left perhaps 200 million chronically ill. Not till 1902 was it known that the organism causing malaria was spread by mosquitoes. And not until after the Second World War did DDT enable us to tackle the mosquitoes directly.

Quinine originated from the South American Andes, from the bark of *Cinchona* trees, which was first brought to Europe in the seventeenth century. In 1820, the alkaloid in the bark was isolated, and demand increased vastly with foreseeable consequences – the trees with the bark containing the largest quinine content, in parts of Bolivia and Peru, were steadily destroyed by the Indian collectors. Both the British and Dutch, with malaria rife in India and Java, tried to collect seeds, young plants and root cuttings and grow them on in those countries. Unfortunately the resulting trees – over a million in the case of the British expedition – were worthless. Clearly, very few *Cinchona* plants contained worthwhile quantities of quinine. Eventually an Englishman obtained seed (illegally) from a grove of trees in Bolivia he knew were very high-yielding, and the Dutch acquired a pound of them for a paltry sum. From this single source, 12,000 trees were raised which yielded quinine in far higher proportion than had ever been recorded and formed the basis of a multi-million guilder monopoly – until the commercial production of DDT and synthetic anti-malarial drugs took over. However, by 1984 the malaria parasite had become resistant to most synthetic drugs in many countries, and quinine is returning as the only currently effective remedy.

Multiple Saviours

Some plants have long stood out in the pharmacopoeia as multiple healers, effective against many ills, and a number of these have yielded modern drugs with correspondingly diverse uses.

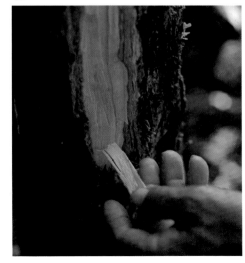

Quinine, still the most effective anti-malarial agent, comes from the Cinchona trees of the Andes, above. The Jesuits of Lima first introduced the ground bark to Europe. Known to the Indians as quinaquina, "the bark of barks", quinine is obtained by stripping the bark from the trees, below – a process which eventually kills them. Some other alkaloids such as quinidine also have pharmaceutical applications.

Above *The value of ephedrine, an alkaloid extracted from species of Ephedra, was discovered for the west by two American pharmacologists who visited a Peking pharmacy in 1923. Their research into Chinese medical literature, and experiments, confirmed the efficacy of the Chinese Ephedra extract, mahuang – especially in raising blood pressure.*

Below *Rauwolfia serpentina grows from India to Indonesia; the anti-hypertensive reserpine is obtained from its roots.*

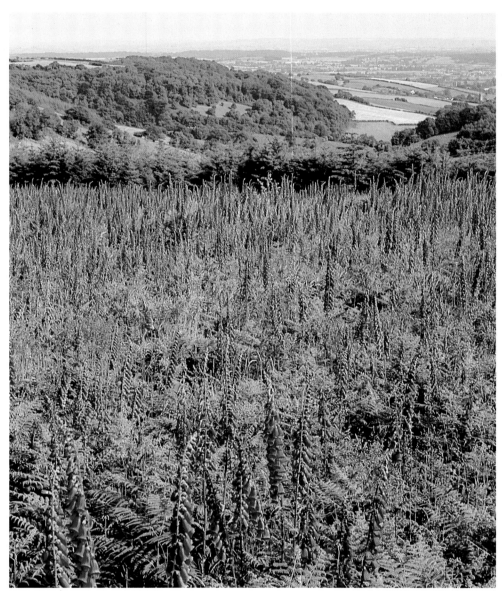

The Foxglove (Digitalis purpurea) has a long history of herbal use, and it was this that led to discovery of its potential as a heart medicine. William Withering, who spent much of his time treating the poor, visited an old woman suffering from dropsy, seemingly far gone. A few weeks later, he found her much improved; he discovered she had taken a herbal remedy and that one of the herbs in it was Foxglove. Withering spent ten years looking into its potential against dropsy, before he suspected its real value. Much later it was confirmed that Foxglove acts on the heart; the improved circulation that results steps up the performance of the kidneys, which in turn clear the accumulated body fluids which our ancestors called dropsy. Foxglove was not apparently known to the ancients. Instead they recommended for heart problems Monkshood, its relation the False Helleborine and the Sea Squill of Mediterranean coastal areas – all highly toxic plants. One should add that Foxglove is poisonous too: Withering spent a long time getting the dosage roughly right. An excess leads to a number of unpleasant symptoms.

One of the earliest was Ephedra, used by the Chinese 5,000 years ago; they made a tea of the twigs to allay fever and coughs, and to increase blood pressure. Today the intrinsic alkaloid, ephedrine, is a valuable multipurpose drug, still made from the plants (which are cultivated) but also synthesized. Ephedrine helps those with low blood pressure, and also has a stimulant action used to treat patients in comas. It prevents the fall in blood pressure which occurs after spinal anaesthesia in surgery, and contains the dizziness and fainting which are symptoms of "heart block". But perhaps the most generally appreciated virtue of ephedrine is in treating hay fever and asthma, for it clears both the nasal and bronchial passages.

By contrast to ephedrine, reserpine – another long-known plant drug – lowers blood pressure, controls arrhythmia and calms the central nervous system. Reserpine comes from the roots of a plant called *Rauwolfia*. The powdered root has been in use for at least 2,000 years in India for those suffering from "moon disease" (lunacy) or other mental illnesses. Not till 1952, however, when the alkaloid was isolated, did its use in western medicine begin to snowball. Probably one of the most effective plant-based tranquillisers, it made the lives of schizophrenics far more bearable. Nowadays, the drug is mainly used to control high blood pressure.

Scores of local folk names attest to the Foxglove's long-standing reputation as a multiple healer; among its many imagined medical virtues were efficacy against fevers and colds, treatment of the King's Evil (scrofula) and, notably, cure of dropsy. It was an eighteenth century doctor, William Withering, who first suspected that Foxglove acted on the heart; but only after his death was it realised that heart disease caused one kind of dropsy.

Today the Foxglove's reputation is justified by results: probably millions of heart-sufferers owe their lives to this charming wild flower. Its active principles, the glycosides digoxin and digitoxin, can strengthen and regularise the heartbeat. They are still derived from the dried leaves, sometimes from the common British plant *Digitalis purpurea* but now, mostly, the European *D. lanata*; the drug has never been synthesized.

Breakthrough on Cancer

Many people know the Rosy Periwinkle as a small pot plant, with showy pink or white flowers. But in various parts of its native tropics this little plant, a member of the poisonous and drug-rich Dogbane family, has a long folk history against diabetes: a tea is infused from the leaves, and patent medicines are still used in the West Indies as anti-diabetics.

Not surprisingly this reputation became the target for scientific testing. In the 1950s a medical research laboratory in Ontario, searching for a substitute for insulin, tested the plant's effect upon blood sugar levels in rabbits. First they were fed with the leaves; then they were injected with an extract from the plant sap. The tests were negative, but many experimental animals died mysteriously. They appeared to have lost resistance to a common bacterium – the Periwinkle extract was reducing their white blood cell count and bone marrow activity. Quite independently, a botanical drug-screening company subjected leukemia-infected mice to Rosy Periwinkle extract – and found that their lives were significantly prolonged.

The Rosy Periwinkle (Catharanthus roseus) is a relation of the hardy evergreen creeping periwinkles liked by Elizabethan gardeners, but has been separated botanically from their genus (Vinca) into the distinct tropical genus Catharanthus. Although naturalised in the tropics, it is often called Madagascar Periwinkle from one of its truly native localities. However, little of the natural vegetation of Madagascar remains and most of the rest is in danger. A close relative of Rosy Periwinkle, Catharanthus coriaceus (also from Madagascar) is critically endangered from bush fires; it too may have valuable chemicals to offer – if it does not become extinct first.

The dainty little Bloodroot (Sanguinaria canadensis), so called because of the red juice that flows from the cut roots, was used by North American Indians to treat several ailments. Modern science has confirmed its value against malignant tumours.

American Mandrake (Podophyllum peltatum), also known as the North American Mayapple, has long been used in the treatment of cancerous tumours and the resin is still the preferred therapy for venereal warts.

The research teams pooled their knowledge, and in 1958 the substance active against the leukemia cells was isolated – an alkaloid, now called vinblastine. In the 25 years since over 70 alkaloids have been isolated – no easy matter since, unlike other alkaloid-containing plants, the Rosy Periwinkle's total content is minute – around 0.00025 percent of dry weight. Fortunately the drug is potent in tiny quantities. Vinblastine was first used in 1960: the patient's large cancerous tumour rapidly disappeared but, after two and a half years' treatment, cancer symptoms began to resurface. Then another Periwinkle alkaloid, vincristine, was tried. Remarkably enough, it started again to control the disease, showing that built-up resistance to vinblastine was not carried over to vincristine.

These remain the two major cancer treatments derived from Rosy Periwinkle. Vinblastine – used in conjunction with other drugs – now produces a remission rate of 80 percent in Hodgkin's disease, compared with 19 percent from previous treatment; vincristine provides over 90 percent remission in acute lymphocytic leukemia, which frequently attacks children. Other types of cancer can also be treated, and further Periwinkle alkaloids are being tried. All share the property of interfering with cancer cell growth.

The hunt for new drugs to fight this disease has involved screening many thousands of plants. The obvious place to begin was with traditional cancer cures in indigenous cultures: Penobscot Indians used the American Mandrake *Podophyllum peltatum* against malignant tumours, other groups the Bloodroot, *Sanguinaria canadensis*. These plants are now being exploited, both for drugs and for knowledge: some of the synthetic analogues of podophyllotoxin are more effective than the natural compound. In India, the Himalayan *Podophyllum hexandrum* is the species used. Several other plants also show promise, including the East African shrub *Maytenus gratius*, the tall American Meadow Rue *Thalictrum dasycarpum*, and the Chinese Plum-yew, *Cephalotaxus fortuni*.

Destruction of vegetation makes this task all the more urgent. Recent studies sponsored by WWF have recorded over 1,000 plants in the rain forests of South America used by tribal people. Among them is *Croton lechleri*, whose bark is used to treat stomach cancer; another is *Jacaranda caucana* which is used for leukaemia. Loss of habitat threatens these and the many other plants whose medicinal properties we may never know.

Contraceptive revolution

One of the most dramatic stories of the last half-century is the development of the contraceptive pill, which has revolutionised birth control. The American who made this possible, Russell E. Marker, was an organic chemist specialising in steroid compounds and, later, in the human sex hormones. Marker was looking for a drug to make up for lack of natural progesterone hormone in women – a cause of miscarriages.

He began investigating plants producing steroid-bearing saponins, including the Joshua Tree of the American deserts and the Sarsaparilla which had long been touted as a tonic and cure-all. Eventually he took the saponin now known as diosgenin, which the Japanese had isolated in 1937, from the yam *Dioscorea tokoro*, and showed how the female hormone progesterone could be synthesised from it in five steps, and the male testosterone in eight. Lack of interest from major pharmaceutical companies provoked him, in 1942, into looking for yams nearer home in Mexico. Out of some 60 or 70 species he finally found four or five which produced tubers of reasonable size fairly quickly. These species provided the basis of the world's contraceptive pill industry – they were both extracted from the wild and cultivated on a large scale in Mexico. Today most oral contraceptive pills in the west are totally synthetic; but in India and China wild yams are still being processed for this purpose.

Marker also searched unsuccessfully for a plant source for the hormone cortisone. By then a well-known drug with enormous remedial value for rheumatoid arthritis, cortisone was being produced commercially from animal adrenal glands, but the process was complex and costly. No commercial plant source of cortisone has yet been found (an African *Strophanthus* liana does contain it, but not in sufficient quantities). However, antifertility drugs based on yams are helping women arthritics who take doses to control pain. This link between sex hormones and cortisone was discovered when women found their arthritis improved during pregnancy.

Many other plants have contraceptive potential, from the Soya Bean, Cotton, and Fenugreek, to cures already known to indigenous cultures. In the species-rich forests of tropical South America, several kinds of tree bark, two arum relations *Dieffenbachia seguine* and *Anthurium kessmannii*, and numerous other herbal sources are used as contraceptives. In Colombia, a woman anthropologist who won the confidence of the Witoto

The South African yam, Dioscorea elephantipes, left, has potential for commercial diosgenin extraction and synthesis of sex hormones. It was in Mexican yams that diosgenin was first found in sufficient quantities to make the contraceptive pill available on any scale. Before Russell E. Marker took his two kilos of yam-derived progesterone to a large Mexican pharmaceutical company in 1942, the drug had been expensive and rare. Marker's yams at once broke the existing monopoly on commercial progesterone, and gave birth to the contraceptive pill industry. Among the many plants now being explored for hormone potential is the ordinary Cotton plant (Gossypium barbadense, far left). Gossypol, extracted from the seeds, is being tested for use as a male contraceptive. Though long tried in China, however, clinical tests have yet to demonstrate that there is no risk to subsequent progeny.

tribe was shown a plant which was given to girls just once at puberty and prevented pregnancy for six to eight years. Another plant was alleged to confer permanent female sterility.

There is a tragic footnote to this story. In northern India, on the foothills of the Himalayas, grows *Dioscorea deltoidea*, reputedly the best known source of diosgenin: not only does it contain high amounts of diosgenin, but it is free from minor steroids. Industrial companies have uprooted large amounts of its tubers from the forests, ignoring strict regulations on exploitation; parts of Kashmir and Himachal Pradesh have been completely denuded. Even more serious, in areas whose plants remain, their diosgenin content is far far lower than before, as big, high-yielding tubers are the first to go. One study found the diosgenin content reduced from over 6 percent to less than 1 percent. An answer, of course, is to domesticate the plant, breeding high-yielding varieties suitable for cultivation, and to conserve the full diversity of the wild ones in strictly managed reserves.

Body as Entity

There are two schools of thought on the role of medicine: one views it as curative, treating specific ailments; the other as preventive – keeping the body well-tuned and resistant to disease. From ancient times Chinese medical practice has been based on the preventive principle. Health-sustaining substances, mild and harmless even in large doses, are regarded as "kings" among medicines, while curative drugs are merely "servants".

The main weapon available to the Chinese has been, for nearly 5,000 years, an ivy relation, *Panax ginseng;* its Latin name means "panacea", all-healing. This thick-rooted herbaceous plant of the ivy family has quite recently surfaced in the west as an invigorating drug, reputedly preventing fatigue and depression, staving off the weakness of old age, increasing sexual potency; also improving headache, amnesia, tuberculosis, diabetes, heart problems and kidney disease, among others. Much empirical work done on Ginseng bears out these claims.

The Russians have a closely related native plant, *Eleutherococcus senticosus* or "Siberian Ginseng", and there are American and Himalayan species. Ginseng can be cultivated but tradition has it that wild plants are more effective; the small gnarled roots indicate the plant has been successful in its struggle for existence and will impart its strength to the consumer. As a result, over-collection is endangering the wild resource – less than 4 kilos were harvested in China in 1981.

In the west, the emphasis on curative medicine and the often theatrical results of new drugs long drew attention away from the potential of Ginseng and other "harmonisers" in medicine, but interest has been growing for some time. A great deal of work, mainly in the USSR but now in the USA too, suggests that these plants *do* improve overall fitness, increase physical performance, and aid mental alertness – especially under stress (as with Soviet cosmonauts). The reason is still obscure but is thought to lie in the combination of chemicals involved. This makes replacement by synthesis difficult, if not impossible. *Eleutherococcus* is now prescribed generally in Russia for convalescence and chronic infection. The Russians have found

Exports to the Orient, where sadly Panax ginseng is an endangered species, are now threatening wild stocks of American Ginseng (Panax quinquefolius, above). Though it once flourished in woodlands throughout the eastern USA, several hundred years of collection have taken their toll, and it has become endangered in some areas. In some States harvesters are required to scatter the seeds of mature plants they pick; in others collecting is totally banned.

similar properties in further ivy relations, the Roseroot (native to Britain and North America as well), and berries of *Schizandra*.

There are many other plants long known for their power to extend human performance without damaging health. Many people use herbal pick-me-ups such as Sarsaparilla, Sage, Yarrow, Mugwort and Dandelion root. Onions were consumed on a prophylactic basis long after most of the traditions of herbalism died in the west. Capsules of Garlic can now be purchased in any health food store, or raw cloves can be chewed. These pungent members of the Lily family are held to reduce the chances of heart attack and stroke by lowering the level of cholesterol in the blood and reducing blood pressure, to stimulate insulin production (thus lowering blood sugar levels), to regulate the menstrual cycle, promote wound healing, suppress allergy, counter asthma, even act as an aphrodisiac. Evening Primrose oil, from the tall-spiked *Oenothera* species, is gaining a reputation which may take it out of the class of panaceas such as Ginseng or Garlic and into mainstream medicine alongside Foxglove and *Cinchona*. It is taken by multiple sclerosis sufferers and hyperactive children, for schizophrenia, migraine, and Parkinson's disease; to counter senile dementia, pre-menstrual tension, benign breast conditions, high blood pressure, and certain types of heart disease; even asthma and eczema. Medical opinion does not support everything said about Evening Primrose; there is guarded enthusiasm but truly rigorous clinical trials are still needed.

Some plants long known in traditional medicine have now surfaced as scientifically based stimulants: Kava Kava from the Pacific islands; Khat, daily chewed by Muslims; Cola nut, favourite West Indian masticatory; and milder tonics like Jujube, Liquorice, Spikenard and Senega have all been profitably investigated. One of the most notorious is the South American Coca plant which is widely cultivated in the Andean highlands. The conquistador Pizarro noted that the Incas chewed the leaves. Indeed the shrub was so highly esteemed that it was considered to be the property of the Incan royal family, and leaves were laid in the graves of noblemen to serve them in the after-life. Coca stimulates the brain and depresses hunger – the Spaniards made sure their Indian slaves had plenty of it. In Peru and Bolivia today, rural people endure the harsh conditions of their lives, carrying loads up and down mountain slopes and labouring at heavy work, by stopping periodically not for food but for the cocada or chewing pause. Coca was distributed to other tropical countries in the late nineteenth century, and the chewing habit has spread to Java, India and Sri Lanka.

The active ingredient, the alkaloid cocaine, was isolated from Coca in the 1840s. It stimulates the nervous system, producing effects very similar to amphetamines but not nearly so long lasting. To maintain a "high", cocaine must be administered frequently. On withdrawal, a habitual cocaine user does not suffer the severe physical symptoms common with some hard drugs, but can become severely depressed, which strongly urges resumption of the habit. In the nineteenth century cocaine was a common addition to elixirs and tonic powders. It was an original ingredient of Coca-cola, though banned from the drink in 1904.

In 1884 a young colleague of Sigmund Freud discovered cocaine's amazing possibilities as a local anaesthetic, in which form it revolutionized surgery. But the potential for abuse was clear, so a substitute lacking the

The leaves of the Coca plant (Erythroxylon coca) have been seen on Bolivia's mountain terraces for centuries, since the days when the plant held religious significance at the Inca court. The physical stamina and relief from discomfort the cocada provides enables people to carry out hard labour on an inadequate diet. The leaves are a source of high income from illegal cocaine. The sight of government officials burning seized cocaine is not uncommon.

Rheum palmatum

Cassia senna

Ricinus communis

Cephaelis ipecacuanha

Aloe vera

Ipecacuanha is the local name of a Brazilian jungle shrub, *Cephaelis ipecacuanha*. One of its alkaloid constituents, emetine, causes vomiting and may be administered in cases of poisoning. It is also useful for amoebic dysentery as well as bronchitis, coughs, whooping cough and croup.

A powerful purge is obtained from the medicinal Rhubarb (*Rheum palmatum*). Although there are 50 species of rhubarb, only a few are laxative; the garden Rhubarb (*R. rhaponticum*), is not. To be effective, plants have to be at least six years old; the dried roots, from which the bark is removed, contain the resinous purging material.

Oil is extracted from the seeds of the Castor Bean or Castor Oil Tree (*Ricinus communis*), also called the Palma Christi or Wonder Tree. It was known to Pliny and, indeed, the ancient Egyptians before him. Besides its value as a purge, Castor oil is used in ointments and eye-drops and has many industrial uses.

Though probably long used by the local Arabs, the merits of Senna, obtained from both the fruits and leaves of a shrub belonging to the large genus Cassia, were first made known by a famous Arabian doctor, Mesue, whom Harun al-Rashid invited to practice in Baghdad in the eighth century AD. It is now grown in India and the Sudan, and imports into the USA are measured in millions of kilos.

As with Rhubarb, so also with Aloes: out of perhaps 250 species only a handful were found to have the cathartic property, one a Mediterranean native, one from South Africa and, the most famous perhaps, from the island of Socotra south of Aden (east of the Horn of Africa) – famous because Alexander the Great, at the suggestion of Aristotle, sent experts there around 325 BC to find out how this drastic purge was produced. Today, however, the flora of Socotra is critically endangered by rising herds of livestock; out of 216 plants which grow nowhere else in the world, 85 are in immediate danger of extinction and some have probably already gone.

stimulant properties was sought. Analysis of cocaine led eventually to the synthesis of a non-addictive chemical substitute, lignocaine, which has largely replaced cocaine in anaesthesia (though cocaine is still used in eye, ear, nose and throat surgery).

Purges

A curious element of humanity's search for health is the long-standing belief that everyone should have a bowel motion once a day.

The Egyptian *Ebers Papyrus* lists three of the classic cathartics then available – Aloes, Castor oil and Senna – all three still used today. The oldest of all recorded purges, however, is Rhubarb – not the familiar garden species, *Rheum rhaponticum,* but primarily *R. palmatum* and a handful of other species, mostly Chinese, in which the purge can be found. Known for 5,000 years in China, Rhubarb came to be valued so highly that in the sixteenth century the French paid ten times more for it than for Cinnamon. The standard North American purge is Cascara, obtained from the bark of a Buckthorn tree, *Rhamnus purshiana.* An early Spanish missionary found the Indians in northern California and Oregon using it; perhaps he was specially cursed by constipation, for he apparently gave it its popular name, Cascara Sagrada, "the holy bark", on account of its mild but highly efficient action. Nowadays its extreme bitterness is usually masked in chocolate-coated pills. Although the tree is cut down to remove the bark, the stump quickly produces new growth, so that – unlike the quinine trees – extinction does not follow collection.

These plant-based purges are ingredients in a good proportion of well over 700 laxatives advertised in the United States alone. In fact, very few people suffer from true constipation as a clinical disease; the rest are indoctrinated by centuries of belief in regularity.

Traditional and Modern

Of the known medicinal uses of plants, by far the largest proportion remains in traditional, folk or herbal medicine. It has been estimated that at least 6,000 plants are involved – in India alone over 2,500 are officially recognised. A great many more are in local use, and may not even be botanically identified. Three-quarters of Third World medical needs are met by herbal preparations – mostly crude medicines in the sense of being "off the tree", pulped or decocted and so on, rather than refined or synthesised.

In the last decade interest in traditional medicine has been renewed, and much is now being done worldwide to give it the respect it deserves – green medicine is being born again. The World Health Organisation (WHO) is trying to incorporate traditional medical plant knowledge into health systems in developing countries, since western health methods are expensive, and often inappropriate. WHO have recognized that it will simply not be possible to replace traditional medicine with western health care for all people, at least before the end of the century. They also recognize the important social function fulfilled by herbalists and bonesetters. For the great majority of people, the local healer offers the only medicine available. The hospital or clinic may be far away, and an alarming place, whereas traditional medicine maintains human dignity, fits in with the culture, and is familiar. So building a national health service out of a synthesis of traditional and modern medicine seems sensible – but it is a great challenge. Above all, WHO seeks to promote plant medicine as chemistry, not magic, by applying scientific analysis to the herbal treatments used. This development has been greatly inspired by the example of China, where the practitioners of western medicine have been made to regard their traditional counterparts as equals, and today herbal medicine and acupuncture are being combined with what are considered the best western methods. Over a million "barefoot doctors" now practise this combination.

The Vietnamese too have a remarkable record. They have had not only to face normal tropical diseases but also horrific medical and surgical demands created by war. Families are being encouraged to grow at least a dozen of the 58 recognised "family medicine" plants. The government buys most of its medicinal raw materials from these gardens, so that villages not only have health care at hand but an extra source of income. In recent years a massive drive to study local plant remedies produced no less than 40 new drugs for disorders as varied as high blood pressure, rheumatism, hepatitis, goitre, coughs, allergy and shock. Other countries producing plant medicines include Bangladesh, Madagascar, Rwanda and Thailand.

In Africa, the daily lives of farmer, raiser of cattle and nomad depend on medicinal plants; in fact 95 percent of traditional drugs come from plants. Their healers serve a long apprenticeship and have great botanical knowledge of local plants, their uses and properties. All this knowledge is in grave danger of being lost, as increasing human and livestock populations put more pressure on natural vegetation.

One man who understands this is Dr Herbert Ushewokuaze, Zimbabwe's Minister of Health. In 1980, soon after independence, he formed a National Traditional Healers' Association and said that traditional healers would be part of Zimbabwe's National Health Service. Six of the healers told him they could reduce surgical operations by 80 percent, using herbal remedies. His answer: "African medicine is part and parcel of our culture. Previous white governments tended to discredit and scorn traditional healers, portraying them as evil by calling them 'witch doctors'". Of course traditional healers have, in WHO's words, to be "weaned away from positively harmful practices". But this can surely be achieved within the context of traditional medicine.

In Pakistan, traditional medicine, known as Unani Tibb, is accepted as a state system alongside modern medicine; it has 36,000 practitioners who are graduates of the nine Tibbi medical colleges. They claim to reach all the rural people in Pakistan as well as many people in the cities. They work under a National Council, which regulates and maintains standards. India too has a very elaborate system of traditional medicine with 900-plus hospitals and 14,000 dispensaries. However, the traditional doctors are regarded as underqualified and subordinate by those educated in western-style practice. Although integrated courses are taken by students, they are inclined to abandon the older Ayurvedic theory when they qualify.

Sphagnum moss, known since ancient times, was widely used in the First World War as a wound dressing, largely for its moisture-absorbing capacity. A Bronze Age skeleton found in Scotland appeared to have a chest wound with a large wad of Sphagnum applied to it. Its healing properties long remained unclear. Recently, analysis has revealed several associated micro-organisms, among them a penicillium, which might explain its apparently antibiotic action. The upper picture shows fruiting bodies; the lower a greatly magnified section to show the highly absorptive cellular structure.

But research into traditional plant drugs is increasing, even in India, as well as in Mexico, the Amazon region, and Ghana, where effective herbal remedies for guinea worm and *Herpes zoster* (incurable by other means) have been found. In time, Third World research into plant drugs may influence western medicine even more strongly. Many such drugs are on the brink of being brought into use – for dysentery, hepatitis, internal parasites, coughs and fevers, and skin diseases, possibly even leprosy.

The greatest virtue of good traditional medicines is their known freedom from side effects, since they have been tested on so many generations. They are also usually cheap and locally available. Most important of all they are acceptable to the patients. However, outside their indigenous areas plant drugs need to be precisely identified, and the best and safest ways of using them worked out. If they are to have wider application, synthesis of the basic compounds may be desirable, partly because this often leads to improved action, but more importantly to prevent the over-collection of the plants concerned. Some are already endangered because of their local use – so much so that in Uttar Pradesh, for example, controls on collection of 13 plants important in Ayurvedic medicine have been imposed.

Scientific examination of the thousands of plants used traditionally seems to be more logical as a first step than random plant screening, which has also been carried out up to a point but is costly and time-consuming. The Russians are far ahead of the rest of Europe and USA in such studies, probably because they never developed widespread contempt for folk medicines. Apart from the USSR, where the extent of screening is not really known, only a few hundred herbal plants have been fully examined for drug potential.

One problem with scientific assay of an indigenous medicine is that it is not necessarily one active ingredient in one plant that makes it "work". The wound-healing properties of Spaghnum moss, for example, are still unclear, after millenia of use. A modern case is the Ghanaian *Cryptolepis sanguinolenta*, which reduces fever including malaria, cures urinary infections and is also a broad-spectrum antibiotic – yet none of the individual substances isolated from it are recognisably antibiotic. It may rather be the combination of several that is effective. This notion runs contrary to western medicine which prefers one problem, one curative principle. Another difficulty is that some local practitioners are, not surprisingly, very wary of western ways. They do not want their remedies snapped up by international pharmaceutical companies, patented and sold back to them in expensive pill form.

There can be no doubt that there are many more drugs to be found in plants and that research into traditional materials will influence western medicine. Furthermore, chemists will never be able to synthesise all the secret substances of the plant kingdom. Thus the future contribution of green medicine strongly depends on the extent to which medicinal plants are conserved, or locally grown, and on the protection of wild environments. Research is urgent, since indiscriminate collection, either for local use or pharmaceutical exploitation, together with wholesale destruction of habitats is seriously endangering not only the plants already in use but those which may be useful in the future. Perhaps most frightening is the lack of knowledge of which medicinal plants are actually in danger.

The tiled walls of this mosque at Isfahan are a spectacular example of the importance of floral decoration the world over.

CHAPTER EIGHT

Objects of Beauty

The story of the Garden of Eden expresses a universal characteristic of humanity – the love of natural beauty. From the Assyrian "Tree of Life" to the Greek Acanthus columns, from the Minoan frescoes of lilies to the lotus of the east, our architecture, arts, artefacts and poetry all reflect the deep impression which flowers and foliage make on the human consciousness. Such appreciation is a luxury, yet given freedom from want and a little leisure, we are all gardeners at heart.

The gardens of the world are a treasure house of botanical skill, the creation of generations of individuals with a gift for beauty, rarity, and understanding of plants. The story of each flower, from its wild origin, through selection and cultivation, is unique and remarkable – though punctuated with some disastrous examples of over-collection and damage to the wild. Today, gardening is a more universal occupation than ever. And the further we are separated from the natural world by our cities and civilisation, the more we fill our flats and window boxes with plants.

Many of these indoor gardens depend heavily on tropical resources. Our northern house plants, which must live in shady, warm conditions year round, are often natives of tropical rain forests, where conditions are similar. But while we recreate tropical habitats in our homes, many of the plants we love are becoming endangered in the wild. The African Violet is as familiar (to northerners) today as the tulip or daffodil. But in its native east Africa, the wild plant is now confined to a few isolated hill forests which are shrinking day by day. In the deserts, particularly of America, illegal collection and sale of cacti – so popular for sunny windowsills and desert gardens – has devastating effects on natural populations, which are slow to regenerate. The rarest orchid species are prized by collectors. And all around the world, wild flower populations are reduced by human impact and agriculture. Traditional garden varieties, too, are being lost, as gardening becomes big business and "new varieties" dominate the market.

When we look at buildings and artefacts of all kinds, it is clear that plants imprinted themselves on the minds of people all over the world early on. The example of temple column capitals is probably the one most often noted by the modern traveller. Papyrus decoration in Egypt, as at Karnak, is replaced with transformations of Acanthus and similar foliages in the various Greek orders which were later taken over by the Romans.

Plants became important to many early civilisations both as symbols and ornamentation. Stylised leaves became habitual on the capitals of temple and palace columns in Egyptian, Greek and Roman architecture, as in this acanthus-leaf capital at Roman Ephesus in western Turkey, above. The Minoans in Crete were great devotees of floral decoration as demonstrated by this unique vase or crater, below, from the period 1900-1700 BC. Instead of the habitual painting on clay the flowers are three-dimensional; perhaps the potter was imitating stone and metal work, as suggested by remnants of a chain hanging from the rim.

Some of the oldest plant decoration is Assyrian and Babylonian, where plant motifs are often highly stylised, showing foliage and trees – the latter often symbolising the Tree of Life. Occasionally these peoples made rosettes, the floral motif more widely used than any other down the ages. It was an integral part of roof decoration in Greece, as can be seen at the great theatre of Epidauros; and so on to the rose symbols of the Tudors and later. The rose can indeed be called the top decorative favourite throughout the world; lilies, pinks and carnations, daisies, violets, crocuses, narcissi, sunflowers, vines and of course leaves follow. In terms of symbolic importance the lotus is the most important: Egyptians, Assyrians, Persians, Indians and Chinese all depict it with reverence.

One of the best sequences of vegetative decoration can be traced right through ancient Greek archaeology starting around 2000 BC when Minoan pottery from Crete began to exhibit its extraordinarily robust decoration, depicting such things as palm trees, irises, papyrus, and often seaweed-inspired motifs. Later the Minoans painted frescoes which can be seen at Knossos in Crete and more recently from Santorini (Thera) (now displayed in the Athens Museum) including beautiful depictions of lilies, irises and Sea Daffodil (*Pancratium*). Some of their later vases carry appliqué flowers reminiscent of art nouveau. In mainland Greece floral decoration surfaces on pottery in the Archaic period (eighth to sixth centuries) and continues on those incredibly detailed vases up to the Romano-Hellenistic period. Foliage represented, apart from Acanthus, includes Oak, Olive, grapes, ivy, and there are also motifs based on the tiny seeds of annual weeds.

In many examples of ancient buildings it is almost impossible not to find plant motifs, whether one is in Italy, Greece, or Moorish countries. Persian flower decoration on tiles and ceramics is notable, while in India inlays of semi-precious stones in marble, as well as delicately carved reliefs, embellish the Taj Mahal (the most famous example). In the Chinese civilization, which matured so rapidly, accurate depictions of flowers appear on porcelain, and in external paintings which embellish almost every surface of places like Peking's Summer Palace, sometimes picking out work in carved relief. Weird objects of plant origin to be seen in some gardens are chairs and bizarre figures made of magnolia roots. In gardens also doors and wall apertures are often in the shape of flowers or fruits, and the persevering can see in the pebble mosaics of the Forbidden City's Imperial Garden all manner of flowers, fruits, and even flower arrangements.

European cathedrals and churches carry relief work of plant inspiration in stone outside and on woodwork within and, gradually, vegetation became used domestically on furniture, panelling and plasterwork right up to Edwardian times. Some strange plants can be found by the discerning: there is the pea-pod decoration in Renaissance work, and stylised catkins decorate many a mantlepiece by Robert Adam. A minor conundrum is posed by their close resemblance to those of male *Garrya elliptica*, but as the last of the brothers Adam died 12 years before the plant (found in 1827 by David Douglas in North America) flowered in Britain, they must just be stylised hazel.

Brief mention must be made of the recurring theme in Persian carpets of a river in the shape of a cross dividing a garden scene into four parts: this represents the cosmic cross whose first reference is in the second chapter of

Conventional flower painting of the Minoan civilisation recently excavated at Thera on Santorini quite recognisably depicts Sea Daffodils, bulbous, autumn-flowering plants abundant on Mediterranean beaches. This fresco, above, dates from about 1500 BC, shortly before the volcanic explosion which destroyed the colony.. Interest in plants as decoration and a subject for painting was even older in China. Many buildings are ornamented with plant motifs, like this painted wooden relief, below, on a Kunming temple – perhaps a tree peony (early favourite of Chinese gardeners) but possibly a waterlily or lotus.

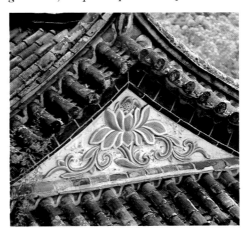

Genesis – "And a river went out of Eden to water the garden; and from thence it was parted, and became into four heads". This symbol can be seen in much garden design, including the Tudor.

The ancient cultures which perhaps took plant forms in everyday objects most to their hearts were those of Central America and Peru. Stone and ceramic objects, some purely decorative, many utilitarian jugs and drinking containers, represent especially the widely used gourds, squashes and melons. The stylised "pineapple pot" has been made for centuries. Stone cacti appear to have been ritualistic.

In even the earliest paintings plants are very frequently depicted, either as symbols – the Madonna lily being a Christian symbol of the Virgin and of purity, for example – as part of a design, or as portraits for botanical purposes or, eventually, for their own beauty's sake. Plant forms exist in every department of architectural design and interior decoration, household objects, and in carpets, embroidery and wallpaper.

Styles of Garden

Gardening traditions arose independently in eastern and western Asia, Egypt, Europe, South America and, probably, Polynesia. The first decorative gardens were certainly made in Egypt by 1500 BC; though the plants in them were utilitarian there were walls, regular beds and pools, and trees featured strongly. Not long after, the Egyptians were including plants grown for their beauty alone, such as the waterlily. A little further east the Assyrians and Babylonians made great tree parks; they were partly for hunting in but also to create, as Francis Bacon put it, "A refreshment to the spirits of man". They built artificial hills called ziggurats to raise greenery above the featureless "land between the rivers"; the Babylonian "hanging gardens" of Nebuchadnezzar II were specifically made for his Median wife who longed for the wooded hills of her home.

In the Far East the first Chinese pleasure gardens certainly existed by the fourth century BC. The Chinese were early devotees of the beauty of individual flowers, and there is a Chinese proverb which says "If you have two pennies left in the world, buy a loaf of bread with one and a lily with the other". Their gardens were very stylised – idealised landscapes where waterworn rocks symbolised those extraordinary pinnacular peaks which sometimes stud the natural landscape.

Japanese gardens, which date from about the third century AD, were far more abstract and with strong symbolic features. Both the Chinese and Japanese regarded (the latter still do) their gardens as a replacement for nature beyond, which was often too awe-inspiring to face and too vast to be disciplined. In India enclosures and water tanks – both for freshness and for potentates to disport themselves – were combined with trees, and quite early on flowers became important.

Climate controlled the design of European gardens when the Dark Ages gave way to the Renaissance. In summer-hot Italy, trees, both naturally "formal" ones like cypresses and sculptured topiary specimens, made avenues and focal points in highly architectural, usually terraced gardens with water and fountains. In France and Germany, where weather was less predictable, people would walk further in great formal parks, from one viewpoint to the next, marvelling at huge expanses of water and grass. In the Mediterranean the Olive, with its combination of shade and life-supporting crop, is widely planted and the Judas Tree with its brilliant pink spring display, and the Horse Chestnut, were early encouraged for shade and flowers.

How Plants got around

As early as 1100 BC we find the King Tiglath-Pileser I writing, "Cedars and Box I have carried off from the countries I conquered, trees that none of the kings my forefathers possessed: these trees I have taken and planted in my own country, in the Parks of Assyria". Even earlier Queen Hatsepshut of Egypt had collected incense trees from Somalia to decorate her temple at Deir-el-Bahri. But such collecting on an international scale was for a long time quite exceptional. Ornamental gardening started in principle with wild plants from the country concerned, and, in the case of Egypt, gardens would commonly contain Date Palms and Sycomore Fig trees, Papyrus and the blue Nile Waterlily.

The earliest plants we now consider ornamentals were, with few exceptions, originally medicinal. This applies to the Daylily (*Hemerocallis*), much prized for its herbal qualities in China, the Prince's Feather (*Celosia*) and the Syrian Mallow (*Hibiscus syriacus*). Like the purgative rhubarbs from China, these travelled as articles of commerce on trade routes like the overland Silk

In dusty Egypt, above left, tall walls and plenty of shade-giving trees, with small, formal water pools, were the rule in 1400 BC. The same applied to many hot countries to the east in later centuries: Islamic gardens were walled for the sake of the women, architecturally constructed with colonnades, formal pools and fountains, and planted largely with trees for shade and some bright areas of colour. Perhaps the finest example of a Moorish garden is at Granada in Spain.

In Kashmir several well-preserved Mughal gardens like Nishat Bagh, above, display their huge shade-producing oriental planes or chenars, regular flower beds filled mostly with annuals, formal pools, canals, and the sloped chiselled chadars or waterslides between different levels. An inscription at Shalamar garden reads "If there be a Paradise on the face of the earth, it is here, it is here, it is here!"

The basis of a Japanese garden – this is the West Garden of the Heian Shrine, Kyoto – was always an island in a lake, with a bridge for access; there might be artificial mountains. Later, planting was usually reduced to a few specially shaped trees among rocks, water or sometimes raked sand in "dry landscape", stepping stones and various architectural features.

In Britain, after stylisation in the Italian manner of Tudor times, the garden became a place for perambulation. Shade was not essential so trees became decorative features or fringes to lawns of grass which the climate encouraged to stay green all year. Fine trees were available but the floral beauty to which we are accustomed today had to await the importation of exotics. Among these the bedding plants, annually renewed, give scope for perhaps the least natural form of gardening, like those which brighten the formally hedged, entirely symmetrical Sunken Garden at Hampton Court.

Gerard, in his Herbal of 1597, was able to refer to 678 groups of plants, many of which comprised many species and varieties. The transition from the practical to the ornamental, however, was rapid: in 1629 John Parkinson was subtitling his equivalent book "A Garden of all sorts of Pleasant Flowers" – its title page is shown above – and his emphasis throughout is on their beauty and garden use.

Route or the ships of Arabian traders between China and Islam. The Syrian Mallow had been established so long in western Asia that Linnaeus thought it a Syrian native, hence its name. From western Asia trade later continued westwards into Europe and brought such plants with it. One early introduction, the double annual balsam, seems not to have any medicinal properties; Chinese ladies used its petals to dye their fingernails. Some plants were traded in the reverse direction: for instance many narcissus species, mostly Mediterranean plants, came into Turkey, and the bunch-flowered *Narcissus tazetta* reached China over a thousand years ago.

Such early arrivals of new plants stimulated the intense botanical curiosity which was a feature of the Renaissance. One of the great stimulants must have been the discovery and conquest of Central and South America by the Spaniards and Portuguese, which led to the importation to the Old World of many esculents, and decorative plants like those now called French and African marigolds (tagetes), dahlias, passion flowers, the Jacobean Lily (Sprekelia), the Tuberose and succulents like Agave and Prickly Pear which are now naturalised features of Mediterranean countries.

All early movement of ornamental plants was between institutions such as the earliest botanical gardens (first Pisa founded around 1543, and Padua in 1545) or between enthusiastic amateurs. It became habitual for government scientific expeditions to carry a botanist – as did Captain Cook (his first and greatest being Sir Joseph Banks) – and to ask sea captains to bring plant treasures back from the countries they visited. Thus around the turn of the eighteenth/nineteenth centuries many camellias and the equally prized Indian azaleas were brought to England by East Indiamen, some on their own account, some for plantsmen like Sir Abram and Lady Hume – one camellia became known as Lady Hume's Blush, while another, a very beautiful form of *Camellia reticulata*, commemorates the captain responsible, Captain Rawes; it is still in commerce.

Nurserymen began to sell ornamentals to paying customers in the seventeenth century, when trade became established between European and Turkish nurserymen mainly in the fleshy-rooted plants like anemones, ranunculus, hyacinths and tulips which the Turks had so remarkably developed from wild species by selection. Horticulture did not become big business, however, until canals in the late eighteenth and railways in the nineteenth centuries eased transport problems. Then, when nurseries arose near all the larger towns, nurserymen began to send people abroad to collect new plants. This was first entirely a European business, with the British, Dutch, Belgians, and French most prominent, although paid collectors also set forth from the USA; and there were a number of freelance collectors.

Most of the collectors were gardeners, not trained botanists, and few had ever been abroad before. It is remarkable how efficiently most of them survived in lands where they could not speak the language and where unimaginable hazards abound, quite apart from privations, and privateers, while on long ship-board journeys. They became devoted to their calling and it was unusual for them to retire while they could still work. Many died on the job, typically of dysentery and tropical fevers or, in the case of David Douglas, by falling into a pit-trap containing a wild bull.

Many house plants are named after people – especially plant collectors and botanists: the great Joseph Banks (1743-1820) is commemorated in the genus *Banksia*; David Douglas in *Douglasia*, a small north American alpine, and the Douglas Fir. This tree's scientific name, *Pseudotsuga douglasii*, was, however, changed to *P. menziesii*, after an earlier botanist.

By the start of the nineteenth century the desire for ornamentals had spread to the middle classes. The first collectors went to North America, for hardy plants were at first most in demand; but the rage for bedding plants resulted from exploration in the tropics, notably South America. This coincided with the vast improvements in glasshouse design, heating methods and the quality of the glass itself. Every British household of any pretensions had one or more greenhouses and a conservatory.

The London (later Royal) Horticultural Society, founded in 1804, also sent out collectors, of whose findings subscribing members got a share. Notable expeditions were those of David Douglas to western North America in 1825 and of Robert Fortune to China in 1842, but plant collecting remained almost entirely in the hands of nurserymen (the only notable exception being Joseph Hooker's important expedition to Sikkim in 1847, which was mainly self-financed). The scale of business may be judged from the payment by Joseph Knight, who ran the Exotic Nurseries in Chelsea, London, of the then enormous sum of £1500 to William Baxter for seeds he had sent during one year from Australia. Without the commercial propagation carried out by the nurseries the work of the collectors would not, of course, have been widely distributed. Apart from disease and physical hazards, there were often political difficulties for the collector to overcome. While Spain and Portugal owned South America it was almost impossible for plant collectors to obtain permission to enter the continent. Apart from a few Jesuit advisers in the eighteenth century, China was inaccessible to Europeans until 1840, while Japan was closed until 1860. A few plants had been obtained from all these countries by interested parties attached to trading missions, but no systematic collecting was possible.

The number of plant introductions gathered great momentum over the centuries. Taking Britain as the example – undoubtedly the country with the greatest long-term interest in plant acquisitions – the number of plants known to be introduced were 84 in the sixteenth century, 940 in the seventeenth, and 8938 in the eighteenth. Hazards diminished, travelling became more reliable, trading in Spanish domains was permitted, and British colonial and political power increased, so that between 1731 and 1763 the tally of introductions doubled; and when Victoria was made Queen in 1831, over 13,000 exotic species were known in cultivation.

The domination of the nurseries in plant collecting diminished in this century with the reappearance of the eighteenth century-style syndicate, the number of subscribers increasing greatly to include growers, nurserymen and botanical institutions. The figure who most clearly demonstrated this was E. H. Wilson, who first opened the rich flora of western China to European and North American gardeners. His first two expeditions were financed by the great Veitch nursery in England, but two later ones, as well as later trips to Japan and Taiwan, were backed mainly by Professor Sargent at the Arnold Arboretum, USA. His successors such as George Forrest and Frank Kingdon-Ward were entirely financed by subscribers who, of course, receive their dividends in the form of plants and seeds successfully brought home, and this practice continues to this day.

The houseplant Sparmannia, the House Lime, was named, with mispelling, after a Swedish botanist, Anders Sparrman (1748-1820) who sailed with Captain Cook on his second voyage. Though an energetic collector, his only remarkable adventure seems to have been his return to his ship stark naked after being surprised by hostile natives while swimming from a Pacific island beach.

The common Corn Poppy (Papaver rhoeas), above, varies slightly in the wild. About 1880 a Surrey vicar found one with a white petal edge; by sowing its seed and selecting unusually coloured seedlings he finally achieved the multi-hued strain – called Shirley Poppies, below, after the Reverend Wilks's home – which are easily grown annuals; modern strains can be either single- or double-flowered.

Plants for Pure Pleasure

As the distinction between useful and decorative plants became blurred, plants were increasingly grown purely for their attractiveness and also oddity: succulents, for instance, were early favoured (and also easily maintained). Increased leisure and the ability to buy herbal remedies rather than having to grow them oneself were important reasons. As interest became focussed on plants for their own sake, increased attention was given to mutations or "sports" which transformed well known flowers (in the same way they transformed crops like cereals). The most pronounced mutation is the "doubling" of flowers, when an abnormal number of petals is produced or, as in the Daisy family, showy ray florets take the place of flat central disk florets. This genetic accident can be seen in the wild from time to time. In Mexico I recall noting how local populations of tagetes here and there had a high proportion of doubles that would not have disgraced the seed catalogues among modern French marigolds. Such mutations can be brought into cultivation and increased by seed or other means.

Parkinson depicts a range of double tagetes which show what we now call French and the bigger African types, names which they acquired during their early peregrinations when people did not know their origin. In this Daisy family other annuals prized more in double than single forms are the Scotch marigolds or calendulas, asters and zinnias, while the perennial chrysanthemum from China and the double dahlias from Mexico are far preferred in general to their single forms. Single pinks are favoured but one cannot imagine their near relative the carnation as other than double; nor has the single stock much appeal. The multipetalled rose is esteemed more widely than the single (even if there are some gardeners who prefer the single's natural grace to the cabbage-like propensity of the double). In the medieval garden the medicinal single peony must have looked attractive, but today's double garden forms (many acquired from China) are objects of surpassing beauty.

There are plenty of exceptions to this statement of course. The double Tiger Lily is a monstrous object and virtually no other double lilies exist. Perversely, the double forms of datura, trumpet-shaped like many lilies, are considered very beautiful. Some flowers seem to have a real propensity for "unnatural" forms. The chrysanthemum and dahlia now have so many that modern competitions are divided into scores of classes to accommodate them. Another example is the camellia, originally a single flower with a prominent central ring of stamens, which has among its huge array of cultivars (largely the products of gardening in antique China) semi-double and fully double forms, the latter either informal in petal arrangement or so geometrical they might have been drawn with a compass; others known as anemone-centred have a central cushion of smallish "petaloids" within ordinary petals.

Sometimes a flower becomes utterly transformed by a mutation. The old-fashioned Lupin, only introduced from British Columbia in 1826 (by Douglas) had a lax spike of down-pointing flowers. A jobbing gardener, George Russell, began to specialise in the Lupin. Among his seedlings he pinpointed a mutation which made the flowers horizontal and hence the spike compact. This he followed by breeding with existing colour forms and incorporating the yellow Tree Lupin in the parentage; but the lucky break was that mutation.

Mutations altering colour are quite frequent. The commonest by far is to a white or albino form, but others arise which, carefully selected, can produce a whole rainbow of colours in a species. The modern race of Shirley poppies with its wide colour range was raised, from about 1880, by the Rev W. Wilks of Shirley, Surrey, who selected and reselected seedlings which arose from a single wild Red Poppy with a white petal edge.

Some of the earliest selections were made, incidentally, by artisan gardeners in the eighteenth and nineteenth centuries. These fanciers, or "florists", established certain stringent rules for their plants, and any seedlings which did not conform were ruthlessly disregarded. One early favourite was the pink, which was the hobby of the weavers of Paisley; other florists' flowers were auriculas, polyanthus, tulips, hyacinths and ranunculus – the last a wonderful flower now only available in limited mixtures, of which over a thousand named sorts were once recorded.

Such florist flowers, perennial plants like the herbaceous peony and shrubby ones like the tree peony or moutan are propagated vegetatively – by division, bulb offsets or by grafting in the case of the moutan. (The latter was, incidentally, one of the earliest speciality plants – in China, around AD 700, a hundred ounces of gold might be paid for a new variety.) In such ways established cultivars would be maintained. Accidents of nature like albinos are propagated likewise. A classic example of such a unique freak is the contorted hazel known as Harry Lauder's Walking-stick (*Corylus avellana* 'Contorta'), spotted in a Gloucester hedgerow in 1863.

Single roses like the variable Eurasian Dog Rose (Rosa canina), above, are undoubtedly distant ancestors of the most popular type of modern rose, the hybrid tea – fully double and perfectly formed according to modern standards – like Chicago Peace, below. However, double roses of various forms arose early in the history of gardening by mutation and spontaneous cross-breeding, from Europe to China.

Chrysanthemums have a very long history. The Chinese grew C. indicum with small yellow flowers about 500 BC and, about a thousand years ago, the white or purple-flowered C. morifolium. Accidental breeding between these two produced the ancestors of our many modern kinds, which include fully double forms much grown by exhibitors and curiosities such as the "spoon-petalled" varieties old and new shown here.

The immensely popular, vigorous and easy-going Clematis jackmanii, below, was created by the deliberate crossing of large-flowered C. lanuginosa from China and small-flowered Eurasian C. viticella, above, by the nurseryman G. Jackman in 1860. Further crosses using the hybrid as one parent, and also mutations from it, have given rise since then to a quantity of large-flowered garden varieties.

An even more peculiar accident (if not a specially beautiful one) is the small tree *Laburnocytisus adami*. This arose in a French nursery in 1826 when the ornamental broom *Cytisus purpureus* was being grafted onto Common Laburnum rootstock to give it more vigour. The *Cytisus* scion was accidentally knocked off except for a tiny piece. This resulted in what is called a chimaera, the Broom tissue being entirely surrounded by Laburnum tissue. The resulting tree randomly produces lilac-purple Broom flowers, yellow Laburnum flowers, or intermediate purplish-pink ones.

Deliberate breeding of garden plants was the next step after selection of seedlings. The first deliberate crossing of two different plants was in 1717, when Thomas Fairchild applied Carnation pollen to the stigma of a Sweet William (both are Dianthus). The result, like a large double Sweet William, was sterile so no more came of it. Amateurs later began to breed garden flowers for "endless interest and amusement" (to quote William Herbert, later Dean of Manchester) early in the nineteenth century. William Herbert specialised in gladioli, heaths and bulbs of the Amaryllis family; contemporaries devoted themselves to delphiniums, petunias, lobelias and verbenas. The ever-popular *Clematis jackmanii* was produced from deliberate crosses in Jackman's nursery in 1862, and the first hybrid lily, *Lilium parkmanii*, was bred in 1879.

Some notable garden plants we owe to the bees, which for instance in 1826, at the chateau of M. Soulange-Bodin near Paris, transferred pollen from *Magnolia liliflora* to *M. denudata* nearby and so gave rise to *M. soulangiana*, the most popular magnolia of all.

Early in the century too the first rhododendron hybridisers set to work (the earliest recorded cross had been made in 1796). Enormous enthusiasm for these large-flowered shrubs or trees had arisen with the introduction of various species; the sendings of early expeditions such as Joseph Hooker's resulted in huge quantities of seeds which germinated like mustard and cress and were planted out in prodigal numbers, arguably ruining a number of British gardens in the process. Early this century, with an enormous influx of Chinese species from Wilson, Forrest and Kingdon-Ward, promiscuous hybridisation became a fashion especially among enthusiastic amateurs, and today there are many thousands of hybrids recorded.

The rhododendron species still exist alongside these, and one can find the parents of the innumerable fuchsia cultivars, but one will seek in vain for the parents of such popular plants as pelargoniums ("geraniums"), petunias, tuberous begonias and hippeastrums (amaryllis).

At first haphazard – as in crop plants – breeding became more precise when the rules of inheritance became appreciated early this century. A true blue rose has never appeared (though there are rumours that some purist breeder suppressed one, considering it quite "wrong" for a rose), but there are now red delphiniums (which a lot of people do not think quite proper either). In aiming for certain characters, like bigger sweet peas with more flowers on a stem, or yet further colour and shape variation in roses, there are often complaints that these habitually fragrant flowers are deprived of scent; but there always remain plenty of cultivars with plenty of perfume. This does show, however, that even with scientific knowledge breeding can be a lottery, especially with flowers of such ancient and mixed parentage as the rose.

In very general terms one can say that hybridisation promotes greater vigour, more variation in flower shape and colour, more floriferousness; with annuals or bedding plants it can ensure regular height. Often the wild parents are more graceful and elegant, but as in all things this is a matter of taste. At the present time, for instance, there is a definite swing away from the biggest dahlias in the world to smaller, daintier blooms, and an urge in several specialist areas to keep to species rather than hybrids.

One curious result of present-day universal travel is the possibility of breeding together plants which could never meet naturally. Among orchids, where this has been practiced to the most extraordinary degree, there are now many trigeneric and a few quadrigeneric hybrids.

Cultivation in gardens and greenhouses allows hybridisation of plants which never meet in nature. Among orchids up to four parent genera have been involved. The Potinara variety, above, is the result of crossing Brassavola digbyana, below, with an existing trigeneric hybrid called Sophrolaeliocattleya, earlier derived from species of Sophronitis, below right, Laelia and Cattleya.

The Tulip

Most important garden flowers, like the Tulip, have a complex history due to their ancestry, human predilictions for their varying natural forms, and their resulting selection and breeding. Wild tulips grow in Europe, becoming more numerous to the south and east of the eastern Mediterranean and Turkey to Turkestan, with a handful in northwestern China.

Though recognised as beautiful in the twelfth century, when Omar Khayyam referred to it, it was not till the sixteenth century that the Tulip began to feature in Persian art. At that time Turkish rulers collected wild bulbs to decorate their gardens. There is a record of an order for 50,000 bulbs in 1574, and no less than half a million bulbs in 1579. This is one of the first examples of ruthless collecting from the wild and it is easy to see how ravages on this scale could render any common species extinct.

The original introductions to Europe came from Augerius de Busbecq, Emperor Ferdinand I's Ambassador to the Turkish potentate, Suleiman the

Magnificent (one of the first to plant wild tulips in his gardens). De Busbecq sent seeds and bulbs to various people, among them being the Fuggers, the bankers of Augsburg; it was their plants of which the famous botanist Gesner published descriptions and illustrations in 1561. In his honour these first tulips were given the name *Tulipa gesneriana*, though this is now recognised only as the name of a group.

Seeds also reached the botanist and horticulturalist L'Ecluse (sometimes known as Clusius); he raised them successfully but asked so much for his bulbs that the best of them were stolen by a group of fanciers and seem to have become the basis for the Dutch tulip industry, soon to give rise to that welter of senseless speculation known today as tulipomania (1634-37). One of the most extraordinary transactions in this mania recorded is the payment, for one single tulip bulb, of – four oxen, eight pigs, twelve sheep, two loads of wheat, four loads of rye, two barrels of butter, a thousand pounds of cheese, two hogsheads of wine, four barrels of beer, a silver beaker, a suit of clothes, and a bed!

Though we cannot trace a precise botanical type of the ancestral garden tulip there is a possible clue. Some of the bulbs imported into Europe, now known as Neo-Tulipae, became naturalised, particularly around Florence, as did others at Aime, on the Little St Bernard Pass in Savoy. Perhaps a cartload of bulbs was accidentally jettisoned here, and some of their seedlings reverted to the appearance of the original species. At any rate, at Aime was found the plant now called *T. marjoletti*, which opens cream and then turns white, the edges of the pointed flower segments becoming edged with rose – the only white-flowered Neo-Tulipa known. It has the pointed segments that the Turkish cognoscenti admired.

Gerard said in 1597 that one might as well try to number grains of sand as to enumerate all the varieties of garden tulip so one surmises that they were already fairly complex hybrids when they reached Europe. They were then further intermixed. Breeders searched for the black tulip, immortalised by Dumas: but as time went on interest became centred on tulips with coloured veinings, the plain ones being known as "breeders". The others had to become "broken" – with feathery markings – to be of any value. We now know that the "breaking" is due to a virus infection; this seems to have done the plants little harm and some early varieties such as 'Keizerskroon', dating from 1680, and 'Zomerschoon' are still in cultivation.

For long the Tulip was a fancier's flower, and there were strict rules as to the form and patterning that were acceptable. But, as bedding out became more popular in the nineteenth century, there arose a demand for a bedding tulip. The Breeders were self-coloured, but no attention had been paid to uniformity of height or of flowering times. These now became desirable qualities and by 1899 tulip breeders were able to introduce the tall, sturdy race of Darwin Tulips which were of level height and flowered simultaneously. These Darwins were in turn crossed with the dwarf Early Tulips, both single and double, which seem to have persisted unchanged since the seventeenth century, to give the mid-season race known as Mendels. Pointed petals, admired of the Turks but ousted by the seventeenth century fashion for rounded ones, reappeared in lily-flowered varieties, while Parrot arose with deep-slashed, garishly mottled petals. Modern Parrots have strong stems but are less fantastic than the originals.

Tulipa pulchella

T. kaufmanniana

T. praestans

During this century something of a tulip revolution occurred with the introduction of previously unfamiliar species from Turkestan. Tulipa kaufmanniana, the Waterlily Tulip, below left, with cream flowers with a red edge, flowers early in the season, and there are now many more seedlings of it and hybrids with other species. One of these is T. greigii, with which it crosses naturally in the wild. This tulip is noted for its purple-striped leaves, and has a large red flower. Its garden hybrids preserve the striped leaves, but the flowers vary from red to yellow, often strikingly marked within, and opening wide in sunlight.

T. fosterana has enormous scarlet blooms, usually opening in April: the most famous variety is 'Red Emperor'. It has been crossed with other tulips, giving rise to yellow, orange and white varieties similar in form to the original species. Between them these three Asiatic tulips provide a host of low-growing, early-flowering and mostly very long-lived varieties before the main range of garden tulips appear.

There are quantities of dwarf species which the gardener can grow, mostly suited to rock gardens, from the European fragrant yellow T. sylvestris to the bunch-flowered T. turkestanica, which may open its flowers in February alongside the violet T. pulchella, top. Others are the scarlet T. linifolia and T. hageri and yellow T. batalinii, while the season ends with the later-flowering T. sprengeri with dull red flowers. Many other wild species are grown by specialists. Most need a summer "baking" without water.

T. praestans, below right, is remarkable for bearing up to four bright scarlet flowers on the one stem, though curiously enough it is not the parent of the modern "multiflora" races which are selections from old Cottage tulips with larger blooms.

Paphiopedilum rothschildianum is one of the striking slipper orchids with very wide-spreading petals. Introduced in the 1880s, it lingered only a few years in the wild because of over-collection and was feared extinct. About 30 years ago it was rediscovered in South-east Asia, but continues to be in great danger from local orchid poachers. However, large numbers could easily be produced by either meristem culture or painstaking pollination and growing on of seedlings, as was demonstrated in 1983 at a Royal Horticultural Society's show when five plants were shown which had been grown from such "selfed" seed. P. rothschildianum may now be saved, in contrast to the similar P. druryi and P. sukhakulii which, stripped from the wild quite recently, are either extinct or nearly so.

Disappearing Beauties

Like early medicinal plants which were wrested out of the ground for local use for trade, ornamentals were treated in the same way. In places with a long tradition of ornamental gardening they were, however, propagated domestically in nurseries: the Chinese Chrysanthemums, Camellias and Tree Peonies are prime examples, where the interesting variants that appeared from seed were increased vegetatively and distributed.

Many of the new species sent back by British and European collectors much later on were in the form of seeds; there was no other way of doing it in many cases. However, things like cacti and other succulents, and bulbs, which could survive out of soil for fairly long periods, were brought back as plants or roots. It was all a matter of convenience, and no-one thought twice about taking live plants out of the ground if that was easy.

Right into the nineteenth century this attitude did not change. Sir Joseph Hooker, travelling in India, remarks that *Vanda caerulea* is "The rarest and most beautiful of Indian orchids". Yet in a footnote he mentions that he collected "seven men's loads" of this plant (few of which reached England alive); he goes on to suggest that collectors with better facilities for getting the plants home "might easily clear from £2,000 to £3,000 in one season, by the sale of Khasia orchids" – and this is just what happened. Collectors swarmed into the forests where the orchids lived, as pinpointed by Hooker, and collected them by the ton, often cutting down the trees upon which they grew as the easiest way of doing so. Few orchids now remain in the Himalayan foothills.

Orchids are among the plants to which most attention has recently been given to prevent such occurrences; as we have noted earlier, they are big business, and a rare orchid is worth a lot of money. Equally big is the business in cacti from the southern United States and Mexico especially, though *Rhipsalis*, succulent euphorbias and aloes from Africa are also endangered. The American deserts are being despoiled of their cacti in the most alarming way by commercial "haulers" who remove every kind of cactus by digging and often pulling out with a chain attached to the back of their truck (which does the plants little good), seeking "ordinary" species for garden use as well as rare specialities. The giant saguaro fetches $20 a foot – much more if it has a rare crested top.

It has been reported that 50,000 rainbow cacti (*Echinocereus* species) are dug out in Texas every *month*. The demand in the US is staggering: in one recent year nearly seven million cacti and succulents were *imported* (this includes a million from Mexico plus plants propagated in nurseries). A lot of the collected cacti are exported to fanciers abroad.

Apart from the local haulers, foreign collectors are equally to blame. A Japanese expedition to Cedros Island, off Baja California, left not one of the native succulents in situ. "Cactus study tours" originating in Europe, have been a cover for collection; a party of German tourists was recently stripped of 3,600 specimens after returning from Mexico.

A few of the other ornamentals which are important in money terms are cycads (primitive, palm-like plants which grow extremely slowly), tree ferns and insectivorous plants. Apart from both American and Malayan pitcher plants (Sarracenias and Nepenthes) the plant most at risk is the incredible Venus's Flytrap: after heavy over-collection in the past it is now recovering well where protected, though drainage of its native marshes still represents a threat.

Large tracts of Portugal and northern Spain are devoid of wild narcissi, so great were the demands for bulbs on their wild populations early in this century. *Narcissus moschatus* and *N. cyclamineus* are very difficult to find, and *N. triandrus* var. *loiseleurii*, local to the island of Glenan, only survives in cultivation. *Lilium pomponium* and *L. chalcedonicum* have nearly vanished.

International trade in many rare plants is controlled by the Convention on International Trade in Endangered Species (CITES), now implemented in over 80 countries. Originally designed to control trade in endangered wildlife products like rhino horn and the skins of jaguars and ocelots, it also covers about 50,000 different plants, mostly on its Appendix II which monitors rather than prohibits trade. This Appendix includes all cacti, orchids, succulent aloes, cycads and cyclamens, among other plants.

CITES has, however, proved difficult to enforce for plants. The trade in wild-collected specimens is highly damaging but it is still small in comparison with the legitimate – and laudable – trade in propagated plants. So it is easy to conceal rare wild-collected plants and evade the laws. Perhaps a more realistic means of approach is to persuade hobbyists and collectors only to buy plants they know have been propagated artificially. Succulent plants societies in the UK have worked hard to outlaw advertising of wild plants for sale in their journals and to persuade their members to follow a code of conduct. After all it is far more rewarding to grow your own plants from seed and win prizes with them than buy in mature specimens, even though some of them such as cacti, cycads and tree ferns, for instance, are notoriously slow growers.

House plants are a good example of a group highly important to commerce where stripping from the wild has not taken precedence over propagation. True, most are easily increased; but one might argue that it takes almost as long to grow a showy bromeliad from seed or offsets as an orchid from very similar treetop habitats.

Fortunately there is a brighter side to these problems. Nature is not always as efficient as she might be. The Monterey Pine, the Flamboyant or Flame-tree, the Philippine Jade Vine and the Horse Chestnut are near extinction in the wild through little fault of mankind's. The Flamboyant, indeed, is only known from a very limited area in Madagascar. The Maidenhair Tree (Ginkgo), *Primula sinensis* and *Malus spectabilis* are unknown as wild plants and only survive in cultivation; the Ginkgo, preserved around Chinese temples, is now grown as a street tree all over North America. The Dawn Redwood was only known from fossils when discovered in 1941 by a Chinese botanist; what is more, the few trees he found were being cut down for timber (more have in fact been found since). Seeds collected were freely distributed and grew readily into fast-growing trees.

The unique succulent Jade Plant or Burro's Tail was spotted in a Mexican market: it has never been found in the wild. The popular house plant *Pilea cadierei*, known as Friendship Plant, was found just once in an Indo-Chinese jungle and never since. Easily propagated, both are now widespread. In the future, establishment in cultivation may well be as important as a few heavily protected plants in the wild.

Narcissus moschatus is distinctive with its creamy white flowers, though now regarded as one of the many natural variants of the Lent Lily (N. pseudonarcissus). Native to the Spanish Pyrenees, its existence in the wild is now open to doubt; like most of the species of daffodils in Spain and Portugal it was heavily overcollected early this century. Bulb merchants paid local inhabitants for narcissus bulbs by the sackful, and the plants were eradicated over large tracts of country.

145

Modern Times

Distinct groups of plants, like bulbs or shrubs, and individual plant genera dominate much modern gardening. In Britain, and much of Europe, the most popular plant is probably the rose. This shrub, with species from most of the temperate world, was a Roman favourite. By that time the rose was already multi-petalled and its long lineage continued unabated, with many species entering in, until the introduction around 1789 of Chinese garden varieties that flowered summer-long – "perpetual" in nurseryman's parlance. These derivatives of *Rosa chinensis* (a species not, incidentally, discovered by Europeans in the wild until 1885) made all the difference to the garden value of roses today. Rhododendrons and azaleas, often accompanied by camellias, are predominant on both sides of the Atlantic. Hobby flowers once thought of only for the rich, but now very much more universal, are the orchids, grown in most countries under glass or in the open according to climate. More than any other plants orchids are big business in money terms.

These and many, many others, have become the subjects of specialised societies – the list is endless. It would seem that whatever one's interest, there is a society to promote it. In Britain the National Council for Conservation of Plants and Gardens has developed the scheme of National Collections of well over a hundred garden genera which have numerous cultivars, so that these will be preserved for posterity. Public, private, national and botanic gardens are all involved.

There are societies too for bonsai, that ancient art of dwarfing trees, and for decorating with cut flowers, both stemming from oriental ritual traditions. Virtually every specialist plant society results in competition at shows and equally in speciality gardens; some people concentrate entirely on say roses, or alpines, or on bedding plants for a summer spectacle. Some connoisseurs search for forgotten cultivars from older days.

Climate is of course a controlling factor. In Britain and northern USA there can be marvellous rock gardens and woodland plantings of hardy trees and shrubs, but in California and South Africa the displays are more likely to be of succulents. The Mediterranean-climate garden always seems to contain bougainvillea, hibiscus, mimosa and climbing pelargoniums, and all round the tropics, public gardens especially display what is fast becoming a rather standardised range of colourful exotics – hibiscus and bougainvillea again, with cassia and flamboyant, allamanda and solandra, fragrant frangipani, lantana and datura; some of striking form like primeval cycad, palms, and the fan-shaped traveller's tree; others with coloured foliage like croton, Joseph's coat and dracaenas.

Those who cannot grow exotics outside cultivate house plants, and these – largely tropical foliage plants – have become a huge trade in Europe and the United States. The house plant fashion reflects the deep-felt internal desire people have to tend something green and living, to get their fingers into soil (even if it is usually a proprietary man-made "mix"), when they have perforce to live without a garden in apartments and flats in cities.

There are few parts of the world, even in poor regions, where you cannot find plants grown ornamentally in some way. Ruskin aptly wrote "flowers seem intended for the solace of ordinary humanity."

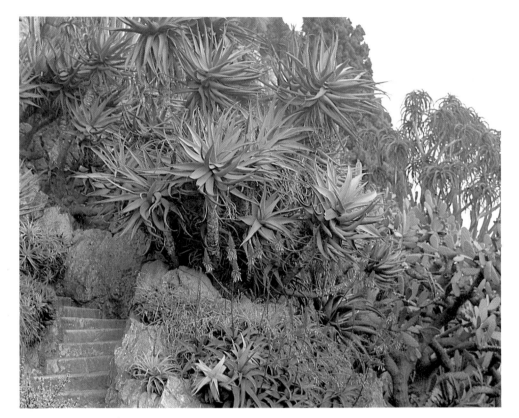

A fine example of a modern speciality garden, Monaco's Jardin Exotique, left, is devoted to cacti and other succulents culled from the drier regions of the world. In some places, like California, climate suggests the cultivation of such plants which are at least much less water-demanding then more orthodox garden plants.

One of the important gardening developments of temperate countries since the late nineteenth century has been that of woodland gardens where exotic plants are sheltered by native trees, or at least the naturalised introductions of earlier generations. Leonardslee in Sussex, England, below, set on steep hillsides around old hammerponds, also exemplifies the specialisation of many present-day gardens, being almost entirely planted with rhododendrons, azaleas and camellias.

The Marsh Arabs of Iraq live in a land of huge rushes which they use for building their remarkable villages and sturdy, often beautiful, houses.

CHAPTER NINE

Plants and Society

It often comes as a surprise to sophisticated citizens of developed countries to realise how much they depend on plants. But is is probably even more astonishing to discover that in many parts of the world whole cultures rely on plants, and their own skills with them, to meet every smallest need. Altogether, millions of people live this way, from the marsh Arabs of Iraq to the Amazonian Indians, from the Bushmen of the Kalahari and the Australian Aborigines to tribal peoples of New Guinea and Indonesia.

Enormous contrasts are explored in this chapter: on the one hand, "primitive" societies based on total involvement with natural vegetation, total awareness of its significance, intimate knowledge of its many uses; on the other, societies which have largely dispensed with natural plant cover and, for better or worse, transformed the land for human domination. Very different from either are cultures where a single kind of plant, with multiple benefits, assumes a unique symbolic and practical value.

These cultural differences shape people's daily lives; more importantly, they shape attitudes and knowledge. The suburbanite tackling a breakfast of cornflakes, sugar, toast, marmalade and coffee is hardly, if at all, aware of eating plants (and tropical forest plants at that); but indigenous people are in direct daily contact with their green life-support systems and thus possess the most enormous store of knowledge about them – knowledge of which we shall be in ever-increasing need in the future. A recent survey of plants used by South American Indians, for example, turned up over 1000 with potential economic value, as yet wholly unused by the West.

The Surinamese say, "In the jungle the Indian knows everything". The Indians of the tropics are indeed intimate with their surroundings, able to live in harmony with their environment, and enviably managing their rich but fragile forests on a sustained yield basis. Until a hundred years ago, the Indians of North America, too, lived this way. Comparing their culture (using British Columbia as an example) with that of present-day Amazonian peoples reveals, in both, an amazingly sophisticated technology. Each shows an intensive knowledge of every plant, its seasons, uses, and preparation. Each shows, too, a respect for the lives, the "souls" even, of the plants. "Look at me friend", prays a woman to the cedar she is about to cut down, "I come to ask you for your dress – for you have come to take pity on us; for there is nothing for which you cannot be used . . ."

Indians of British Columbia

For many centuries before the arrival of European settlers, the Indians of the North American continent trod lightly across the land, leaving it little altered. These resourceful people were able to find a solution for nearly every problem and, ingeniously, a use for almost any material, from their green surroundings. Sometimes one plant, like the Western Red Cedar, served many purposes; sometimes many plants could meet one need – Sagebrush, Pinegrass or Timbergrass, for instance, all provided footwear.

Among its myriad applications, Red Cedar supplied housing – boards and planks for walls, bark for the roof. Cat-tail yielded mats of braided leaves for insulation or for bedding, and offered its fluffy seeds to stuff mattresses and pillows. Spruce, Fir, Sword Fern, Black Cottonwood, Fireweed – all contributed branches, fronds or seeds for warmth and comfort. In the hot summers of the interior, teepees framed of light branches and bark strips were preferred, or huts thatched with Tule Sedge.

The fire-lighting skills of the Indians are celebrated in folklore. These tribes used many fuelwoods, highly prizing the bark of Douglas Fir, and other resinous conifers; for friction drills, they chose Lodgepole or Ponderosa Pines, and Pacific Willow; fungi, Cedar bark and Sagebrush served as fire carriers between camps, rotten willow roots as firelighters.

For weaving of clothing and mats, the versatile Red Cedar once more provided, yielding some of the best fibres. Leaves and stems of grasses and grass-like plants were woven too, on simple looms, or pounded into strands and then twined together. Sagebrush was used for moccasin insoles and Tule, stitched with hardwood needles, for soft fabrics.

A Shalisham speciality was coiled basketry, in which spirals of fibrous materials were sewn together. These, and the woven baskets, were often

The great carved totem poles still stand in many places, silent symbols of one-time tribal coherence. These statuesque poles, recording family history, were made of Western Red Cedar (Thuja plicata), a tree up to 70m tall with strong, light, rot-resistant timber, quite easily worked.

Babies were often back-packed in carriers, made from the pliable stems of the Vine Maple (Acer circinatum, right) or its relations – as were snowshoes and a range of open-work baskets. To mop up urine, nappies or diapers would be provided by shredded cedar bark, cat-tail, seed-fluff or rotten aspen wood. Absorbent branching lichens and Sphagnum moss were also used, the latter widely known also for dressing wounds; while wormwood (Artemisia) could heal nappy rash.

decorated by intermingling strips of naturally or artificially coloured leaves or bark. Bitter Cherry's tough, shiny, reddish-purple bark was often used in this way, sometimes dyed black. Some of these containers were so tightly woven that they were watertight. So too were the elegantly decorated Red Cedar boxes used for storing foods or to boil or steam them. The beauty of these Indian designs and artefacts has not been entirely lost, but passed into the modern tourist and craft industries. Red Cedar also made the large (up to 60-seater), ocean-going canoes. The trunks were hollowed out in age-old dugout fashion. For light canoes, the river people (immortalised in Longfellow's *Song of Hiawatha*) looked to willow or cedar for flexible frames, to birch bark for the one-piece skin, and to conifer resin or pitch to caulk any cracks or seams. Some builders were so skilful that their canoes could be dismantled for portage.

Indians of the Amazonian Jungle

The once numerous tribes of Central South America inhabit the richest and most diverse forests in the world. Their skills echo those of the colder north, but with a completely different and much wider range of species. In every chapter of this book, plants from these jungles feature – food crops and spices, oils and fibres, medicines and contraceptives, orchids and houseplants. And in most cases, their "discovery" arose from local peoples' use of the plants concerned. Such contacts, however, have only brushed the surface of the Indians' knowledge of the forests. In their daily lives, plants provide everything.

The jungle has many discomforts, from parasites to vast numbers of irritating insects – tiny midges, mites which burrow into the skin, giant

Only a handful of the plant-based artefacts of these sophisticated people can be mentioned here, but this quotation from "Plants in British Columbian Indian Technology" by Nancy J Turner lists other uses of Red Cedar wood by Coastal tribes – "Dishes, arrow shafts, harpoon shafts, spear poles, barbecuing sticks, fish spreaders and hangers, dipnet hooks, fish clubs, masks, rattles, benches, cradles, coffins, herring rakes, canoe bailers, ceremonial drums, combs, fishing floats, berry drying racks and frames, fish weirs, spirit whistles and paddles. Ritual objects are typically of wood like the North American shaman's rattle, left, in the shape of a bird with a human figure and a frog, and the Pueblo Indian kachina doll simulating a supernatural being, above.

The orange dye from the seeds of Bixa orellana, below, known variously as urucu, achioto, annato and by other names, is widely used to colour thread, ceramics, implements and weapons, but most of all to paint the body and hair. Colorado Indians use it to colour the hair and, applied thickly, to create helmet-shaped hair styles. It gives magical protection from the spirits of the forest; its oil also acts as a mosquito repellant. Dyes are obtained from a variety of plants to colour feathers and material used for baskets, and to paint tools, wooden containers and calabashes, often mixed with palm oil. The xagua or tapurita (Genipa americana), whose sap becomes dark blue after exposure to the air, is widely used both for dyeing and body painting.

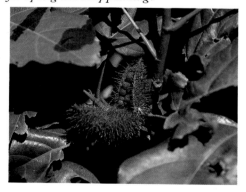

cockroaches which swarm round habitations; many plants are used to counter these pests, and the illness they may bring. Rainstorms have leached virtually all minerals out of the soil, so the area has no salt; a brownish salt substitute is sometimes made by boiling up the ashes of certain trees, especially palms, to evaporation point. The fire is started with a drill, and rapidly boosted by adding lumps of rubber from latex-bearing trees, or other resinous material.

Many of these peoples wear few or no clothes. Women may have a band of bark cloth, men a penis sheath woven from palm leaflets. Without clothes, personal ornaments take on great importance. The black, shiny nuts of *Astrocaryum* palms are widely carved into beads and earrings; beads are also made of fragrant woods such as the incense-scented Pau, Santo, or Holy Twig. For personal care, soaps and shampoos are made from several plants, notably several species of *Sapindus*; parasitic worms and mites are dealt with by smearing the skin with rubber latex, which suffocates the parasites. The Xingu Indians know a wild grass which is used as razor blades, and the Tapirape tribe used the crested fruits of a *Streptogyne* grass as tweezers to pluck hair.

As in the north, twine and ropes are vital. Various thicknesses are obtained from fibres, typically extracted by soaking leaves and picking out the strands. The common palm *Mauritia flexuosa* is a main source of cord, and other palms such as *Astrocaryum* and *Bactris* species provide the fibres used for sleeping hammocks, nets, and fish traps. The familiar raffia comes from several species of *Raphia*, especially *R. farinifera*. Many jungle Indians use fibres from the epiphytic bromeliads which cluster on the trees; in the uplands, the similar rosetted leaves of agaves are rotted in water to expose the fibres. Agave leaves usually have a fine hard point at the end and with care this can be extracted complete with the internal fibre leading to it, providing a needle and thread in one.

The jungle arsenal holds bows and arrows, spears, clubs and blowpipes. The most remarkable is the blowpipe – a tube about two metres long, bored from a palm stem – from, in the upper Amazon, the Paxiuba Palm. In Guyana, blowpipes have an inner barrel for extra accuracy. The outer tube is made from the Yurua Palm and the barrel is formed by the stem of a rare giant grass, *Arthrostylidium schomburgkii*. This plant comes from one area only and has only twice been seen by a white botanist. These components do not grow together: the giant grass is harvested only by the Machiritare tribe of the Pakaraima Range; the Yurua Palm by lowland Indians. Other tribes again hollow the palm stems and fit the inner barrels to them, after which they are traded back for specialities, such as cassava graters.

The dart, a sliver of wood perhaps 20cm long, is fitted at the base with a wad of cottony material from the fruit of *Bombax globosum* or *Eriodendrum samauma*; the sharpened tip is usually dipped in curare. The Indians have great knowledge of poisons for many different types of hunting: an ethno-botanist recently discovered a potential heart-surgery drug among the forty or more different fish poisons used by Indians of Guyana; the toxin stunned, but did not kill the fish, and on investigation proved to be temporarily stopping the heart without killing the organ.

The lives of these forest Indians are intimately linked with the jungle and all its plants. Perhaps they should be recognised as its best guardians. One

Most houses are small, their frames made of relatively light poles lashed together and a thatch of palm leaves covering the roof and walls. Some, such as those of the Yanomani, illustrated, are communal and may be very large: up to 30 m long, 20 m wide and 8 m high, with slats of bark, often painted with designs, for the walls. In the Upper Xingu, roof and wall curve continuously like an aircraft hangar: these are made of lashed poles and are thatched with grass.

group, the Kuna of Panama (Kuna is a local species of palm) have taken the bull by the horns and initiated a rainforest reserve in their own area – understanding that to preserve their culture, they need to preserve the forest, and that to achieve this, the best hope is a national park, partly open to research and tourism, the rest left wild.

One Plant, Many Uses

Some peoples have depended so greatly upon a single genus, even a single species, for their daily needs that these uniquely useful plants have acquired a special status, as symbols of the culture they serve. Such is the Date Palm (*Phoenix dactylifera*), grown since time immemorial in India, westwards to Mesopotamia, Palestinian lands, and North Africa, and most important in Egypt until very recent times. Other palms, too, have influenced whole cultures, from the Coconut to the Nipa Palm. But the Date has the longest and most illustrious history of all. There are now large plantations in Arizona and Southern California.

The fruits can grow to 12-15 cm long. They are classified into three types: soft, to be eaten fresh and ripe, and containing only a little sugar; semi-dry, which are sun-dried and packed loosely, keeping a long time without fermentation; and dry, smaller dates containing a high proportion of sugar which, after sun-drying, keep indefinitely.

This last type, particularly, is consumed by the Arab people. Desert nomads find them especially valuable for their long-keeping, depending on their store of dates to supplement their standard diet of camel's milk. The dry dates are softened by soaking in water: rich in sugars and starches (up to 70 percent), they also contain fats and essential protein. Dates are used in confectionery too, in preparing pastries, and as an alternative to honey. The nuts are roasted as a coffee substitute, and the ground seeds are also used as camel fodder. Nomads even sometimes ate the growing tips as "palm cabbage"; but this destroys the tree.

Arabs have a saying that there are as many uses to the Date Palm as there are days of the year; the Babylonians referred to 360 uses — a mystical number. Mysticism aside, it appears that some 800 uses have actually been recorded, many of them involving the wood, which is used for building huts and houses, and for any number of implements which can be cut and carved from it. The fronds are used, entire, for thatching; individual leaflets and the long hard leaf stems provide fibre, for ropes, cords, and baskets; stem fibre mixed with camel hair is woven into cloth, especially for travelling tents; mats are woven from the leaflets or their fibres.

The Date Palm is monoecious — it bears the flowers of each sex on separate trees. The knowledge of this is ancient; there are cuneiform texts of around 2300 BC from Ur, recording the necessity to carry out pollination. The traditional method is to cut male flower clusters when the pollen is ripe, climb each female tree, and tie a piece of the male cluster among its flowers. Mahomet taught his followers: "Honour the Date Palm, for she is your aunt on your father's side; she is made of the same stuff as Adam, and she is the only tree that is artificially fructified".

People have found even more uses for the ubiquitous bamboos of the Orient than for the Date Palm. First, many bamboo species provide food: the young growing tips of new culms (stems) are highly prized, especially those which are not bitter; the larger bamboos may have tips many centimetres across. Secondly, bamboo has special values as a material: light, but very tough indeed, with enormous tensile strength, the biggest kinds are virtually rigid, the thinner ones flexible. It can be split easily, but only in one direction. If heated, it can be bent, and on cooling retains any shape thus created. Artefacts can be made from the entire culm, reduced into sections where necessary (as for cylindrical containers), or by carving the wood into any shape or form; the split culm can usually be bent and woven, or reduced to strips of fibres of varying thickness, even to thread-like proportions. The long papery leaf-like sheaths formed at every joint on the noded culm are used to make hats and fans, roofs and as food wrapping. A few species are currently used for paper-making and also to form window panes.

Today, visitors to China, industrial Hong Kong and Japan will see tall buildings being erected with bamboo scaffolding (using some of the vigorous species which can reach 25 m tall); garden buildings made entirely of bamboo; and, in wood-framed houses, bamboo serving as walls, roofs, window lattices, in garden gates and doors, and as fences both ornamental and utilitarian. Bamboo supplies many surprising products, too, including ski sticks, vaulting poles and shuffleboard cues. Thomas Edison even used bamboo fibres as filaments in his early electric light bulbs before tungsten was available, and the plant once supplied gramophone needles!

Bamboo is one of the four noble Chinese plants, (the others are the orchid, chrysanthemum and plum tree). Perhaps its most ancient association is with writing. The first Chinese books were handwritten, using a bamboo brush, on strips of bamboo lined with silk. It is also the subject of innumerable paintings, where in earlier times it served a moral purpose, to symbolize straightness. The brushwork needed to paint bamboo – there are a dozen prescribed basic strokes – is intimately related to calligraphy in both China and Japan. Bamboo remains integral to the cultures of these countries at every possible level: as the Chinese poet Pou Sou-tung wrote, 800 years ago, "Without bamboo, we lose serenity and culture itself".

Modern Times – Crops Versus Vegetation

Modern commercial agriculture has a very different attitude to plants from that of the cultures we have just examined. Instead of living off the natural vegetation in harmony with its cycles, agricultural peoples remove the original plant cover, and replace it with their own. Widespread cutting of trees and pasturing of grazing animals lead to irrevocable changes. Dense forests become broken into parcels, to be replaced by lighter woodland for coppicing, or by fields, until the forests vanish; all over the world, this process has continued for millenia. Fields were at first small, often irregular, separated by hedgerows or fences, and bearing many mixed crops. In the last couple of centuries, however, and mostly very recently, the development and use of cultivating machines has swept away the hedges, turned small fields into great tracts, many kilometres square, and encouraged vast monocultures. Where animals are grazed in large numbers, equally vast extents of grassland have been opened up, as in New Zealand.

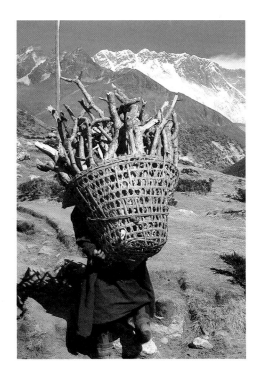

An English traveller wrote in the 1860s "What would a poor Chinaman do without the bamboo? Independently of its use as a food, it provides him with the thatch that covers his house, the mat on which he sleeps, the cup from which he drinks, and the chopsticks with which he eats. He irrigates his fields by means of a bamboo pipe; his harvest is gathered in with a bamboo rake; his grain is sifted through a bamboo sieve, and carried away in a bamboo basket. The mast of his junk is bamboo; so is the pole of his cart." He ends sombrely "He is flogged with a bamboo cane, tortured with bamboo stakes, and finally strangled with a bamboo rope".

The giant bamboo, Dendrocalamus giganteus, is still used for rafts in shallow turbulent rivers; while Phyllostachys pubescens is singled out as the source of cables. The stems are split and twisted together and, in lines up to 500 metres long, used by teams of men to tow junks up the rapids of the Yangtse gorges. Cables 65 cm in circumference are recorded as supporting a bridge nearly 250 m long and 3 m wide.

In Nepal bamboo is used for baskets, above; for matting to protect livestock, right; and for the Pakhola Bridge, far right.

Masses of people join in the final stages of the rice harvest in Bali, as they have throughout the processes of cultivation. Bunches of rice plants, cut by sickle, are banged on the ground to release the seeds; chaff is removed by sieving and winnowing by hand before the grain is bagged up. It is possible to mechanise rice cultivation on level terrain up to a point, but not on the steep-terraced paddy fields prominent in many parts of the Far East. More importantly, the large population, living in villages dotted all over the countryside, need the work. To introduce automation into such situations is folly.

Much modern crop cultivation is featureless; among the flat cereal-filled plains of North America, the only prominent features are the circles of bright green crop which indicate the range of huge rotary sprinklers.

The greatest areas of cereal cultivation, notably Wheat, are in North America and USSR. Only flying above these apparently unbounded fields really brings home their immensity. Every aspect of cultivation, including the addition of fertiliser, is done by machine; weed and pest control are typically carried out by spraying from aircraft. Those who tend these vast crops live in farmsteads or small communities great distances apart, a lonely life in which the understanding of machinery and chemicals still remains harnessed to the controlling march of the seasons.

Where fields remain small, and where there is plenty of labour, most aspects of cereal cultivation are carried out by one person behind an animal, or one person on a tractor. In China Wheat is cut by sickle, threshed often by laying the crop on tarmac roads so that passing vehicles do the hard work, winnowed by pairs of girls throwing the grain up in huge wicker baskets, and finally ripened off on mats in the sun. A great number of people are employed, which makes nonsense of the present attempts to introduce combine harvesters into over-populated places like Bangladesh.

Rice, the staple cereal of the tropics, is grown and harvested mechanically in developed countries, but in the steep-terraced fields of the Far East, where the paddies may be only a few feet across as they follow the contour lines, hand labour is the only possible way. In China work starts by carrying night-soil to the main fields and pouring it in. Then a plough pulled by a water buffalo turns the soil over, both man and beast wading deep in the mud. In separate small paddies where the seed has been densely sown, the workers gather the young plants into bundles. Taken to the cropping paddies, these are placed in position one by one, again by stooped workers with arched backs. Weeding during the growing season is often carried out with the feet; it has been truly said that the peasant knows every inch of his soil. Come harvest, the grain is cut with a sickle, threshed and winnowed and ripened much like Wheat. Some warm zones can grow two or three crops a year, so the task here is literally endless.

Tea and Coffee

The tea shrub, a close relation of the garden camellia, is planted in long straight lines over the undulating hills of Assam, Sri Lanka, Indonesia, Japan and China.

Tea is almost always grown as a monoculture but I have seen cabbages interplanted with it in China; shade trees are also sometimes grown among the bushes. The plant can grow quite large but under cultivation it is kept a little above knee height by pruning and, in particular, regular plucking of the young shoots which pickers cast into baskets slung on their backs; their labour is endless and even more monotonous than that of the rice cultivators. After picking, the leaves go to factory buildings where they are withered, rolled, crushed, fermented, fired, sorted and finally packed. Villages around the plantations are often entirely devoted to the routine of tea, which is continuous in monsoon climates.

Coffee comes from the berries of a large shrub. Picking needs as much precision as tea, because only ripe berries must be taken from clusters which ripen over a period, and the picker has rather more searching to do up and down the plants. After the berries are collected, they may be dried so that their flesh can be rubbed off or pulped entire to remove it mechanically. The stones are then dried, during which time the final remains of the flesh ferment; this fermentation improves the appearance and also the quality of the final cleaned-up product.

Fruit Trees

The widely cultivated Apple and Pear, grown since ancient times in temperate climates, have been very labour-intensive since their early beginnings. These are idiosyncratic trees; although mainly grafted (the selected variety being scions on a stock selected for uniformity and, nowadays, to control ultimate tree size) they develop irregularly, and need annual pruning. But they are grown in rows, which facilitates mechanised weeding and feeding and the application by tractor-hauled blowers of the numerous sprays needed by these insect- and fungus-prone crops each season. Harvesting is almost entirely by hand, for bruising associated with mechanical picking causes fruit to rot quickly. Large areas are often put down to fruit farms and a lot of casual labour is brought in at picking time.

157

The Olive, with its gnarled, often perforated trunks, irregular growth habit and restful greyish colouring is picturesque in the Mediterranean heat. Harvesting is done by hand, often by women armed with long sticks, with children to gather the fruits. Nowadays it is usual to cover the ground below with plastic sheeting. After harvesting the fruits are taken to oil presses: once worked by circling donkeys these are now almost all motor-powered. Olive groves are usually worked by local villagers who often also maintain flocks of sheep or goats.

In contrast to the Olives, citrus fruits present a regimented appearance. Like apples they are grafted plants, but the rounded trees planted in endless rows in the Mediterranean and North America, grow more regularly. Again, spraying against the many enemies of this monoculture is essential, and the easily damaged fruit is also picked carefully by hand. Citrus plantations are usually under the control of a handful of experts with picking done by casual labour. In America, the migrant pickers move steadily northwards following the ripening of the crops.

The Grape

Wine has been made since very ancient times – perhaps as long ago as 8000 BC; Noah is traditionally reputed to have been the first vine-grower. Nowadays there are well over 10,000 cultivars, from which the astonishing range of different wines is derived.

The grape-vine is another very labour-intensive plant, needing expert pruning and training, difficult soil-cleaning operations in often stony ground, and a good deal of chemical spraying. Vine growing is a family affair, or involves small collectives with whole families working over generations. Most attention is by hand, notably picking. Because of the plant's end product, harvest is normally a time of gaiety, laughter and song (a French saying is that "a mouth busy with song is not busy with the bunch"). In places where the best vintages have been grown for centuries, wine production has stamped the land and its people; little else is grown over large areas. The fields, often terraced and divided by low stone walls, occupy all suitable sites; local variations of soil, situation and aspect all contribute to different end-products from the same grape varieties. In France especially the wine "factory" is often a chateau, itself the centre of social and economic interest. As the grapes mature their progress is the main topic of local conversation, and if disaster strikes – perhaps a heavy rainstorm just before harvest – the neighbourhood is united in despair.

Vines also, of course, are grown for dessert fruit in several warm countries, and sultanas and raisins are grapes preserved by drying. Currants come from the small, mostly seedless grapes, and take their name from Corinth, where the ancient variety Black Corinth is still grown.

Ultimately, all human societies depend on plants. The destructive nature of modern agriculture, with its vast monocultures, and prowling combine harvesters, does them much damage. Worse still, the acculturation of primitive peoples, ever accelerating in pace, often takes their irreplaceable knowledge from us for good. The plant world can probably supply

The symbol of the enormous wheatfields of the northern hemisphere – the world's breadbasket – is the combine harvester operated by a single man. In this land without a vestige of the original vegetation, machines, fertilisers and chemicals against pests, diseases and weeds dominate the giant cultivation operation. Density of population is tiny, for workers live in small communities great distances apart, while the crop goes largely to feed the multitudes packed into cities, mostly divorced from any contact with plants or the land.

answers to some of our most urgent problems – but we have to know where to look. Faced with the task of random screening thousands of untried plants, the botanist is like a person fumbling for a key in the dark. The indigenous peoples, however, have hundreds or thousands of years of knowledge to draw on. They hold the key to the plant storehouse.

But though their knowledge is deep, it is not inborn. As communities die out, or are absorbed into the wider society, the oral tradition is broken. When, for example, missionaries in 1959–60 came to aid the Tirios of Suriname, who were being decimated by introduced diseases, the medicine they offered persuaded people to abandon their old way of life. The Tirios have now virtually ceased to use their old cures; the adults recall some details, but the children know practically nothing of the medicinal properties of their own flora. Recorded botanical knowledge is slight, so once the Indians have forgotten, centuries of research will be lost.

Can concerned people act to secure this knowledge? To a degree, we can; and it is greatly in all our interest to do so. Ethnobotany is becoming a priority science, but it is running late in the race against acculturation, and is poorly appreciated. Even if the plant lore of some peoples is saved, the loss of the Indians, holistic philosophy, of their understanding of the forest, is to be mourned. They have much to teach careless western society about the value of plants. According to the South American Indians, legend tells that "The forest supports the sky. Cut down the trees and disaster will follow". We should heed them well.

Imperial Chemical Industries' Pruteen plant at Billingham, England — the protein-maker of the future?

CHAPTER TEN

Improving the Resources

Few people realise how vital wild plants and primitive crop varieties or "land races" are to plant breeders. Yet our hope for the crowded world of the future rests on just such plants, and the untried virtues they may offer of disease resistance, drought or salt tolerance, ease of harvesting, or soil improvement. We can only guess how many of these potential saviours are in danger; the majority grow in countries of rapidly rising populations and extreme poverty, where the pressure on them increases year by year.

One way to save these plants is by in-situ, "on-the-spot", conservation – protected areas like nature reserves and national parks. Another is ex-situ, either "in cultivation" or "in-the-refrigerator", conservation – gene banks for seeds that will remain viable in cold storage, especially important for maintaining the seeds of cultivated varieties.

As long as we can protect these resources, there is hope that the part-nership of modern science and the plant kingdom can flourish, and continue to provide all we need. New skills exist in breeding and manipulating plants to suit uncongenial environments or to supply specific food or industrial requirements. Laboratory techniques, too, offer the prospect of breeding large numbers of plants at once, or of persuading them to mass produce their valuable chemicals for us.

There even is the possibility, in some measure at least, of increasing food production and supply of industrial substances, without putting pressure on land, by turning to products made by micro-organisms. Imperial Chemical Industries, for example, are now cultivating bacteria to provide an animal feedstuff in a massive fermentation plant. As foods, micro-organisms are not as unfamiliar as they may sound. Yeasts and other fungi have been involved in the production of bread, cheese, yoghurt, beer, wine and vinegar since ancient times. In Indonesia, fermented Soya Bean and Peanut cakes make up a third of the protein requirement; the similar bean curd is widely eaten in China. The use of the blue-green alga *Spirulina* as food has been described on p.81.

Bio-engineering, bacteria, algae – these high-tech solutions can, at best, only serve to reduce the pressure of hungry populations on our remaining untouched natural vegetation. Without the wild plants and ancient land races, we have no wealth for the future. Conserving these, in one way or another, is the first imperative.

The Age of the Bug

Modern biotechnology, the *industrial* processing of materials by micro-organisms, has achieved much in its fifteen year history – new foods and nutritional upgrading of traditional foods; antibiotics, vaccines and drugs for human and animal use; enzyme technology for industrial and clinical purposes; energy and fuel production; pollution management; extraction of metal from waste and low grade ores; and polymers for use in food, textile and heavy industries.

Biotechnology is a profitable industry. Japan, at the forefront in this field, earned over £5 billion from it in 1979 (5 percent of the gross national product), the amino-acid industry producing more than 100,000 tonnes of glutamic acid alone. In Britain, ICI's Pruteen fermentation plant is capable of producing 150 tonnes per day of single-cell protein for animal feedstuff, by culturing the bacterium *Methylophilus methylotrophus* which multiplies extremely rapidly.

It also makes sound ecological sense. One million tonnes of Pruteen could, in theory, be produced on a land area of 100 hectares – compared with two million hectares required to grow the protein equivalent from Soya Beans. This space-saving aspect of biotechnology is one of its most important features; another is that it can use discarded oil residues, or wastes left after processing plants for other purposes, for raw materials.

Test Tube Plants

Many plant substances highly prized in medicine or industry require long and complex extraction processes. Some day, perhaps, these may be manufactured in test tubes, by plant cells. If a piece of plant is disinfected, broken down to single cells or small groups of cells, and grown in a carefully composed nutrient medium, a mass of undifferentiated tissue will form (in the right conditions). With luck, these cells will release the desired substance straight into the culture medium.

The possibilities are enormous. The pharmaceutical industry, for instance, derives a quarter of all prescribed medicines in the western world ultimately from plants – more in the east. The Rosy Periwinkle (p.121), used against cancer, has already been grown in a test tube: the cells synthesise the valuable alkaloids, scarce in the plants, at high rates and secrete them directly into the culture material, thus greatly simplifying extraction of the drug. Contraceptive pills could also be manufactured this way, using cell cultures of the hormone-producing yam species (p.123) – particularly desirable in view of their increasing rarity in the wild.

Many factors induce drug firms to invest in cell culture: unpredictable harvests at limited times of the year; unpredictable supply in changing political situations; the cost of importing plant materials from the other side of the world. But the science is still in its infancy. Successful culture media are often hit on by trial and error, rather than knowledge and the only industrial product so far (apart from the Rosy Periwinkle alkaloids) is shikonin, a red dye with anti-bacterial qualities. Made in Japan from cell cultures of the roots of *Lithospermum erythrorhizon*, it costs £2,000 per kilo.

Tissue culture has other exciting applications, too. If the cells multiplying in culture are encouraged to reorganise, it is theoretically possible to produce plantlets – and so breed up huge numbers of plants. This process, known as cloning could help us reafforest huge areas, regreen denuded lands, take pressure off exploited wild plants, and increase food supplies.

All the cereals, however, belong to the monocotyledons – a group that are notoriously awkward customers when it comes to tissue culture, and do not regenerate at all readily. It is only recently that a breakthrough has come: scientists are now regenerating palms (also in this group, and normally only grown from seed) in culture. Cloning a high-yielding individual oil palm in this way may increase yields by 20 to 30 percent; yields from cloned coconut could be increased five-fold.

One special kind of tissue culture is meristem propagation, in which almost microscopic shoot tips, like miniature cuttings, are placed in flasks of growing medium, constantly turned to remove gravitational effects. Each tip rapidly produces clusters of tiny plants, which are later divided and grown individually. The method has been used successfully with orchids, enabling growers to build up stocks of new, expensive hybrids quickly.

Breeding for Improvement

Until recently, the only means of improving plants has been to select those with useful natural mutations – a process which has been going on in farmers' fields for millenia – and then deliberately hybridise (cross-breed) the best cultivars which emerge. But today, the fledgling science of genetic engineering offers the prospect of inserting foreign gene material directly into a new host. Scientists are working on techniques which will cross the barriers of sexual reproduction, perhaps even straddle the divide between the different kingdoms of plant, animal and micro-organism. Inducing cereal crops to take on the nitrogen-fixing properties of the legume-*Rhizobium* symbiosis (p.104) is one – at present distant – possibility. But though full of unexplored possibilities, which will certainly surface in the years ahead, genetic engineers can only supplement the standard methods of improving plants: we cannot create genes, and so still need to use existing plants to derive new strains.

There are two important considerations in breeding. The first is obvious: in crossing two plants, each with distinct desirable characters, the breeder hopes to combine the virtues of both in their offspring. Sometimes the attempt is to breed just one valuable character (a specific disease resistance being the most obvious example) into an existing cultivar which is otherwise excellent. The second purpose of breeding is to create an F_1 (first generation) hybrid: if two selected cultivars are crossed to produce seed, the plants grown from this seed often (though not necessarily) have hybrid vigour, displayed in improved stamina and increased yield. The catch is that the F_1 hybrid cannot be reproduced from its own seed; the second generation would show very great variation. The cross to produce F_1 seed has to be repeated annually (it usually applies only to annuals – garden flowers and most cereals). This places the propagation of an F_1 strain in the hands of its creators – the farmer must buy new seed each year.

Scientists now use laboratory techniques to save endangered plants. Here, seedlings of the rare Australian orchid, Pterostylis fischii, are ready to be planted out, having been raised in test tubes. The orchid seeds, produced in abundance, are tiny and only germinate in the presence of a fungus which provides essential nutrients. The scientists' method involves growing the seeds in a weak porridge inoculated with the fungus. Six endangered Australian orchids have been bred by these techniques, and re-introduced to nature reserves after their brush with extinction.

Plant breeding and production of new strains have been vastly stepped up recently partly because computers can now monitor enormous numbers of crosses, and a wide range of characters. In its 350,000 test plots, Shell Oil can monitor the progress of over a million plants.

Genes from the Wild

All cereal crops have in the past acquired improvements through accidental breeding with wild relations, and most have been deliberately improved, too, with genes from the wild. Even so, this resource remains partly untapped. Breeders will resort to the wild only if the crop to be improved is rather uniform and therefore offers insufficient genetic wealth (known as variation) for selection, or if the desired qualities are much more pronounced in the wild forms than the cultivated. It can be very difficult to make a fertile cross using wild material; and even if a cross is achieved, it may not be easy to get rid of the weedy characters associated with the desired quality. Besides which, the cultivated forms are so much better known and more readily available.

The Tomato (*Lycopersicon esculentum*), owes its enormous commercial success almost entirely to its wild relatives. With a little help from its friends, the crop has gained: resistance to the fungus *Fusarium oxysporum* (borrowed from *L. pimpinellifolium*); a change to the fruit stalk that adapts it for mechanical harvesting (from *L. cheesmanii*); intensified colour and increased soluble solids (from *L. chmielewskii*, among other species, even though *chmielewskii* is green); higher beta carotene (*L. hirsutum*) and increased vitamin C content (*L. peruvianum*). The Tomato is a rather unusual crop in that it apparently was first domesticated not in its ancestral home in Ecuador, but in Mexico where it had travelled as a weed in maize crops. This alien origin deprived its first cultivators of access to the wealth of genetic variety normally available to a species.

The genetic wealth, or gene pool, of a crop comprises all the genes from all the varieties and species that could possibly breed with it. The *primary* gene pool consists of domesticated varieties, the wild original, and related wild species that breed readily with the crop to produce fertile offspring; the *secondary* gene pool includes the species that will cross with the crop using conventional methods to give some fertile progeny, but many sterile. The *tertiary* gene pool requires the special techniques of the twentieth century to persuade the reluctant parents to breed; even then the hybrids will usually be completely sterile. Tomato and Cotton at present stand alone in having had genes added from all three pools.

The wild genes most widely used are those for disease-resistance, usually major genes which confer vertical resistance – that is, protection against a specific race of pathogen. The wild potato species *Solanum demissum*, for example, from the secondary gene pool, was used originally for its major gene resistance to Late Blight. However in 1936, races of the disease arose against which the gene proved ineffective, so breeding with *S. demissum* was largely abandoned. But then it was noticed that varieties with *S. demissum* in their background were generally a little more blight-resistant than those without. Generalised or horizontal resistance of this kind is conferred by many minor genes, and is now considered an important safety net to prevent new races of disease wiping out crops.

Genes from the wild have been used in all of the big three cereals. Bread wheat has already obtained considerable benefit, including resistance to Eyespot disease (*Cercosporella herpotrichoides*) from Goatgrass, *Aegilops ventricosa*, and frost resistance from *Agropyron*. Commercial maize has been improved only with genes from the wild *Tripsacum dactyloides* (p.76).

The wild input into rice has also been limited to one improvement, but with spectacular results. The big new paddies of the Green Revolution, cropping rice all year round, greatly suited the ecology of the Grassy Stunt Virus, which never found itself homeless, as it might if there had been a break between crops; the rice was also an abundant food source for the virus's carrier, the Brown Plant-hopper (*Nilaparvata lugens*).

Grassy Stunt appeared almost from nowhere as an important disease. In the early 1970s, 116,000 hectares of rice in Indonesia, India, Sri Lanka, Vietnam and the Philippines were destroyed by epidemics of this virus. Immediately, the hunt was on for a high-resistance gene. Screening of the 6,273 samples of rice kept in the collection of the International Rice Research Institute revealed that only *one*, the feeble *Oryza nivara*, had the required character; as a bonus, it was also resistant to Blast, another major disease of rice. This sample had been collected from central India in 1966, a time when no-one could have guessed that it would ever be of value – Grassy Stunt was of no importance then and the wild rice had lots of bad points – weak stems, low yields, with a head that shattered at maturity to scatter the seeds. Now, thanks to *Oryza nivara* (fortunately in the primary gene pool that breeds readily with the crop) the disease has gone back into obscurity, and IR36, the rice variety with the wild genes, is planted across 11 million hectares. Of course, this record is far *too* good, and scientists are busily breeding new rice varieties with different genes, to introduce before the pests and diseases catch up with IR36 and overrun it.

Cocoa provides another intriguing story. Most is produced in Africa from old plantations of unimproved stock; but since demand for the commodity is still rising, the trend is to develop new, high-yielding hybrids. However, Cacao cultivation spread around the world so quickly that all the crops were derived from just a few wild ancestors, and so suffer from a lack of genetic variation. Faced with this, commerce had to go back to nature: wild and semi-wild Cacao material has revolutionised cacao breeding, providing vigour, resistance to the crop's three main diseases, and greatly increased productivity. The wild trees grow in the tropical forests of the Amazon, with greatest diversity along the eastern fringe of the Andes, as in Ecuador. But in the past 10 years, with the discovery and exploitation of important oil fields, these once remote jungles have started to disappear under roads, airstrips and towns. The cocoa resource is disappearing, and collectors are now travelling the Amazon region on an ever more urgent mission to find wild Cacao and bring back planting material.

Twenty-four of our major world crops have been improved with wild germplasm: rice, barley, oats, sweet potato, sunflower, oil palm, sesame, tomato, carrot, bell or sweet pepper, grapes, apple, strawberry, sugar cane, sugar beet, rubber, cacao, cotton, maize, potato, cassava, peas, tobacco and wheat. The use of wild species in sunflower breeding has helped to raise yields by 20 percent, and in sugar cane breeding has almost doubled the cane yield and more than doubled the yield of sugar. The list of important crops yet to receive commercial benefit from their untamed cousins is limited to soya beans, cabbages, coffee, tea, jute, bananas and citrus fruit. Of these, several are now being worked on; others, such as the Cabbage tribe, already have so much variation among the cultivated types that it may not be necessary to resort to the wild. Yams are similar but wild species have much potential. A number of minor crops, too, have benefited from their uncultivated relatives, including hops and gooseberries.

Land Race Genes

Even more important to the plant breeder are the land races – the traditional varieties of crops that evolved under human use over the centuries. Developed in an environment with relatively low levels of cultivation, fertilization and plant protection, these varieties experienced selection pressures for hardiness and dependability, rather than productivity. Moreover, the genetic diversity found naturally within each land race provided the farmer with insurance against climatic extremes and disease epidemics. Traditional varieties, in fact, are often able to withstand conditions which would seriously harm many modern lines; but they may be so closely adapted to their particular locality that they do not do well in other environments.

Within these land races lay a wealth of genes, just waiting to be sorted into the right packages; so the first purposeful selections led to greatly improved yields. In the minor crops, especially in the tropics, there is even now considerable scope for selection directly from land races. But the greatest benefit they offer today comes from the individual genes they contain, which can be inserted singly into ailing crops to revitalise them. Land races have been described as the product of human genius, and their survival has depended upon the caring hand of rational agriculturalists down through the generations.

Naturally enough, the centres of genetic diversity of crops and of their pathogens (disease organisms) often coincide – the Old World cereals, and the rusts, are an example. The diseases develop to exploit the plants, and the plants adopt counter-measures to combat the diseases; but they manage to rub along together. It is not in the interest of the disease to exterminate its host; the two co-evolve. Disease resistance can also develop in land races far from the crop's centre of origin. A survey among the 6689 samples of Barley in the US Department of Agriculture's world collection revealed only 117 with resistance to Yellow Dwarf Virus – 113 from Ethiopia, three with Ethiopian parents, and one from China; but the crop originated in the Near East. It can safely be assumed that this rare asset arose in Ethiopia, not in the crop's original home.

In 1974 a group of scientists went to the mountainous areas of northern Moravia and Slovakia. They gathered material from fields, gardens and farmers' stores and found 247 different cereals, grain legumes, vegetables and medicinal plants. The expedition was in the nick of time; the remaining material is vanishing fast. The old land races are disappearing everywhere, overtaken, and ousted, by the introduction of "improved" and F_1 strains.

The Soya Bean depends on a slim genetic base. In the USA most varieties are derived from just 11 lines. Hitherto the increase in production has been brought about largely through increasing acreages; but with only a finite amount of land available for the crop, agriculturalists now wish to raise the amount produced with genetic improvements. The worry is that the variation does not exist within the crop, and that the oriental germ plasm base needed for the improvements is fast vanishing. The homelands of the Soya Bean's wild relatives are being covered by building and industrial developments and land races are being displaced by higher-yielding selections.

The new high-yielding varieties of wheat and rice are causing special concern in this respect. As the Green Revolution varieties of wheat and rice spread around the world, farmers eat the seeds of their old land races, and plant the new. As geneticist Garrison Wilkes has said, this is like "building the roof with stones from the foundation". In Pakistan, all the areas to which access is easy, by road or path, have reportedly been planted up with the new cultivars. Even in the Himalayan valleys, isolated by high mountain ranges, the ancient races of wheat are being replaced with high-yielding lines from the south. In Nepal, the wheat-growing area has increased dramatically, with 80 percent given over to the new varieties.

Collectors must push ever further on to remote places to find old races, and breeders will have to look sharp to collect the surviving range of types before they are exterminated. In the last 40 years, 95 percent of native wheat varieties have been eliminated in Greece. There has been equally catastrophic genetic erosion in Afghanistan, India, Iraq and Turkey; and this great loss has all occurred in the last 20 years.

The threat to wild crop relatives is equally alarming. Take maize, for example: the cleared forests and verges of new highways, opening up across Mexico and Central America, may sometimes provide a temporary habitat for its weedy relatives, the Tripsacums and teosintes; but in the course of construction, the ancient stands of these wild grasses may be destroyed, and human settlements following the roads continue the attrition. The up-to-date farmer uses pure, hybrid seed in large, weed-free fields, destroying all the old varieties and squeezing out the weedy erstwhile bedfellows on the old field margins. In some places in Central America, maize land has been cleared and planted with more lucrative cash crops, notably strawberries, for export to the United States.

Genetic loss is occurring in many other crops. Recent reports have pinpointed wild relations of cocoa, coffee, sugar cane, sweet potato, tomato, some pulses, pepper, onions and brassicas as all seriously endangered. This wild germplasm is the fundamental resource of biological engineering – and in real danger of being the limiting one. No one can (as yet) *create* genes with specific attributes.

The world over, wild relatives of crops are being decimated, from cabbages in France and Italy to cotton in the US, Ecuador and Peru. The oats of Morocco and Spain are under threat, sunflowers in the US, avocado in Ecuador, olives in North Africa, oil palm in South America, beets in Portugal, Greece and especially Turkey, safflower in Morocco, and coffee in Ethiopia. In western Asia the wild pears, cherries, pistachios and other fruit and nut trees are being felled for timber and fuel. In South-east Asia the lowland tropical rain forest, home of the wild relatives of mango (*Mangifera*), durian (*Durio*) and rambutan (*Nephelium*), is being cleared.

The current loss of genetic resources, both land races and wild crop relatives, can be attributed to three main causes. The chief of these is loss of habitat, the second is over-exploitation, and the third competition or predation by introduced species. Of the 250,000-plus flowering plant species known to science, about 1 in 10 is threatened with extinction. Who knows how many of the threatened 25,000 are potentially useful to us? This unknown quantity of useful plants is in danger of genetic erosion before domestication has even begun. And there are also species that have only just entered our catalogue of value, and as yet differ little from the wild, such as the Monterey Pine. There are only five small populations remaining in its native California, yet it is an important plantation tree in Australia and New Zealand. The remaining Californian specimens are clearly a great genetic treasure. The wild Douglas Fir of the Pacific coast is threatened by plantations of the domesticated form which, shedding their pollen into the common pool, could reduce the diversity of the indigenous population.

Conserving the Resource: In-situ

Wild crop relatives can be conserved in-situ by setting aside the areas where they live as reserves, with facilities for study and collection of germplasm under licence, if necessary maintaining the vegetation in its existing sub-climax state. This is a novel use of reserves – most protected areas in the past have been set up for scenic beauty, to protect individual species, or to maintain representative ecosystems. An important part of current conservation efforts is to develop management methods and goals for in-situ gene conservation.

Not surprisingly, very few areas so far have been set aside for this sole purpose. There is one in the Kopet-Dag mountains of Turkmen-SSR, to protect fodder grasses, apricot, pistachio and almond, and one in the Caucasus for wheat and fruit trees. Sri Lanka has a reserve for medicinal plants and India is planning reserves for banana, citrus, rice, sugar cane and mango. Most reserves also serve other purposes – a good thing since then the price of protection can be spread across other objectives, such as amenity and watershed protection. It is helpful to the breeder to study the ecology of the plant in its proper habitat. But the greatest strength of in-situ conservation is that the crop relatives continue to evolve alongside their pests and pathogens, under the pressures of natural selection. They thus provide the breeder with a dynamic source of genes.

In-situ reserves are ideal, too, for plants whose germplasm is difficult to store artificially. Some seeds cannot be dried, or have brief viability; some plants seldom produce seeds; some seeds rarely germinate. These genes have to be stored as roots, tubers, cuttings, or whole plants, which occupy too much space for a good range of genotypes to be held. They are more easily conserved in the wild.

Conserving the Resource: Ex-situ

The loss of genetic variety that has taken place in the last few decades has underlined the need for places where plant genes can be stored for safe keeping and future use – "gene banks". The first great collection of germplasm was assembled by the Russian botanist N.I. Vavilov and his colleagues in the 1920s and 1930s. He and his successors set a great example which has been emulated the world over, but not always with equal success or scientific rectitude.

The collections are usually made up of seeds, and they need to be kept in cold storage at very low humidity, if they are to keep well. Unfortunately,

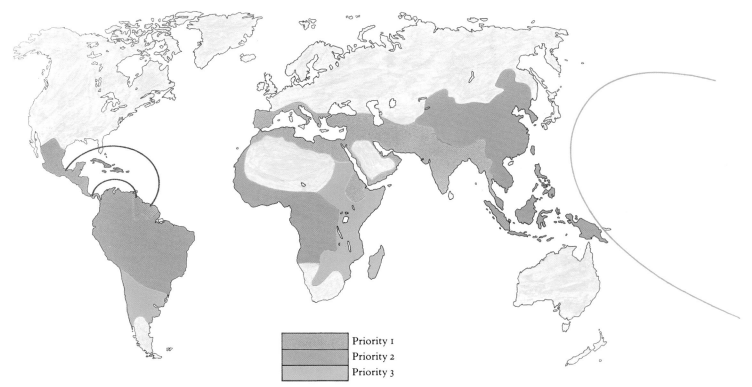

	Priority 1
	Priority 2
	Priority 3

Priority Regions for the Conservation of Crop Genetic Resources

The map indicates where irreplaceable genetic diversity of important crops is threatened. The priority areas for conservation cover not only the centres of crop evolution as envisaged by De Candolle and Vavilov but also secondary centres with a rich heritage of land races. It was drawn up in 1981 by the International Board for Plant Genetic Resources, an organisation which works in close association with the Food and Agriculture Organisation of the United Nations.

this introduces a new and important selection factor – the ability to withstand the very conditions of storage. Thus, particularly at the end of an unusually long period, the remaining viable seed will probably be adapted to storage, and not be a fair reflection of the original sample.

The seeds of most species will keep in cold storage for a number of years, but they are living organisms, and must be tested for viability regularly and also sown and grown (known as growing out) once in a while or they will die. Self-pollinated crops can be grown out in garden plots, but open-pollinated species need to be raised in bee-proof glasshouses and hand-pollinated to ensure that the lines remain unadulterated. Even some very famous collections lack the facilities to plant out as regularly as they should, and it is rumoured that some seed banks now contain large amounts of rotting or dead material.

Other, more obvious, troubles are caused by pathogens attacking both seeds and vegetative material. Losses occur too from causes like refrigerator breakdown, electricity failure, transferring material in unsuitable conditions, or growing out in the wrong way (one maize strain has been killed off by being grown at the wrong altitude). It has been calculated that only 11 percent of gene bank storage is truly long-term.

Seed material is generally preferred because it occupies little volume. But some seeds, notably those of certain tropical plants, have no dormant period and will not keep beyond a few weeks, so germplasm from these must be stored as vegetative materials (roots, cuttings, etc.). Cassava and yams, for instance, are banked as this way; so are bananas, and some peanuts, both of which practically never produce seed. Most tropical fruits and most medicinal plants are maintained by growing specimens from cuttings. Vegetatively produced materials are no problem as far as genetic purity goes, since they are produced without the sullying influence of sex, and are always identical to the plant from which they were taken. Even so it appears that much variability can be lost between each growing out.

Many working collections kept by plant breeders have only the small range of varieties likely to be easily assimilated into the breeding programme. Sometimes the assemblage lasts only as long as the different lines are being investigated, and the collection is abandoned once the final selections have been made; it takes time, space and money to maintain a good collection. At the other end of the spectrum are conservation collections such as those held at the National Seed Storage Laboratory in the USA and the N. I. Vavilov Institute in Leningrad, which cover a substantial part of the genetic variation of a wide range of species.

There are now national gene banks in some 60 countries, as well as private seed companies, and specialist crop research centres. The International Potato Centre in Peru, for example, was set up to find a mutation that would enable potatoes to flourish in tropical lowlands. Based on the dry coastal plain, it runs several other stations where the wild potatoes are grown, both in their natural habitats and in experimental ones, such as tropical forest.

Rice also has its own bank: out of an estimated 120,000 strains in the world, about half are held at the International Rice Research Institute in the Philippines. But its Director-General, M.S. Swaminathan, is not satisfied with this already good collection, and aims to complete it to "preserve for posterity the fruits of thousands of years of natural and human selection".

The centre for world maize and wheat collection, with 120,000 entries from 47 countries, is the International Maize and Wheat Improvement Centre in Mexico. Sorghums and millets are kept at the Indian Agricultural Research Institute at New Delhi. The Asian Vegetable Research and Development Centre on Taiwan holds mung beans, common bean, Chinese cabbage, cauliflower, mustard greens, radish, pepper, tomato and sweet potato. The National Vegetable Research Centre at Wellesbourne, England, has the world's first comprehensive vegetable gene bank. It holds seeds of cabbage, sprouts, calabrese, cauliflower, carrots, celery, beetroot, turnips, swedes, parsnips, onions, leeks, rhubarb, tomatoes, lettuce and smaller quantities of other vegetables, including those from the tropics.

Some rather special gene banks have been set up in various parts of the developed world by people wishing to preserve traditional crop varieties in the face of economic or political opposition. The European Economic Community, for instance, has a draconian ruling that varieties of vegetables not on their approved list can neither be sold nor even given away. The list excludes hundreds of old varieties mostly because they are supposedly synonymous with modern types. One current British seed catalogue lists a number of such cultivars with the comment "Sorry, available outside EEC only". In a few cases, like the disallowed huge and popular tomato Ultra Boy, the seed merchants sell "plantlettes" – seed already sprouted because the regulations say nothing about this. Nor do they include "borrowing". Thus a seed-lending "library" has been set up, with such accessions as the Irish Potato Onion (which reputedly does not make your eyes water when you peel it), and Cook's Delight Beet (which can grow to over 2 kilos without becoming woody). The borrower is supposed to let some of the crops go to seed, harvest this and return it to the library.

The British Ministry of Agriculture, when drawing up their national list for the EEC, considered the onion Up-to-date as synonymous with Bedfordshire Champion; yet in older Ministry lists the former is specified as being specifically resistant to Downy Mildew, the latter as having least resistance. Confusion and insensitivity seem to have reigned supreme in making out this list. To get on to it with a new variety involves testing at a cost of about £600 before registration, and £70 per year thereafter. No wonder small seed firms are being forced out of business.

Several British stately homes have been prevailed upon to become vegetable sanctuaries, and start growing "heritage" seed. In the USA, old vegetables discontinued by the commercial firms are handled by small "heirloom" firms, trading maizes, for instance, that rejoice in such names as Bloody Butcher, Gila Indian, Aunt Mary's Sweet, Extra Early Adams and Pencil Cob. Enthusiasts can join clubs, such as the Seed Savers Exchange, to swap their heirloom varieties.

Some gene banks are in commercial hands, and so subject to vagaries of profit and loss. The only world collection of banana germplasm, for instance, is owned by United Brands – who are closing it down, as an unwarranted expense. Others are poorly or unsuitably housed: the world's only collection of the 250 major wheat races occupies a small North Carolina shop, sandwiched between a restaurant and a hardware store – fire in either could destroy it. The US official seed bank is sited between a nuclear reactor and a munitions factory!

Good gene banks cost a lot; most of the money and effort in gene conservation – about $50 million worldwide annually – goes into ex-situ, not in-situ, conservation. But the international community surely needs to upgrade them, establish new ones, and safeguard their resources. Perhaps we should place all seed banks under the auspices of the United Nations. Even governments may cut expenditure, and political upheavals of any kind may spell disaster.

Who Owns the Genes?

Quite suddenly, it seems, those who control and cultivate world food crops are realising that all is not as it should be. In attempts to improve existing crop varieties, breeders seek land races and weed relations which contain the biggest potential, or often the biggest safety net – only to find that the new seeds of the past few years, the modern ways of cultivation, have removed immense numbers of them from the earth forever.

Even so, many old strains remain with us. Some are now lodged in gene banks or in reserves; some still exist in the wild, and should be sought out. But just who do the genes belong to? For example, in the 1960s, wheat crops in North America were attacked by the deadly disease Stripe Rust. Breeding from wild wheat found in Turkey produced new strains resistant to the rust, so that yields were not just maintained but increased. The US Department of Agriculture has estimated its resulting annual saving at $3

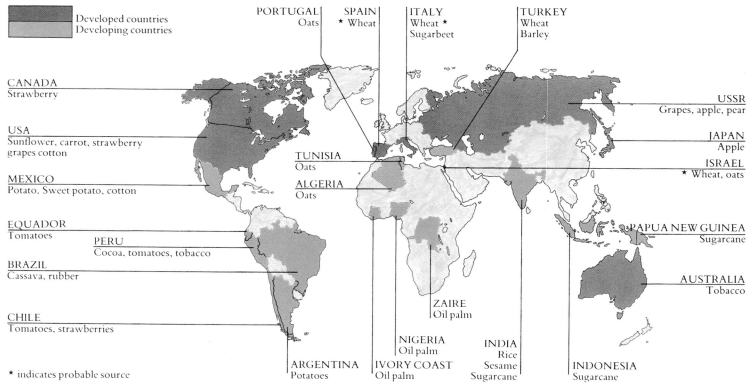

Developed countries
Developing countries

PORTUGAL
Oats

SPAIN
★ Wheat

ITALY
Wheat ★
Sugarbeet

TURKEY
Wheat
Barley

CANADA
Strawberry

USSR
Grapes, apple, pear

USA
Sunflower, carrot, strawberry
grapes cotton

JAPAN
Apple

TUNISIA
Oats

ISRAEL
★ Wheat, oats

MEXICO
Potato, Sweet potato, cotton

ALGERIA
Oats

EQUADOR
Tomatoes

PERU
Cocoa, tomatoes, tobacco

PAPUA NEW GUINEA
Sugarcane

BRAZIL
Cassava, rubber

CHILE
Tomatoes, strawberries

AUSTRALIA
Tobacco

ZAIRE
Oil palm

NIGERIA
Oil palm

INDIA
Rice
Sesame
Sugarcane

ARGENTINA
Potatoes

IVORY COAST
Oil palm

INDONESIA
Sugarcane

★ indicates probable source

Sources of Wild Germplasm used in Crop Improvement

Some experts have stated that the rich countries – the North – are relatively gene-poor while the developing countries – call them South or Third World – are gene-rich. They argue that the North is stealing from the South, because they can afford the research and have more expertise.

However, an opposing analysis suggests that this is not quite the case. Of the top 20 world crops which have been improved with wild germplasm, three have wild gene pools entirely in developing countries and 12 mostly there, the latter including vital foods – Rice, Maize and Potato. Two come mostly from developed countries and three – the very important Wheat, Soya Bean and Sugar Beet – are evenly split between the two areas.

It is clear that the North is somewhat dependent on the South in respect of valuable genes, and Third World countries certainly think in these terms, creating a situation which has aroused a great deal of acrimonious discussion and, indeed, political action.

million. But Turkey has not been paid for its wild wheat genes. Or has it? Since 1970, when the improved wheats were made available to Turkey, their cultivation there has doubled yields; farmers have received more cash, the Turkish government has presumably benefited from profit taxes, and more people have been fed.

Other examples include wild cherry material, collected in northern China, which has virtually resuscitated the cherry industry in Britain, and wild lucerne material, collected in Libya quite recently, which one Australian breeder has said is worth millions to the country's livestock industry.

Some countries are already creating administrative obstacles to foreign botanical collecting teams. Mexico has actually banned the collection of most wild plants, and Ethiopia has legislation to stop coffee germ plasm leaving the country. At least 55 percent of all Third World crop genetic resources in storage are housed by the developing nations. The germplasm has been sent on the assumption that it will be freely exchanged; but this is not necessarily the case, and many countries limit flow. The reliance on the germplasm of other lands has been described by the US Department of Agriculture as serious and potentially dangerous to the welfare of the nation: the US considers all germplasm it receives for safe-keeping as federal property. Where such an attitude prevails, transfer to hostile or intractable regimes could be withheld. Sadly germplasm is a new weapon with political clout. Already the political situation in Libya and Afghanistan has resulted in wheat genes originating in those countries (and now no longer to be found there), being withheld from breeders there.

Large companies are buying up seed firms so that they may each control large numbers of breeding and distribution arrangements. Ten major companies now control a third of all the cereal cultivars listed by the OECD. In 1983, Shell controlled 68 seed firms directly and 3 indirectly which market seeds in Europe, North and Latin America, and large parts of Africa: it is now the biggest seed company in the world.

Less profitable varieties in the seed lists of the seed firms bought up can be lost for ever, despite their genetic potential. These varieties are often those best suited to limited areas of cultivation.

The involvement of large seed companies in pesticide and herbicide manufacture has led to concern that they might stop trying to incorporate genes for resistance against diseases, eelworms etc. into crops, and then direct customers to their own-brand pesticides when disease threatens. They might furthermore design seeds so that only their own-brand chemicals are effective: others could even be toxic to the crop. At the very least, they might offer the farmers packages of seeds and chemicals, thus encouraging heavy use of pesticides. Credit, and cultivation facilities like irrigation, may also be linked to the use of specific seeds, when offered to the farmers by Third World governments who deal with these companies.

One result of such package deals is the coated seed. A disturbing example is that of grain sorghum marketed by one of Ciba-Geigy's seedsmen: it is coated in three chemicals, two of which protect against grass invasion and the third against Ciba-Geigy's own herbicide "Dual", which is toxic to sorghum. Apart from such extraordinary situations, there is always the danger that in times of famine, seed grain gets eaten – and if it is coated those who eat it will join the 10,000 peasants who die from pesticides each year, or the 375,000 who become ill from their misuse.

Plant Breeders' Rights (PBR), or plant patents, have been in force since the 1930s, and have now been established in some 25 countries. They allow plant breeders to obtain royalties, either from seeds they have produced or from plants themselves. It seems reasonable that years of careful research and breeding should be rewarded, but the potential damage against the genetic resource is unfortunately considerable. Minor varieties are ignored, because PBR demands a unique factor in the new cultivar. This also works against the production of "multi-lines", strains which are uniform and stable but have enough intrinsic variability in matters like disease resistance to be preferable to a single strain. One cannot patent a multi-line, only its components, which is very expensive and seldom done.

Further, many grow-outs needed regularly by gene banks are handled by commercial firms. In this way, unfamiliar genes are in effect offered to commercial breeders to assess. Seed from grow-outs, and also from International Agricultural Research Centres, has undoubtedly been purloined, grown on and patented by seed firms, with no credit or payment.

PBR is difficult to police. Some traditional cultivars and some land races have certainly been patented in developed countries and, as they stand, the PBR laws encourage such poaching. Even entire botanical species can be "protected" in this way so that, for instance, a deep-coloured heliotrope has, after selection from the offspring of collected seed, been granted PBR with the result that Guatemala now cannot export this quite common wild flower to the US.

Whoever owns the genes, whether copyright or common heritage, they are a precious resource and need conservation *now*.

Annihilation of forest by fire, practised all too frequently, kills every living thing and exposes the soil to erosion

Saving the Plants that Save Us

Not long after the Pilgrims had landed in North America in 1620, an early traveller described riding across prairies where "the strawberries grew so thick that their horses' fetlocks seemed covered in blood". What an evocation of an all but virgin land! A land whose bounty the Indians used so lightly that it regenerated when they had passed. Today only about one percent of the prairies remains as the settlers found it.

The world's natural vegetation is in deep trouble, and with it the soil that sustains humanity. The major cause of this ruination is "the paving over, digging up, ploughing under, overgrazing, chopping down, poisoning, flooding, burying, blasting and trampling of natural ecosystems". And the agents are people – ever-increasing population, with the consequent spread of habitations and the other human appurtenances like roads (cities are expanding and fertile ground disappearing at a rate of 65,000 sq km per year), the need for food and all the other demands we make – for firewood, for animal fodder, for raw materials – plus a good deal of sheer greed.

Much emphasis has been placed on the tropical rainforests. In their amazingly complex ecosystems, the plant and animal life is unique. They may contain as many as half the world's stock of species. Many of us still think of the rainforests as huge, inviolable and everlasting. Alas, they are perhaps the most fragile, easily ruined ecosystems on planet earth. Not long ago they covered 1160 million hectares. They are now being cut, burned or chemically defoliated at the rate of roughly 11.4 million hectares annually, which is 21.6 hectares every minute – every year an area the size of the British Isles. Estimates as to their potential survival vary from 20 to at most 50 years, if this destruction continues unabated.

In some areas the situation is even more acute. Brazil's Atlantic rainforest, which extended about 2300 km in the nineteenth century, is reduced to a number of totally separate fragments, covering not more than 2 percent of its former area; it is now the subject of major international rescue efforts. And nearly all the lowland forests of peninsular Malaysia and the Philippines are likely to be logged by 1990. Twenty years ago, who would have predicted that the rain forests of the world, once symbolic of remote places, would be in danger? The speed of loss is incredible.

The motive for destruction may be timber extraction – the demand for tropical hardwoods shows no signs of diminishing, let alone that for wood

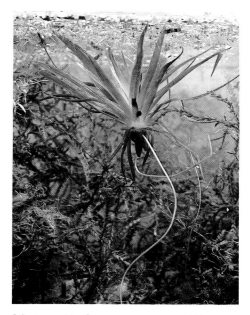

Most aquatic plants are very susceptible to chemicals and very low pH due to acid rain. Water Soldier (Stratiodes aloides) is one such plant; it inhabits ponds and ditches, sinking to the bottom in its winter resting period, probably by accumulating calcium carbonatein in the rosetted leaves. A local plant, it is diminishing in many parts of its range in Europe and North-west Asia because of drainage and water pollution.

chips for paper, board, and chipboard – or clearance for cattle-ranching grassland, or crops of various kinds, including trees. Even if forest is logged and left, regeneration of secondary growth is of indifferent life quality: the trees of the mature forest may not grow again, if only because their seeds have very short viability, and it has proved almost impossible to nurture and plant out most of these trees of ancient lineage.

Island floras are particularly vulnerable. In Madagascar 80 percent of original rainforest cover has already vanished. To blame are slash-and-burn agriculture, frequently resulting in uncontrollable fires (quite often deliberately allowed to go as far as possible), plus unbridled exploitation of trees and forest products. On smaller islands, human activities and the depredations of various animals – many of them introduced, either accidentally or deliberately for food, like goats (as on so many of the Galapagos Islands) – cause ever-increasing destruction of the often tiny populations of rare endemic plants. The situation is so grave that on one island, Rodrigues (near Mauritius, Indian Ocean), all but two of the 34 endemic plants are extinct or endangered. Exotic plant species, introduced for whatever reason, also endanger native flora. Galapagos, Juan Fernandez, Seychelles, St Helena, Mauritius, New Caledonia, Hawaii – all are threatened.

Of course the rainforests and the island floras are not the only great natural systems at risk. Many northern woodlands have been turned into long-term tree monocultures, while the savannas of the African Sahel countries have ecosystems as fragile as the rainforest.

Natural meadow and prairie are becoming rare: there is hardly any meadowland left in Britain – it has either been made rich for grazing and poor for plant life by fertilisers, or has been ploughed up for crops. Hedgerows, admittedly "artificial", have largely been swept away, and with them a wonderful flora and fauna familiar only a generation back. There are still primroses in Britain, but how few they have become. Drainage of marshes and wet grasslands for agricultural improvement irrevocably destroys a further range of temperate flora. And prairies are replaced in North America by endless, enormous, cereal fields.

Even where forests are left more or less alone, the lesser plants they share the ground with can readily be overgrazed or overexploited. The contraceptive-producing yam is almost extinct in the once forested Himalayas, the fabled ginseng endangered in China.

In areas which have long been cultivated in traditional ways, modern methods, machines and herbicides wipe out wild "weeds" and, more importantly for our own future, antique land races and ancestors associated with crops.

The world's coastlines and estuaries are vulnerable too. Algal beds, coral reefs and coastal estuaries provide vital hatcheries of fish, crustaceans and molluscs; but we take too little care of them. The dredging of shipping lanes completely alters the sea bed; silt from eroded lands damages reefs, smothering the fragile coral; sewage leads to blooms of marine algae which consume all the oxygen in the water. The 9 million tonnes of sewage from New York and New Jersey dumped each year have degraded all marine life over a horrifying 12,000 sq km.

Even the valuable mangroves, which not only protect tropical coasts but also nurse rich fisheries, fare no better. It has been plainly demonstrated that fish and prawn production in the vicinity of mangrove belts diminish greatly if they are removed. Yet throughout the tropics mangroves are in danger – from refuse and solid wastes often dumped in swamps, from river silt, mine wastes, sewage and chemical effluents, and from oil discharged by ships. Vast areas are being destroyed, either intentionally or as a secondary result of other activities. The largest single cause of destruction is clear-felling, usually for fuelwood.

All over the world the pressures on wild plants, and more especially on large areas of natural vegetation, mount literally week by week. Too often their removal is carried out with no planning for maintenance of the denuded soil, with the result that we are soon faced with terrain which is either infertile, over-steep, too wet or too dry, or simply has no topsoil to sustain any plants at all, let alone useful ones. The consequences of such mismanagement are often irreversible. In the next few years we shall surely see a series of ecological catastrophes.

It has been estimated that some 25,000 plant species – a tenth of the plants of the world – may be dangerously rare or already under threat of extinction. This is a conservative estimate: if present trends continue, as many as 40,000 species may be lost before the middle of the next century.

So far 15,000 of the threatened species have been catalogued. It is encouraging that, since 1970, most developed countries have prepared lists of their threatened plants in their famous Red Data Books, as a guide and stimulus to action; it is less encouraging that few have done much to implement these gloomy findings. There is a tremendous role here for volunteers and activists, taking action at local level to save their own wild plants and natural heritage.

But the hard fact is that in most tropical countries, especially those with rain forest, it is usually not possible even to identify individual threatened species. The plants are too numerous, too scattered in distribution and too little known. In some cases they will become extinct before we even know they were endangered. Here the emphasis has to be on identifying not the threatened species but the sites where the most species can be saved.

One scientist estimates that for every plant species made extinct, up to 10 to 30 other non-plant organisms may go with it. They depend on the plants for food, or some part of their life cycle (as indeed many plants depend upon animals). Large-scale forest or grassland destruction wipes out literally thousands of animal species of every type, large and small. Conservationists have mostly publicised the dangers of the extinction of large, picturesque animals – the panda, the tiger and the polar bear, for example. It is time to realise that every living creature depends on a habitat which is primarily constructed by plants. Today we see these ecosystems being diminished, degraded or, more usually, utterly destroyed. The rates of destruction and extinction are unprecedented in evolutionary history. In previous "extinction spasms" species are estimated to have disappeared at the rate of perhaps one in 1000 years. In 1980, some scientists have estimated, the loss rate was at least one species a day; by 1990 the projected loss rate has been put at possibly one species an hour, if destruction is not halted.

In a mere 10,000 years or so we have succeeded in ruining the equilibrium of a major part of our own habitat – ruination now accelerating, apparently quite out of hand.

The King River in Tasmania has been severely polluted by the effluents from copper mining in Queenswood. Aquatic plants are particularly susceptible to copper, which is in fact used to control blanketweed and other algae in ornamental pools. Like most pollution, such occurrences could be prevented by adequate control measures – but industry generally considers that these cost too much to be undertaken.

Of course, changes are a part of life: as the poet Oliver St John Gogarty put it, "Everything changes/Time deranges/Men and women/And mountain ranges...". But Gogarty was contemplating past millenia, when life forms had the chance and the time to adjust by the processes of evolution; they no longer do.

There is a deep-seated feeling among people that nature is ever bountiful and land ever plentiful. The less favoured, desperate simply to keep alive, can be forgiven for looking little further than their noses. But the first-worlders seem also extraordinarily reluctant to face facts. A flight over Toronto, to choose just one modern city, will demonstrate the lavishness of highways and enormous flyover junctions, while a run along the Queen Elizabeth Highway from Toronto to Niagara shows how the absence of legal constraint has resulted in ribbon development and a considerable loss of some of the area's most fertile land.

Much of the destruction borders on the irrational. It has indeed been called subsidised vandalism. There seems to be something irresistible about the chainsaw. Away from forests, power machinery is equally damaging to vegetation: often, work is carried out (on drainage projects, for instance), simply to keep the machines employed. The impact of machinery on the world's wildlife in the past century, and most of all in the last 20–30 years, has to be compared with the greatest cataclysms of the geological past.

The species of plants being extinguished by our activities today represent the genetic heritage of aeons; their going represents biological massacre. The destruction of forests and other natural habitats stops evolution dead in its tracks. "Of the events in the 1980s," as Dr E. O. Wilson has said, "the one our descendants will most regret is not limited nuclear war, nor energy depletion, nor economic collapse, but the loss of genetic and species diversity." Because this loss will take millions of years to compensate for – longer, perhaps, than the span of humanity itself.

Polluting the Air

It has been recognised for a considerable time that factory chimney effluents are capable of damaging vegetation severely, but the effects have usually been considered relatively local. Today it is abundantly clear that this is not so – the effects can range far afield. The words "acid rain" are now in common usage; they describe the damaging, polluted rainfall which results from the emission of sulphur dioxide from chimneys and nitrogen oxides from vehicles. In the air, these form sulphuric and nitric acids; and winds can carry them hundreds of miles, to fall as rain.

The acidity of this rain is commonly around pH 4.6 – the same as orange juice; but levels of pH 2.0 – stronger than vinegar – have been recorded.

Scandinavian countries have known for over a decade that acid rain, blown from Britain across the North Sea, is making their lakes so acid that there are now no fish in many of them. All aquatic life is affected by the damage inflicted on freshwater plants, particularly in those freshwater lakes and rivers on granite. Such waters, naturally low in mineral nutrients, (especially calcium), have no buffer resistance for acid rain; the increased acidity quickly makes them unsuitable for a wide range of organisms.

Only crustose lichens if any
Heavy pollution (150 units)

Crustose lichens and a few foliose lichens (70-125 units pollution)

Lichen flora increasing
60 units pollution

Beard lichens occasionally found
Pollution low (40-50 units)

Rich lichen flora
35 units pollution

25 species plus on large trees
Pure air (under 30 units pollution)

Lichens are unique in being composed of two organisms, algae and fungi, which form a close symbiotic association: the fungus greatly benefits by the alga's ability to produce chlorophyll and thus to photosynthesise. In return fungal tissue protects the alga from intense light, drought and heat. Together they are able to colonise harsh environments. But lichens' efficient absorption mechanisms make them highly susceptible to contamination – especially sulphur dioxide. Their presence or absence is therefore a useful indicator of atmospheric quality. The map shows increasing lichen-richness away from industrialised areas. The unit of pollution is the mean winter level of sulphur dioxide in microgrammes per cubic metre of air.

Lecanora conizaeoides

Pannaria rubiginosa

Parmelia caperata

Teloschistes chrysophelmus

*Around this hamlet in the north of Kordofan
Province, Sudan, all trees except the leafless
baobabs have been cleared for firewood. The
baobabs may survive, for they have very
extensive horizontal root systems which will
glean any available surface moisture; but in
principle the area is in an advanced state of
desertification. The need for firewood,
coupled with the rapacity of grazing
animals, are the main causes of tree
destruction in many arid areas.*

Acid rain has damaged large tracts of forest in Norway and Sweden and in the Black Forest, Germany, where the proportion of damaged trees rose from 8 to 34 percent in 1982-3. Los Angeles smog has killed or damaged over a million of the Ponderosa Pines in the surrounding forests. Governments generally are unwilling to lose tax revenue by enforcing remedial measures on the perpetrators: industrial chimneys and the motor car.

Acid rain apparently attacks tree foliage directly, and then has a further effect on the soil: the sulphates in the rain bind with essential plant nutrients in the soil, such as calcium and magnesium, which then link up with water and leach away – becoming unavailable to roots. Magnesium deficiency causes leaf yellowing, and eventually acute poisoning sets in from aluminium, manganese and other elements which inhibit the division of cells in the roots of trees, so exposing them to disease pathogens. Tree death occurs through a combination of starvation, disease and poisoning.

Atmosphere is further polluted by forest burning. Some parts of Brazil have atmospheric conditions resembling those of Los Angeles because the smoke of burning trees produces photochemical reactions exactly like those of industrial smog.

Desertification

Besides the problems of pollution, there are the other effects on atmosphere which were outlined in Chapter 2. Destruction of forest and vegetation cover is at the basis of a scenario of eventual doom, due either to the warming up the globe because of too much carbon dioxide in the air (the "greenhouse" effect) or to the cooling "albedo" effect of greater reflection of solar radiation, due directly to less vegetation cover.

What is abundantly clear is that the destruction of forest, and corresponding reduction in water vapour transpired, reduces the amount of rainfall in a given area in an often drastic manner. The effects just mentioned must almost certainly induce large-scale climatic change.

One of the places where this appears to be occurring is the northern part of Africa, especially the Sahel belt including the countries of Mauritania, Chad, Niger, Mali, Senegal, the Gambia and Upper Volta. The southern edge of the Sahara desert has in recent years crept southwards; rainfall has decreased and in particular been much less regular, often arriving unseasonally and even missing whole years. The desertification here has been accelerated by human activities – with famine, hardship, and the disruption of wars and refugees all playing a role.

Lands become unnaturally barren in several ways. If too many animals are put on sparse rangelands – not only cattle but goats and thorn-relishing camels – they destroy the plant growth, except a few remnants of inedible scrub, and trample the soil into dust. Coupled with this shortage of forage is shortage of fuelwood, so people strip and cut down trees in ever-widening circles from their settlements. Such activity allows eventual loss of topsoil, due to wind and the occasional torrential downpour which causes a sheet of water to move across flat areas (this is known as sheet erosion).

Another certain way is by ploughing up and down steep slopes without terracing; this puts the topsoil at risk in heavy rain. Slopes over 35 percent should not be cultivated without special protective measures. And, further, barrenness can follow in the wake of ill-conceived irrigation schemes which deposit salts, and create a saline wasteland.

Desertification as a result of vegetation destruction without replanting is occurring in many places; some on the edge of existing natural deserts like the Sahara, others creating new arid lands. Land totally, incapable of supporting life, now covers 6 percent of the land surface; arid lands with less than 250 mm rainfall per year, and semi-arid ones with 250-600 mm rainfall (FAO definitions) account for 14 percent. A recent United Nations Environment Programme survey suggests that a third of the earth's surface is in danger of gross degradation or desertification within the next 75 years; 470 million people living in these arid zones – over 10 percent of world population – are at present badly undernourished or actually starving.

Present-day desertification, and indeed destruction of natural vegetation in general, worldwide, are inextricably tied up with the apparently inexorable increase in population. The population bomb, first defined by Malthus in 1821, is still ticking implacably.

There is more than enough food produced worldwide to feed everyone, but at present enough food aid is most certainly not reaching most of the 800 million destitute. And as long as people are destitute they will, as in Africa, continue their reliance on local resources or, as in Amazonia, lay waste to primary forest in order plant subsistence crops, while those better off try to raise cash from beef cattle, Oil Palms, or Bananas.

It seems that the world's population will at least double in the next century or so; if the UN estimate of 30 percent degradation of the land is true, how many more will then be destitute? Developed countries have got their growth rate down to about 1 percent or below; in most of the Third World it is between 2 and 3.5 percent, reaching a peak in Kenya of 4.4 percent. Birthrate can be reduced: the Chinese now have the rule of one child per family, while in Thailand less draconian control has cut the growth rate from 3 to 2 percent.

I hold the strongest possible view that a massive reduction in the rate of growth of the population is a prerequisite for adequate comfort and nourishment and the conservation of what is left of our green inheritance.

Solutions

There are two main approaches to saving plant cover, both urgently needed. The first is to halt degradation and rehabilitate land already damaged, so those who live there can continue to use it. The second is to conserve as much as possible of the remaining natural vegetation – not just as a living museum, but as a resource which can provide for the future.

Some remedies to prevent degradation are glaringly obvious. Protecting the air from factory effluents is simply a matter of installing filters; it can be done – at a cost. Protecting water is, equally, an expensive matter of curbing the dumping of untreated effluents and oil.

In poor countries suffering desertification, the solutions are again obvious in principle. Trees and other growth can be protected by reducing the number of grazing animals, or by fencing in areas for new plantation or

Franklinia alatamaha, above, found once by the Alatamaha river in Georgia, now survives only in cultivation.

The African Violet (Saintpaulia ionantha, below) symbolises WWF's international plant conservation efforts because it is severely threatened in its East African jungle home, a habitat of steep rock surfaces in dense shade endangered by forest clearance.

regeneration. To stop erosion on slopes, if cultivation terraces are too difficult to create, the simplest remedy is to plough along contours, and dam gullies to trap water in heavy rain. Sheet erosion can be prevented by ridges as little as 20 cm high across gentle slopes, while a semi-circular ridge on the downhill side of newly planted trees traps water, and greatly increases their chances of survival.

Reafforestation, by the planting of seedling trees after clear-felling, is an accepted part of the logging cycle in industrialised countries, but is seldom practised with tropical forests. Holders of felling concessions may complain that their leases of only 15-20 years are too short to provide incentive, but in fact most foreign logging companies like to extract timber as fast as possible and get out. Some of these exploiters seem now to be developing a conscience; the Japanese, who have now over-exploited South-east Asian forests, have proposed a regulatory organisation which would channel funds and expertise into reafforestation and all aspects of forest management. The loggers are not solely to blame; timber rights are let to the highest bidder, without control or direction for reinstatement by governments forced to take short-term actions to satisfy immediate human needs – food, shelter, water.

In some places, selective logging has been a deliberate policy in the expectation that this would not harm forests materially, and would allow them to regenerate. In practice it is impossible to avoid severe damage overall; even if only a few large trees are taken here and there, the trails needed for getting at them and pulling them out open up remote parts of forests to poaching and illegal exploitation of trees and minerals, which is equally destructive. Some tropical trees are known to suspend their growth for up to 20 years if disturbed: no-one yet knows why, or how. Any removal of trees alters the species complement of the forest, which is almost always detrimental in the long term. In principle such disturbance ruins tropical moist forest.

Tree plantations are an obvious improvement for logged or otherwise degraded land, and many countries have schemes in operation; the Chinese government, for instance, funds the growing of young trees in nurseries, and their distribution, and local people then plant and tend them.

It is expected that 17 million hectares of plantation will be established in the tropics by the end of 1985 – though deforestation at the current rate will exceed this by ten to one. Many kinds of trees are used including arid-tolerant Acacia species in savannas, notably *A. albida*. Eucalyptus are the classic fast growers, but Lamtoro (*Leucaena leucocephala*) is now a serious contender. It grows very rapidly to a height of 20 metres and each hectare can produce 30-40 cubic metres of biomass a year. Out of the 42 million hectares in Indonesia needing re-greening, Lamtoro is reported to have rehabilitated 3.7 million hectares in four years. Its merits include controlling erosion and resisting drought; providing forage, firewood of high fuel value, timber, windbreaks and shade; and improving the soil (being leguminous it has nitrogen-fixing bacteria on the roots). Despite all such merits, plantation trees are much less efficient than big forest trees in producing oxygen and, more importantly, transpire only from one-tenth to one-fifteenth as much water, so rainfall in replanted areas, though it will improve, will never be as much as over rainforests.

Parks and Reserves

By far the biggest threat to plants is that the habitats in which they grow – rainforest, desert, savanna – are themselves in danger. So a top priority is to build a network of protected areas – national parks and nature reserves – covering representative samples of the best habitat types. These will protect populations of species and also serve for scientific and historical study – future generations will only have these to appraise. They may be the only areas of true wilderness left on earth.

Above all they will protect wild genetic resources, which, as we have seen throughout this book, are so important to human welfare. The present view of conservation is a change in emphasis from conservation for its own sake to conservation for the benefit of people. Conservation bodies such as WWF are now making special efforts to safeguard plants used by people, whether or not these enter the monetary economy of governments. In so doing, it is hoped such conservation will also support those peoples that still live in harmony with their environment, with their invaluable knowledge, and maintain habitats for the innumerable animals that would otherwise vanish with the plants.

Below *The lower reaches of the Gordon and Franklin rivers have been in the news, as the Tasmanian government had plans to flood this area of considerable biological and archaeological importance. Conservationists were in uproar, especially as the area had been declared a World Heritage site, nominated by the Australian federal government for protection under the Unesco World Heritage Convention. TV botanist David Bellamy was incarcerated for his protest – to good effect as the dam was eventually banned. This area is one of the last remaining temperate rain forests, dominated by Southern Beech (Nothofagus). Two-thirds of the island's endemic plants live there and 18 species would have been threatened if the scheme had gone ahead. Among these is the Huon Pine (Dacrydium franklinii) – 35 percent of its habitat would have been flooded.*

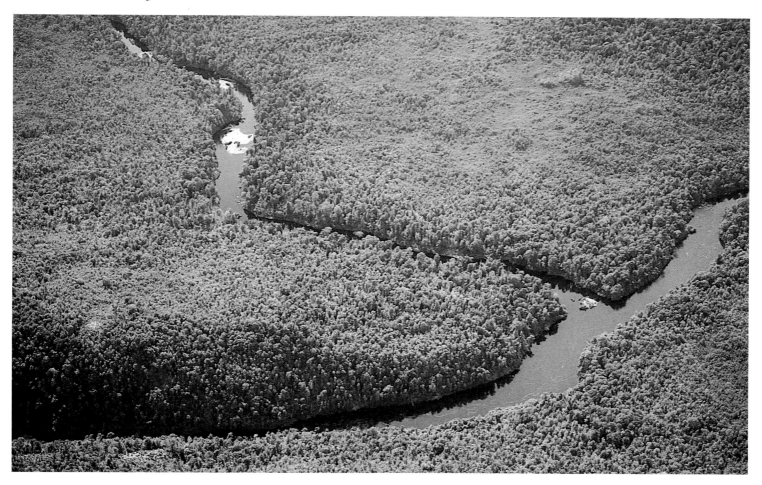

Along with this is a recognition that conservation organisations, with limited funds, can achieve most not by concentrating on a single species, but by focusing on a type of habitat, like the rainforest. Because vegetation is being lost so fast and because of the sheer number of species threatened, it is neither possible nor sensible to plan a reserve for each species.

Clearly a priority is to find those areas with the most diversity, and protect them. Setting up one big rainforest reserve could alone save hundreds, if not thousands, of species. In some cases, the areas are those believed to have been the refugia of tropical vegetation during the late Pleistocene era, when much drier conditions than today's affected the tropics, and the forest retreated into small pockets which became centres of species-making. In the Amazon basin, for example, Brazil has based its protected area plan upon studies of these Pleistocene refugia, which are the chosen areas for the big parks Brazil is creating. Yet the impressive total of 10 m hectares declared in Brazil is only 1.2 percent of that vast country. Conservationists' targets are nearer 10 percent.

In some cases a single species acts as symbol and rallying point for a whole programme of habitat conservation. Project Tiger, which WWF-India supported with a major campaign, led not only to an increase in tigers from about 1800 to over 3000 but, even more important, to a revitalising of India's protected areas network, with benefits to all the numerous plants and animals with which the tiger shared its habitat. Building on this, the Indian Government is planning an ambitious programme to create a further network of large reserves, covering perhaps the last great areas of natural vegetation. These areas will continue to provide a home for tribal people, but gross modification, such as clear-felling by outside contractors, will be forbidden. The participation of local people in management, education and training should make the Indian project a model for other countries.

Many of the threatened Indian plants occur in plots of vegetation too small for habitat reserves. For them, conservationists in India are planning to invite caretakers – schools, colleges, botanic gardens and even village *panchayats* – to look after enhancing public awareness of the need for conservation.

Yet it has to be realised that the creation of protected areas is principally a means of buying time. There cannot be effective conservation in the middle of over-populated, poverty-stricken and largely hungry agricultural communities; the pressures and temptations are too great when protected areas become lush – but forbidden – pockets of vegetation, in a sea of degraded and transformed land.

Concerned at this development, enlightened park chiefs are changing their tactics. They understand that in developing countries, meeting human needs – food, health and shelter – has to be the primary goal. Rather than set the area aside, they want to protect it so that its benefits continue to radiate out into the surrounding countryside – migrating meat for the pot, fresh water in the streams, markets for local handicrafts. A key concept is that of the buffer zone, a broad and fuzzy edge between the park and the neighbourhood; here people could get firewood and wild fruits, graze limited numbers of cattle, and perhaps gather medicinal herbs – many Africans feel that saving their valued medicinal plants is perhaps the best justification of all for having national parks.

Ever since the United States declared Yellowstone National Park in 1872, parks have been created all over the world. In the decade between 1972 and 1982, major protected areas, excluding the smallest, rose from 212 million hectares to around 386 million hectares – an impressive 55 percent increase. Yet this covers only a small proportion of the earth's surface, at a time when vegetation is being destroyed faster than ever before. It is a race against time: most areas will have to be declared before the 1990s – after that it will be too late in many parts of the world. The timescale for global conservation is as short as that.

Desperately needed are the skills and resources to create and manage protected areas, and to implement the still very new concepts, of the park in harmony with its neighbourhood, and making a contribution to national development. Worldwide, park managers form a community of conservationists who have perhaps the most important and urgent job of all. Money is important, but trained and skilled manpower is even more vital. One of the characteristics of the conservation movement is how one persistent person on the ground can safeguard an area far better than any intervention from outside or any passing interest. Intelligence, persistence and above all enthusiasm – with these one can work miracles.

The Place of Botanic Gardens

There are about 600 botanic gardens around the world, and they have an important job in certain aspects of plant conservation. As far as the public goes, these gardens, many near large towns, are the only places where large numbers of people can see exotic and unfamiliar plants. They are ideal places to tell the public about conservation and what people can do to help, especially where gardens have museums and exhibition centres. They should be the shop windows of plant conservation.

These institutions can undertake rescue operations to places with many threatened endemics, where habitat conservation is difficult or impossible, like Socotra and Somalia, and bring examples of the plants into cultivation. Botanic gardens can save seeds in gene banks, nurture plants which cannot be cold-stored, and increase stocks of endangered species. Ideally every rare and endangered plant should be cultivated in at least one garden, and their genetic material be in at least one seed bank; that is a minimum. With modern methods of propagation, like meristem and tissue culture, endangered plants can be increased for dissemination to other gardens. Perhaps even more important with specially desirable ornamental plants, commercial markets can be flooded with specimens at low prices which will undercut the trade in wild-collected, often poached plants. Gardens can equally introduce, propagate and disseminate plants of economic importance. Currently there are several efforts underway to co-ordinate botanic gardens as the ex-situ network for threatened plants and to encourage them to take up this new role.

Experts can correlate existing strategies for conservation and regeneration, and experiment in new ones. Well co-ordinated data-collecting methods will vastly increase information capacity, as botanic gardens communicate with each other and build up knowledge worldwide. In this

The ginkgos – primitive, deciduous conifer relations – came into being about a quarter-million years ago and fossils confirm their worldwide distribution. The present-day Maidenhair Tree (G. biloba), little changed from its ancestors, was last seen in the wild in the Tien-Mu range in China, but was re-introduced to the world in the eighteenth century from Chinese and Japanese temple gardens. It was grown for its unique foliage, stately growth habit and longevity, and also for its edible seeds. Now it is widely planted in parks and gardens and as a street tree in many North American towns. Mostly these are a narrow upright form known as "sentry" which, being male, have no fruits; but in some places female trees have been used and their malodorous seeds are a menace in autumn. In towns ginkgos put up with the aridity of pavement planting and severe air pollution with such tolerance to inimical conditions it is a mystery why they almost became extinct.

connection, one should not underestimate the existing storehouse of plant species in public and private gardens.

Already botanic gardens hold around 3000 of the 15,000 or so listed threatened plants. Even a few species believed extinct – like the toromiro, Easter Island's only tree – have turned up in botanic garden collections, their unique value not appreciated until recently.

A Final Word

Ahead of us is one of the most difficult tasks which we have ever faced – comparable with that of avoiding a nuclear holocaust. Nations need to agree, and act together to curb the unbridled destruction of remaining tracts of natural vegetation – stop it altogether if possible. It will be a hard struggle indeed for people of such different needs, wishes, outlooks and backgrounds all jostling with their own points of view – let alone for politicians, who seem never to consider any moment but the present. But if the destruction continues unabated, the earth will become largely covered first with crop plants and then, probably, barren lands, and no-one has ventured to predict what this might do to the life-support system of planet earth and the future well-being of its inhabitants.

The pragmatic new attitude of international conservation efforts, such as those of the WWF and International Union for Conservation of Nature, towards plants as resources must surely make governments think again about conservation. We are making a start towards saving plant life – Saving the Plants that Save us.

Few will deny that there *is* a moral issue here: a simple enough axiom that we should not, for our own immediate comfort and gain, destroy plant life so wantonly and with so little thought for the future. For ourselves, and how much more for our descendants, there is a high need to leave something at least of the world we inherited, its plants and the animals they support, for the future to comprehend, enjoy and benefit from.

It is surely possible for us now to strike a balance. Technologically we have the means. It is incredible, really, to consider that so many billions of dollars are being spent on space research, that we know more about the moon than some parts of the Amazonian forests. Is it not time to divert some of these scientific and financial resources to our biosphere? The stars will still be there in 20 years time; tropical forests will not.

We now have the technological capacity to plant those land areas already modified for agriculture with sufficient crops, of every conceivable kind, to feed, house, and clothe everyone well – making it unnecessary to destroy what remains of natural vegetation. Besides thus providing for our physical needs, plants can also provide solace for the mind. They are endlessly fascinating, exciting, wonderful – even fabulous is not too strong a word, and they are diversely beautiful too. And this fascination is greatest when one can see plants interacting with each other in the intricate web of life which botanists call an ecosystem, adapting themselves to every habitable niche on the earth's surface.

It is surely time we sealed a non-aggression pact with these remarkable planet-sharers and lived with them in a harmonious relationship.

Facing page *Harmony of nature and human needs, as in these Balinese rice fields, is something we must aim for all over the world.*

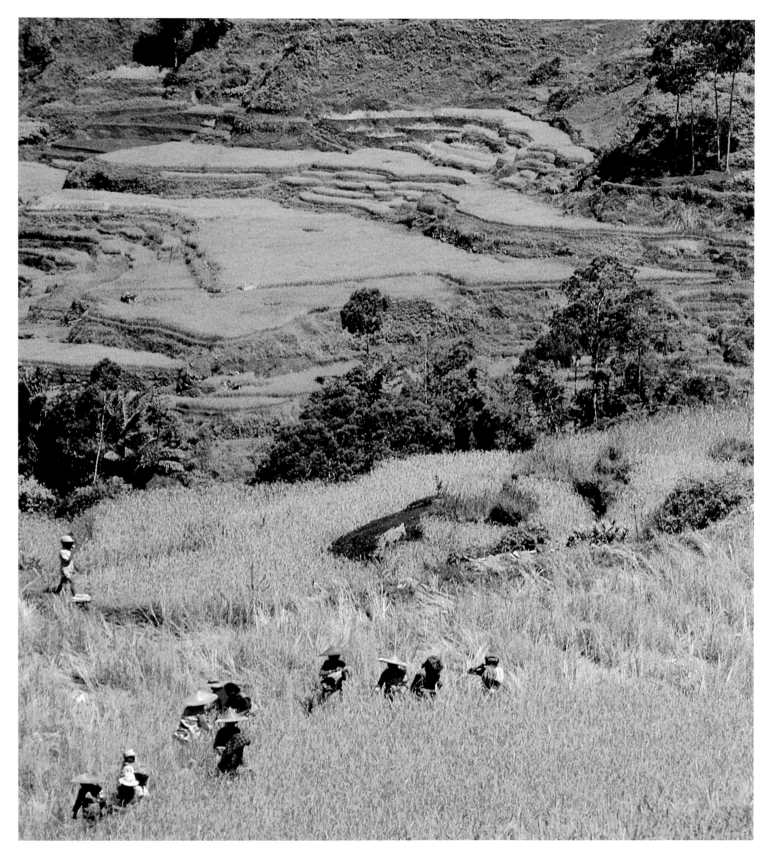

The WWF/IUCN Plant Conservation Programme

We often forget just how important plants are. Individual plants feed our world, cure our ills, provide materials for industry, and enrich our spiritual lives. As vegetation, plants form the earth's soft green "security blanket" which protects fragile soils from erosion, regulates the atmosphere, maintains fresh water supplies for agriculture and prevents formation of deserts. Without plants, oxygen-breathing life could never have evolved on earth: without plants it cannot hope to persist.

Because many important and valuable wild plants and plant communities are endangered, WWF and the International Union for Conservation of Nature and Natural Resources (IUCN) have launched an international programme for plant conservation – to save the plants that save us. This book has been published as a part of that effort.

From March 1984 to September 1985, most of the 24 WWF National Affiliates will focus on plants. They will tell people about the importance and fascination of plants and explain how and why plants are now endangered. Many of the national WWFs are already running plant conservation programmes in their own countries. But the heart of the WWF system is the support WWF gives to conservation in the developing, mainly tropical, countries which, for the most part, cannot afford to implement conservation programmes or lack technical expertise. Yet it is here where the threats to plants are most acute.

This international plant conservation programme has six main objectives. The first is to build public awareness to help stimulate action by pressure on governments and industries, by citizen action, and – last, but not least – by encouraging donations. WWF will also attempt to reach beyond the countries of the 24 national WWF. They will support struggling citizen groups in developing countries and will work with the Scout Movement in preparing plant conservation projects for scouts. They plan to mount intensive 2 or 3 year awareness programmes in carefully selected countries where the main impediment to conservation is lack of understanding. And their news service will get the message out to TV, radio and press all over the world.

The second objective is to help build the capacity to conserve – to persuade other organizations to conserve plants. It is essential to provide them with the tools to do the job – not so much spades and jeeps but books and manuals incorporating the latest and most creative thinking, and above all information on what plants are threatened and where they grow. Only in this way can a 2–3 year programme have a continuing impact in the years to come. This programme includes projects to prepare a book on the principles of plant conservation, projects to promote training and projects to make better use of law in conserving plants.

The third objective is to promote the conservation of plant genetic resources – IUCN and WWF will work with organizations such as the International Board for Plant Genetic Resources (IBPGR) to prepare programmes for conserving *in-situ*, and thereby balance the major *ex-situ* programmes already underway. These include plans for *in-situ* gene banks in the plant-rich areas of Colombia, Ecuador, Peru and Bolivia, the homelands of many of our major crops.

The fourth objective is to promote the conservation of economic plants, in particular medicinal plants. Here WWF/IUCN will work with the World Health Organisation in planning a model programme to monitor, conserve and use sustainably the medicinal plants of a chosen country. The Programme includes support for IUCN's Conservation Monitoring Centre, which provides an international database and information service on all aspects of conservation, including plants. IUCN will expand its monitoring of the status of economic plants, in particular the medicinal plants and wild crop relatives which may disappear before we have explored their full potential.

The fifth objective is to boost the conservation work of the 600 or so botanic gardens around the world. WWF/IUCN will encourage them to be more active in conservation, try to ensure that every threatened plant is maintained in cultivation, and above all, assist the botanic gardens in more effectively telling their large publics about the need for conservation of plants.

The sixth objective, for which most of the funds are required, is support of plant conservation in 24 selected countries (IUCN and WWF cannot realistically mount projects all over the world). Most of the projects are to support and encourage the declaration of large protected areas, and to secure the future of those areas protected on paper but not yet on the ground. As examples of the former, WWF/IUCN are assisting in the establishment of 130,700 hectare Sapo National Park, Liberia's first park located in an untouched rain forest. They are supporting the creation of three massive parks in lowland Cameroon, perhaps the richest place for forest plants in Africa. And they are backing the development of park networks for the whole of Kalimantan (Indonesian Borneo) and Irian Jaya (the Indonesian portion of New Guinea), the two most botanically diverse areas in Southeast Asia. To secure existing parks, they are continuing to support the massive Manu Park in Peru – a rain forest bigger than Northern Ireland with more birds, and perhaps more plants, than any other park on earth.

The Programme also covers many islands: on Mauritius WWF fund plant conservation surveys, on Madagascar re-establishment of critical reserves. Off South America there are plans to rescue the beleaguered flora of the Juan Fernandez Islands and to conserve the plants on the Galapagos Islands.

Perhaps most exciting of all is the programme in India. Here IUCN experts have combined with Government of India scientists to design an ambitious programme to save India's plant life, with emphasis on those plants needed for development, eg. medicinal plants, and those on which tribal people depend. After approval by the Prime Minister, WWF/IUCN will contribute outside expertise, where needed, to implement the plan.

The international IUCN plants programme will cost about US $4 million, this in addition to those funds needed for national WWF plant conservation programmes. This is not a great deal of money in international terms, but considerably more than WWF can provide without a major increase in donations. The problems facing the world's plants are serious, but they can be solved. You as an individual can help. Together, we can make a difference.

WWF invites you to become part of the worldwide movement to save our green home. Send your donation to your local WWF office, or write for further details of the WWF Plant Conservation Programme to:

WWF
Membership Secretary
World Conservation Centre
1196 GLAND
Switzerland.

or:

WWF United Kingdom
Conservation Department
Weyside Park
Godalming
Surrey GU7 1XR
U.K.

For references to national plant Red Data Books see Synge (1981) or, for more detail, IUCN Conservation Monitoring Centre (1984). News on plant conservation is published in *WWF News* (write to your national WWF office), and *IUCN Bulletin* (write to IUCN, CH-1196 Gland, Switzerland).

Eckholm, E.P. (1976). *Losing Ground: environmental stress and world food prospects*. 223 pp. Norton, New York.

Ehrlich, P. and A. (1981). *Extinction: The Causes and Consequences of the Disappearance of Species*. 305 pp. Random House, New York.

Hoyt, E. (1988). *Conserving the Wild Relatives of Crops*. IBPGR/IUCN/WWF.

IUCN (1980). *World Conservation Strategy: Living Resource Conservation for Sustainable Development*. Prepared by IUCN with UNEP, WWF, FAO and Unesco. Available from IUCN, Gland.

IUCN Conservation Monitoring Centre (1984). *Plants in danger: what do we know*. IUCN, Switzerland. Available from IUCN Conservation Monitoring Centre, 219c Huntingdon Road, Cambridge, U.K.

Jain, S.K. and Mehra, K.L. (1984). *Conservation of Tropical Plant Resources*. 243 pp. Botanical Survey of India, P.O. Botanic Gardens, Howrah-71103, India.

Lewington, A. (1990). *Plants for People*. The Natural History Museum, London.

Lucas, G. and Synge, H. (1978). *The IUCN Plant Red Data Book*. IUCN, Switzerland. 540 pp. IUCN Conservation Monitoring Centre.

Mabey, R. (1980). *The Common Ground*. 266 pp. Arrow Books, London.

Myers, N. (1979). *The Sinking Ark*. 307 pp. Pergamon Press, Oxford.

Myers, N. (1983). *A Wealth of Wild Species – Storehouse for Human Welfare*. 272 pp. Westview Press, Boulder, Colorado.

Prance, G.T. and Elias, T.S. (1977). *Extinction is Forever*. 437 pp. New York Botanical Garden, Bronx, New York.

Prescott-Allen, R. and C. (1982). *What's Wildlife Worth? Economic contributions of wild plants and animals to developing countries*. 90 pp. Earthscan (10 Percy Street, London W1P 0DR).

Prescott-Allen, R. and C. (1983). *Genes from the wild. Using wild genetic resources for food and raw materials*. 101 pp. Earthscan.

Simmons, J.B. *et al.* (Eds) (1976). *Conservation of Threatened Plants*. Plenum Press, New York.

Synge, H. (Ed.) (1981). *The Biological Aspects of Rare Plant Conservation*. 588 pp. Wiley, Chichester, U.K.

Synge, H. and Townsend, H. (Eds.) (1979). *Survival or Extinction*. 250 pp. Bentham-Moxon Trust, Royal Botanic Gardens, Kew, Richmond, Surrey, U.K.

World Plant Conservation Bibliography (1990). World Conservation Monitoring Centre, Royal Botanic Gardens, Kew, U.K.

WWF (1989). *WWF Conservation Yearbook*. Available from Isobel Greenfield, WWF United Kingdom Conservation Dept.

Index

Acknowledgements

Author's Acknowledgments
This book has been very much a collective effort and I gratefully acknowledge the immense help provided by the editorial team, especially Joss Pearson. Richard Gorer and Juliet Bailey helped greatly with research on several chapters. The basis for the account of North American Indian ethnobotany came from the book *Plants in British Columbia Indian Technology* by Nancy J Turner, who has kindly permitted the direct quotation made on p.151. Quotation has also been made briefly from *The Law of the Seed* by P R Mooney (in Development Dialogue, 1983, 1-2), which provided invaluable background material for chapter 10. I must also thank my wife Alyson who typed most of my initial handwritten draft.

Photographs
Ardea London: 183; 178 (Jean Paul Ferrero); 118 top left (A Green Smith); 101 bottom (Francois Gohier); 15 bottom right, 159 (John Mason). *Aspect*: 125 (J Matthews). *BBC Hulton Picture Library*: 150 left. *Biofotos*: 14 left, 17 top, 53 bottom right, 135 top (Heather Angel); 180 (Murray Watson). *British Museum*: 60 left, 134 left. *Stefan Buczacki*: 99, 101 top, 102 top (Vietmeyer). *M Clements*: 163. *Bruce Coleman Ltd*: 24-5, 129; 118 top right, 147 top (Eric Crichton); 68, 75 bottom right (Cameron Davidson); 10-11 (Jack Dermid); 90 (Nicholas Devore); 15 top (M P L Fogden); 63 top (Michael Freeman); 35 left (C B Frith); 107 top, 147 bottom (Jennifer Fry); 66 (David Hughes); 63 bottom (O A J Mobbs); 157 (Norman Myers); 174-5 (Mike Price). *Mary Evans Picture Library*: 89 top. *C Grey-Wilson*: 15 bottom left, 17 bottom right, 34, 155 bottom right. *Susan Griggs Agency*: 148-9 (Tor Eigeland); 21, 58, 75 top and bottom left, 153 (Victor Englebert); 54-5 (Ivan Polunin); 187 (Joseph F Viesti); 82-3, 130-1 (Adam Woolfitt). *David Hall*: 81, 97. *Robert Harding Picture Library Ltd*: 39 top; 57 (C Grey-Wilson). *John Hillelson Agency*: 37 (George Gerster). *ICI Agricultural Division*: 160. *Michael Holford*: 67 top right; 107 bottom, 112 bottom left, 151 top right. *Anthony and Alyson Huxley*: 46 top, 49 left, 60 right, 62, 85 left, 89 bottom, 134 right. *Mansell Collection Ltd*: 77, 112 top left, middle, bottom top, bottom right, bottom right, 113 bottom. *Tony Morrison*: 30 top, 31 bottom, 32, 33, 102 bottom left, 108 top, 119 bottom, 152. *Natural Science Photos*: 53 bottom left (H E Axel); 88 top left (P J K Burton); 117 bottom right (M Chinery). *Nature Photographers Ltd*: 41 (S Bisserot). *Christine Osborne*: 39 bottom. *OSF Picture Library*: 53 top (Liz & Tony Bomford); 176 (G I Bernard); 14 right (Sean Morris). *Joss Pearson*: 17 bottom left. *Ann Ronan Picture Library*: 46 bottom left, 50 bottom left, 51, 52 top. *A D Schilling*: 155 top and middle. *Seaphot*: 2-3, 6 (Jorge Provenza); 31 top (Ian Redmond). *R Sheridan*: 67 middle left; 113 top. *Harry Smith*: 135 bottom, 138 bottom, 139 bottom, 140 bottom. *Tony Stone Worldwide*: 68. *Survival Anglia/OSF*: 46 bottom right; 111 top (Cindy Buxton and Annie Price); 111 bottom (Jeff Foott). *Vision International*: 132 top (D Warren). *World About Us/Richard Taylor*: 35 right.

Publisher's Acknowledgments
Gaia gratefully acknowledge the help of WWF, the International Union for Conservation of Nature, and the Royal Botanic Gardens, Kew. Their advice, assistance, and provision of access to research data and the library and art collection at Kew have been invaluable. In particular, we would like to extend special thanks to the following people: Paul Wachtel and Peter Palmer for all their support; Hugh Synge, Jeremy Harrison, Steve Davis, Stephen Droop and all the staff of the IUCN Conservation Monitoring Centre at Kew; Gren Lucas, Sylvia FitzGerald, John Flanagan, Marilyn J Ward, Hilary Morris, Tudor Harwood, Milan Svanderlik and all the staff of the library at Kew. Dr Paterson and Professor David Hall of King's College, Amory Hubbard and Linda McMahon of WWF US; Libby, Juliet, Bridget, Tony, Imogen, Elly and Anita for all their work; Bob Christie for controlling the production; George Greenfield and the staff of Van Leer and Rommerts, Mike Jarvis, Allan Ticehurst and Bob Aldridge of SX Composing, On Yer Bike, Lesley and Sue for much weekend typing; Dorothy Frame for the index.

Botanical Plates
Franz Antone, *Atlas Phyto-iconographie bromeliaceen*, 32. Vicente Martin de Argenta, *Album de la Flora medico-farmaceutica é industrial, indígena y exótica*, 19. R Bentley and H Trimen, *Medicinal Plants*, 87, 125. F Cassone, *Flora medico farmaceutica*, 116. Crown copyright: reproduced with permission of the Controller of Her Majesty's Stationery Office and the Director of the Royal Botanic Gardens Kew, 18, 19, 48, 58, 60, 79, 80, 100, 104, 123, 144, 185. Curtis's Botanical Magazine, 32, 68, 124, 137, 139, 141, 143, 145, 182. Joseph Descaisne, *Le jardin fruitier du Museum*, 84. M Greshoff, *Nuttige indische planten*, 120. Hedrick, *Plums of New York*, 69. Sir Joseph Hooker, 19. Nicholaus Jacquin, *Floral austriacae*, 19, 167. Fr. Eugen Kohler, *Medizinal-pflanzen*, 93. Lindley and Paxton, *Flower Garden*, 52. Thomas Nuttall, *The North American Sylva*, 150. J Parkinson, *A Garden of all sorts of Pleasant Flowers*, 136. Joseph Plenck, 48, 61, 84, 117, 139. Pierre Joseph Redouté, 92. Francois Regnault and Genevieve de Nangis Regnault, *La botanique mise a la portee de tout le monde*, 50, 69, 76, 87, 91, 92, 93, 108, 109, 115. John Sibthorpe, *Florae graecae*, 120. J T I Syme, *English Botany*, 85. Tanako Citrus Studies, 78. Ventenat, *Jardin de la Malmaison*, 182. William Woodville, *Medical Botany*, 138.

Illustrators
Sandra Pond
Andrew Macdonald
Alan Suttie
Ann Savage
Endpapers devised by Tony Spalding and painted by Peter Morter

▼ Strelitzia
Birds seeking nectar in the centre of the Bird-of-Paradise Flower, (Strelitzia reginae) stand on a strong trough-shaped platform, unaware that stamens in the trough are pressing pollen onto their feet ready to be transferred to the stigma of the next bloom visited.

▲ Mimosa
Leaves and stems of Sensitive Plant (Mimosa pudica) collapse at a touch from raindrops, strong winds, or animals. The speed of collapse over a whole plant is about 3 cm per second; the collapse "message" is probably carried chemically, but electrical charges may also be involved.

◄ Durian
Durian fruit combines revolting smell with delicious flavour. The smell attracts animals of all sorts who help disperse its seeds – elephants, rhinoceroses, tigers, pigs, monkeys, bears and squirrels – and people who have acquired a taste for it. Durian is pollinated by a single bat species, now in decline.

▼ Argyroderma
A number of succulents of the Mesembryanthemum family resemble the stones of the South African deserts in which they live. This Argyroderma is mimicking white or quartzy stones. Other "living stones" are grey, brown, yellowish or green with granite-like speckling.

◀ Jade vine
The spectacular Jade Vine
(Strongylodon macrobotrys),
almost unique in flower colour,
is severely endangered in its
native habitat, the Phillipines.
Fortunately it readily takes to
cultivation in tropical gardens
or under glass, as in the Palm
House at Kew, England.

▶ Cycad
Half tree, half fern in
appearance, cycads like Cycas
revoluta are in danger from
collectors, as ornamental
plants. Known as fossils from
200 million years ago, their life
span measured in thousands of
years, these ancient plants grow
only from seed.

▶ Gingko
The deciduous Maidenhair
Tree (Gingko biloba) once
flourished all over the world,
but dwindled to near-
extinction, except in Chinese
and Japanese temple gardens.
Gingko is now widely grown
for ornament and even as a
street tree in North American
towns.

▼ Welwitschia
One of the most bizarre plants
in the world is Welwitschia. It
has two ever-growing leaves,
up to 9 metres long, which split
to give the impression of many
more, and absorb moisture only
from sea mists in its native
South-west Africa.

▶ Coco de mer
The Double Coconut or Coco-
de-mer is the biggest seed in the
world, weighing up to 30 kg. Its
shape once made it prized as an
aphrodisiac, when washed up
on far-off beaches. The palm is
at risk in its only habitat, one
valley on one island in the
Seychelles.